SURVIVE AND RESIST

THE DEFINITIVE GUIDE TO
DYSTOPIAN POLITICS

AMY L. ATCHISON
SHAUNA L. SHAMES

Columbia University Press

New York

Columbia University Press
Publishers Since 1893
New York   Chichester, West Sussex
cup.columbia.edu
Copyright © 2019 Columbia University Press

Library of Congress Cataloging-in-Publication Data
Names: Atchison, Amy L., author. | Shames, Shauna Lani, author.
Title: Survive and resist : the definitive guide to dystopian politics /
    Amy L. Atchison and Shauna L. Shames.
Description: New York : Columbia University Press, [2019] | Includes
    bibliographical references and index.
Identifiers: LCCN 2018058580 (print) | LCCN 2019006482 (ebook) |
    ISBN 9780231548069 (e-book) | ISBN 9780231188906 (cloth : alk.
    paper) | ISBN 9780231188913 (pbk. : alk. paper)
Subjects: LCSH: Dystopias in literature. | Authoritarianism in literature.
    | Politics and literature. | Fiction—20th century—History and
    criticism. | Fiction—21st century—History and criticism. |
    Dystopias. | Authoritarianism. | Popular culture—Political aspects. |
    World politics—21st century.
Classification: LCC PN56.D94 (ebook) | LCC PN56.D94 A73 2019
    (print) | DDC 809.3/9372—dc23
LC record available at https://lccn.loc.gov/2018058580

Columbia University Press books are printed
on permanent and durable acid-free paper.

Printed in the United States of America

Cover image © plainpicture/Cultura

SURVIVE AND RESIST

Shauna: In memory of Rebecca Faery,
who first inspired me to love dystopian fiction

⬤ ⬤ ⬤

Amy: For my dad, who watched *World News Tonight*
with me every night and taught me why it matters

Contents

Acknowledgments

The authors gratefully acknowledge input and assistance from Lisa Alston, Jane Atchison, Dawn Bartusch, Phil Carbo, Caelyn Cobb, Chelsea Coccia, Anna and Susannah Ettin, Johanna Ettin, Kim Fields, Steve Gowler, Marc Grossman, Carter Hanson, Richard Harris, Cathy Jenkins, Annalisa Klein, Julia Kudler and the other Vaughn-Kudlers, Howard and Susan Levinson, James Loxton, Jane Mansbridge, Nicole Niemi, James Old, Kathryn Owens, George Pati, Jennifer Piscopo, Beth Rabinowitz, Richard and Karilee Shames, Gabriel Shames, Gigi Shames, Robert Sheppard, Jim Spencer, Miranda Stafford, Daniel Tague, Sue Thomas, Louise Tindell, Andrea Tivig, Shelby and Chris Topping, Vanessa Williamson, Christina Xydias, and Rebecca Yowler. We would also like to thank several anonymous reviewers for their helpful comments, our classes at Valparaiso University and Rutgers University–Camden, and the Valparaiso University Faculty Writing Circle. The authors would also like to thank each other; author listing is alphabetical.

Preface

Are you:

- Wondering if your government is inching (or hurtling) toward dystopia?
- Interested in the concept of dystopian government but lacking the time to read the hundreds of excellent works in this ever-growing genre? Wanting to connect them to real-life examples?
- Pondering that eternal question of human existence, how in the world can we create a government for ourselves that is neither totalitarian nor useless?

This book is for you.

We are two feminist political scientists who have a passion for democracy, good public policy, and horribly depressing visions of the future. Let us guide you through some of our favorites, tying them to real-life examples and pointing out key patterns and trends.

Dystopian government happens all the time, in both fact and fiction, and it has all kinds of recognizable "hallmarks" and major weaknesses that you should know about. Some of these examples are truly terrible, but there are also some useful examples of resistance that are important and uplifting. These are what give us hope for the future of democracy and, well, the human race.

Ultimately, this is our message to you: Be not afraid.

Maybe that is overstated. Okay, be a little afraid. This is not a normal moment in modern history or politics. Right-wing populists are gaining strength in the United States and Europe, and left-wing populists have done fairly well in Latin America. Both have done a *lot* of pandering to people's worst instincts to stir up fear, hatred, and resentment. But don't let the fear overwhelm you. Worse threats than this have been faced down and overcome, and the human spirit has a way of shining through in the darkest moments.

The resistance has already started. All over the world, regular citizens are standing up for the basics of democracy, like free speech, freedom of religion, rule of law, the right to vote, and checks and balances. Their strength gives us courage for the battle ahead.

SURVIVE AND RESIST

Introduction

I t's no coincidence that two dystopian classics—George Orwell's *1984* and Margaret Atwood's *The Handmaid's Tale*—shot to the top of best-seller lists in the wake of the 2016 pro-Brexit vote in the United Kingdom and the 2016 U.S. presidential election. Novels, like other art forms, can help people make sense of the world around them. In this case, it is political fiction helping readers parse the political world, with frightening futuristic visions serving to amplify, explain, or warn us about current trends. The government that controls Oceania in Orwell's *1984* is a Stalinesque communist nightmare centered in what was formerly London, England. The Party, led by the dictatorial Big Brother, keeps its members under control through constant surveillance and intensive language and thought policing. In Atwood's *The Handmaid's Tale*, the Republic of Gilead is a theocratic (religion-based) totalitarian government that controls the Northeast of the former United States; it parcels out its most precious resources—fertile women—among powerful men for purposes of enforced reproduction.

Key themes link Orwell's and Atwood's otherwise quite different visions of totalitarian government, including surveillance, fear, hierarchy, rules about sex and reproduction, violent repression, and a deep concern with language and its connection to thought control. This is also not a coincidence; these are some of what we will later discuss as hallmarks of dystopian government. A good dictator, if he or she knows what's what, will be concerned with all of these. And those who might want to resist such governance should also know and understand key concepts about dystopian government.

Democratic self-governance is difficult, tedious, easily corrupted, and prone to failure. History is littered with failed democracies (ancient Greece, Rome, multiple Italian city-states, current abortive attempts at democracy in the Middle East, Latin America, Africa, Russia . . . and the list goes on). As Aristotle noted more than two millennia ago, democracies often devolve into dictatorships, which can then be overthrown in favor of democracies, and so on; political scientists refer to this as regime cycling.[1]

Since Aristotle's time, many political theorists and philosophers have helped us clarify the negatives of both tyranny and mob rule and tried to form political philosophies that would strike a balance. No government, they have concluded, is perfect—but even so, some government is better than no government at all. In these sentiments, political theorists are joined by writers of dystopian fiction, who delight in pointing out the myriad problems both with the presence of government and with its absence (the pure state of nature). It is a paradox: we need government, but it often sucks. Democracy, however, can be seen as an attempt at stopping dystopia.

In this book, we try to give you (relatively) short answers to large and longstanding questions: Why do we even have government if most governments either under- or overreach? Short answer: like bad pizza and bad sex, a bad government is better than no government at all. Second, why do some people choose to live under authoritarian rule? Short answer: democracy is scary, and it's hard freaking work. Next, why would democracy prevent dystopia? Short answer: because no one gets exactly what they want in a democracy. Finally, is resistance futile? Short answer: of course not. But some forms of resistance are more realistic than others, and we'll mostly look at nonviolent resistance.

The premise of this book is fairly simple. We believe that dystopian fiction can help us explain and make sense of key concepts in political science—that is, the study of government, governance, state power, public policy, people's political behavior, and social movements, importantly including resistance to authoritarian rule. Political science taught in a purely theoretical way can be dry indeed; using dystopian fiction, especially popular books and films, like Suzanne Collins's *The Hunger Games* or even J. K. Rowling's Harry Potter series, helps put some meat on the bones. And art gets under the skin and into the soul in a way social science, journalism, and outright legal argument just cannot do. For all the abolitionist arguing for over a century, it was Harriet Beecher Stowe's *Uncle Tom's Cabin* that spread the antislavery message across the United States—the book was so influential that Lincoln called Stowe "the little lady who caused this great war."[2]

The approach we take blends fictional examples of bad government with concepts from comparative government studies and adds a dash of political theory. Fiction is a good lens for concepts because it insulates us from the horrors being presented in the narrative and sometimes helps us see our world in a new way. For instance, it is not too far a stretch to compare those seeking to consolidate and wield power in real-life states to the "Death Eaters" trying to control the Ministry of Magic in Harry Potter's world. Dystopia, however, is far from a fictional concept. Real-life examples of dystopian government, while useful, and which we will use throughout the book, can be downright distressing.

This book, we hope, strikes the right balance between humor and political science, a blend that invites you to better understand bad governments and why they do what they do, and we hope it does so in a way that is ultimately empowering and even inspirational—or at least not tedious. The good news, as you will soon learn, is that every dark dystopian vision has at its core a little ray of sunshine.

WHAT IS THIS BOOK? WHAT WILL IT DO? HOW? WHY?

In this book, we'll be using dystopian fiction to explain what good governance looks like and how to resist bad governance. You probably had to read at least one dystopian novel in high school (*1984*, we're betting), and you would have to have been living under a rock to miss *The Hunger Games* mania that swept the United States a few years ago. There have also been several dystopian TV series—notably cult hits like *Jericho* (2006–2008) and Joss Whedon's *Firefly* (2002–2003), the reboot of *Battlestar Galactica* (2004–2009), as well as newer shows like CW's *The 100* (2014–2018) and Amazon's *The Man in the High Castle* (2015–).[3]

But dystopias show up in some unexpected places, too. For example, who would expect to find an Orwellian nightmare in a hilarious and seemingly perky kids' film? Yet you'll find one in *The LEGO Movie*. The movie is a brilliant depiction of a dystopian Lego Universe in which happiness comes from obeying The Instructions. It gives you an oppressive authoritarian ruler (Lord/President Business) who rules with an iron fist, lies to his people regularly, keeps/tortures political prisoners, and uses gimmicks to distract his subjects from the reality of their oppression and impending doom. See also Disney's *Wall-E*, a somewhat soul-crushing but cute indictment of the disposable elements inherent in today's consumer culture.

There is also dystopian poetry. For example, Bruce Boston's 2008 poem "Dystopian Dusk," about a society gradually sliding toward fascist rule, ends with "and a bare reflection of the sun's last rays heralds a fascist night."[4] Then there's dystopian music—Pink Floyd's "Another Brick in the Wall," Black Sabbath's "War Pigs," and Judas Priest's "Tyrant" and "Metal Gods" come to mind pretty quickly.[5] And for those of you who aren't metal fans, the Pet Shop Boys' 2006 song "Integral" explicitly references Yevgeny Zamyatin's *We*; the song is meant "to register [the band's] hostility toward the Labour government's plan to require national ID cards containing individuals' biometric data."[6] Most recently, dystopias are appearing in video games, too—for example, the dystopian cities of Columbia and Rapture at the core of the first-person-shooter series Bioshock.[7]

There has been considerable speculation in the popular press as to why dystopian fiction has become so popular—maybe it's because so many dystopian stories show an everyday person fighting back against oppressive government. Maybe it's because the magnitude of the surveillance state in many countries has made the stories relatable to people. And maybe it's just that there are just some damn good stories in the genre. Honestly, we don't really care *why* people like it. We're just excited that people have gotten into it, and in this book we hope to help people translate their familiarity with dystopian societies into an understanding of modern authoritarian and other horrible forms of government.

It is worth mentioning, too, that those who make dystopian fiction, in whatever form, are not just trying to tell a good story (although they often do). It is the creators' objective to get us to think critically about a current pattern or trend in our world, project where it might go in the future, and then (hopefully) take steps to avoid it. You can almost hear Bruce Boston screaming at us in that poem, à la Dylan Thomas, to not go gentle into that dystopian night.

A key element of this book's approach will be comparing governments; throughout, you'll see several "Comparing Dystopias" boxes. In them, we contrast real and fictional dystopias, using the fictional to highlight key elements of the real. We report a Freedom House score (0 to 100, with 100 being most free) for each state—real or fictional. Freedom House (an international nongovernmental organization, or NGO) provides that score for each real state, and it also provides its methodology for arriving at a score. We've used Freedom House's methodology, including its "Freedom in the World 2017 Checklist of Questions," to score the fictional dystopias we've used in the comparisons.[8]

Here's how the book works: in chapter 1, we do the set-up work for the rest of the book. First, there's some basic stuff about dystopian fiction that you just have to know. Also, a bit of history. (Truly, just a bit.) And then you have to understand a little about political theory, which is that branch of philosophy focused on governing, politics, and the state. We promise we will make all of this interesting. But it's impossible truly to appreciate dystopian fiction without knowing some of the theory and history behind it.

Chapter 2 dives into some examples of dystopian government, of both the fictional and the real-life variety. The goal of this chapter is to define dystopian government and understand its hallmarks. And then in chapter 3, we switch to the role of economics in real and fictional dystopian states.

Starting with chapter 4, we delve into the strategies and tactics that dictators use to achieve and then maintain their power. (Have you ever wondered what the difference is between a strategy and a tactic? Stay tuned.) We examine survival and resistance; there are a variety of ways for people to survive in a dystopian state, some of which work better than others. Chapter 5 explores individual strategies for survival and tactics that you can use to keep yourself sane while (hopefully) undermining a dystopian government.

In chapters 6 and 7, we look at the theory and practice of collective resistance to dystopian government. Specifically, we examine *nonviolent* resistance, and we do so for two reasons: first, nonviolent resistance works better, and, second, a successful nonviolent resistance campaign is more likely to result in a new democracy than is violent resistance. That brings us to chapter 8, which tackles rebuilding your society after you bring down an oppressive dystopian regime. In this chapter, we want you to think about what type of society you want, what principles the government should uphold, and what institutions you could use to build a strong, sustainable, and just government and society.

Ultimately, this book acknowledges the visceral power and popularity of modern dystopian fiction and seeks to use readers' interest in it as a hook to draw them into deeper analytical thinking about the concepts, questions, and answers that political science can offer on the topic of good versus bad governance. Our epilogue suggests that there is still reason to hope, even in dystopian darkness. Fictional works about bad governments can be enormously useful as case studies; they help us know and name what we are seeing, perhaps avoid it if we see it coming, and find the way out if we are trapped.

SPOILER ALERT

Before we go too much further, we should probably give you one very large spoiler alert. We are going to give away major details of many books and movies. Sorry. But now that we've given you fair warning, we can move on to giving away plot twists and endings!

We hope you enjoy and learn from this book. If it does nothing else, we hope it gives you a greater appreciation for that clumsy but ultimately hopeful system of governance we call democracy, which we argue is the antidote to dystopia. Although the fictional visions we use to explore bad government can be dark indeed, keep this in mind: someone bothered to write them, and millions have read them. That means people care enough about what bad government is to want to change it. Through the fiction, they are giving warnings for the future. Think about it: that's hope.

1

Malice in Wonderland

Every utopia since Utopia has also been, clearly or obscurely, actually or possibly, in the author's or in the readers' judgment, both a good place and a bad one. Every utopia contains a dystopia, every dystopia contains a utopia.

—Ursula K. Le Guin

The basis of utopian literature is the idea—the *hope*—that humanity can create a better world, one in which we all live better lives and get along with one another. From the seventeenth century on, one of the major themes in utopian fiction was the promise of science to deliver this better world—and of scientists to rule it.[1] The "utopia of science" idea was at its height in eighteenth- and nineteenth-century socialist utopian fiction, in which there is a clear belief that we *will* overcome human limitations (science!), humanity *will* flourish (higher consciousness!), and the perfect cooperative society *will* emerge (communal bliss!).[2]

Dystopian fiction—depicting horrifying societies—is an offshoot of the utopian genre. Logically, it would seem that a dystopia would be the exact opposite of a utopia: dark versus light. As if malice had crept into Wonderland.[3] In reality, though, dystopias are what we nerds call the reductio ad absurdum of utopian ideas—by extending ideas to their logical and potentially absurd extreme, dystopias demonstrate some of the potential dangers that lurk inside these so-called better worlds.[4]

In short, utopias and dystopias are two sides of the same coin. Your utopian dream might just be our dystopian nightmare.[5] What we typically see when someone imposes their utopian ideal on others is that the people who make the rules are living their dream, while the people living *under* those rules are trapped in a nightmare.

Another way to look at it is like Le Guin does in this chapter's epigraph: every utopian dream contains elements of dystopia, and vice versa.[6] Take

Thomas More's **Utopia** (1516), the book that lent its name to the whole genre. More's ideal society isn't really all that great for everyone—the society uses slave labor to do all of the dirty or dangerous work; everyone's daily work is assigned based on gender rather than ability or interests; there is free time but it must be spent "wisely"; and deviance, like laziness or premarital sex, is not tolerated.[7] We're betting that this doesn't sound ideal to you, but it seems to have been appealing to people in sixteenth-century England.

Utopia, by Sir Thomas More, was written in 1516—apparently he coined the term with some sense of mischief, drawing on two different Greek words: *eu-topos*, meaning a good place, and *ou-topos*, meaning no place. "Utopia," in other words, is a good place that does not really exist. *Dystopia* as a genre took its name from its opposition to utopia; think "dysfunction."

In some ways, much of the early dystopian fiction was meant to show the flip side of the utopian coin; it was a reaction to the unfettered science-inspired optimism of the utopian authors.[8] Yevgeny Zamyatin's *We* and Aldous Huxley's *Brave New World* can be read as direct critiques of H. G. Wells's uncritical and somewhat naive belief in the benefits of science and the benevolence of scientists.[9] The early dystopians saw considerable reason to fear the advance of science, and, to be fair, if you look at what came next, they weren't wrong to be cautious.

THEN THE TWENTIETH CENTURY HAPPENED

The early twentieth century dealt blow after blow to utopian ideals, particularly the belief that science would lead us to bliss. It's in this century that we see a serious turn toward dystopian depictions of the future.[10] The century started with the genocide of the Herero and Nama peoples of Namibia. Then came the mechanized warfare and chemical carnage of World War I (oh, science). Then the Armenian genocide, the Great Depression, World War II, the Holocaust—wherein the Nazis achieved murderous efficiency through science—the nuclear bomb (science again), the killing of millions of Russians by the Soviet government, and the Cold War. Whatever happened to achieving higher consciousness and communal bliss?

The dystopians express a profound pessimism about the ability of mankind to control itself, much less its destructive scientific creations.[11] (Think *Dr. Strangelove*.) No more odes to the promise of science to free humanity and lead us all to enlightenment. No more paeans extolling the virtues of perfect communal societies. Instead, the dystopians emphasize the potential of science and technology to stifle imagination and creativity (*We*), to oppress the citizenry (*1984*), to control women's bodies (*The Handmaid's Tale*), and, ultimately, to strip us of almost every emotion that makes us human (*Brave New World*).

In addition, as the twentieth century wore on and the oppressive and homicidal nature of the Soviet and Maoist states became clear, the belief that socialism could bring about a more just and beneficial society eroded. In response, the dystopians created fictional governments that were harsh, rigid, and oppressive in their pursuit of their goal of creating happiness for the masses. We see this desire to make people happy at the core of Huxley's *Brave New World*, Zamyatin's *We*, Ray Bradbury's *Fahrenheit 451*, and even Atwood's *The Handmaid's Tale*.

Zamyatin arguably puts it best in this proclamation from the One State: "If they won't understand that we bring them mathematically infallible happiness, it will be our duty to force them to be happy."[12] It's a very narrow vision—a specific type of *societal* happiness that can only be achieved through oppressive government enforcement of uniformity, efficiency, and stability. Thus, many of these early dystopian novels were cautionary tales warning the reader of the horrors of socialist or totalitarian societies. In real life, such societies, of course, were the communist-totalitarian Soviet Union and fascist-totalitarian Nazi Germany—and if ISIS were actually to achieve their goal of founding a caliphate, the government would be fundamentalist-totalitarian (akin to the theocracy in *The Handmaid's Tale*.)

PARALLEL UNIVERSES: DYSTOPIAS
IN FICTION AND REALITY

We're going to get into the specifics of authoritarian rule in the next few chapters, but for now we're going to talk about how to recognize a dystopia in fact or fiction. Dystopian governments take any number of forms, so it's not like there's one standard model. Like the U.S. Supreme Court justice Potter Stewart once said, we may not have an explicit definition, but we know it when we see it.[13]

The big clue that you're in a dystopia is the absence of personal freedom—what we commonly call civil liberties. Civil liberties, such as freedom of speech, religion, and assembly, are supposed to guarantee that you are "liberated" from government interference in those areas. You may say what you'd like, worship (or not) as you'd like, and associate with whomever you like. Authoritarian governments rarely allow civil liberties because then citizens might interfere with a government's ability to control things, and we can't have that, now can we? Having freedom gives people ideas. They start to think that they can do whatever they'd like. And, like Westley says in *The Princess Bride*, "Once word leaks out that a [dictator] has gone soft, people begin to disobey you, and then it's nothing but work, work, work all the time."

Dictators in dystopian fiction know all too well the power of the press. Consider the position of President Snow in Collins's *The Hunger Games*, for instance: Totally muzzling the media would look bad, and Snow's power depends in no small part on the attention of his easily distracted citizens being focused elsewhere (preferably on the Games) and not on his actual policies and practices. The ideal situation for him—which luckily, coincides with the desire of the press—is represented in the character of Caesar Flickerman. Flickerman is more than happy to have attention riveted on him and his "news" coverage while Snow's actual governing goes unmentioned; this suits both fine. But things are not always so easy for fictional dictators; the Big Brother government in Orwell's *1984*, for instance, spends most of its time framing official government and press statements to say the "right" things in the "right" language.

In real life, allowing, say, freedom of the press means that (a) an authoritarian government cannot operate with relative impunity and (b) that people would see things that make them critical of the government. This is why Vladimir Putin worked quickly to muzzle the press after his election in 2000—by 2003, he had shut down every independent news station in Russia.[14] Denying civil liberties, such as free speech, is one of the main ways authoritarian governments maintain their strangleholds on the citizenry. The path to dictatorship often starts with rolling back freedom of speech or otherwise making it more difficult for the press to operate.

Civil liberties are not to be confused with *civil rights*—which are more about equality than freedom. Theoretically, democratic governments will do their best to ensure that people are given equal treatment under the law. Nondemocratic dystopias, however, are often (but not always) created on a foundation of societal inequality. Typically, the citizens are exploited to make the leaders' extravagant lifestyles possible—and the leaders institutionalize that exploitation so that it just seems normal to the citizens ("your misery is right and proper, and you have no option but to obey"). We see this in multiple dystopias, from Fritz Lang's 1927 film *Metropolis*, where the underclasses literally live under the city, toiling away to make a comfortable life for the people on the surface, to today's young-adult Red Queen series (by Victoria Aveyard), where the underclass (the Reds) has been trained to believe that their servitude to the ruling class (the Silvers) is the natural order of things.

Although we tend to think of the servant culture as a relic of earlier eras (for example, the feudal system or the upstairs-downstairs culture of *Downton Abbey*), servitude—more accurately, slavery—is more prevalent today than most people realize. Modern slavery takes multiple forms, including sex trafficking, debt bondage, forced labor, and forced marriage. In 2017, the International Labor Organization estimated that more than 40 million people are enslaved around the globe; the vast majority of the enslaved are women and children.[15]

Even when the dystopian society is nominally founded on the premise of equality among citizens, as in the USSR or Maoist China, that never lasts long. It's the *iron law of oligarchy* at play; no matter how egalitarian your group, organization, or society is supposed to be, it will inevitably develop a hierarchy because people want leadership.[16] The leaders may keep up the rhetoric about equality—as the Soviets did—or about valorizing the peasants—à la Mao—but it's like the pigs say in Orwell's *Animal Farm*: "All animals are equal, but some animals are more equal than others."

THAT GOVERNMENT IS BEST WHICH GOVERNS NOT AT ALL. OR IS IT?

Given our discussion of dystopian states, it's easy to see why the poet-philosopher Henry David Thoreau might have preferred life without government at all.[17] But we beg to differ. It's not that we think governments are all great, it's that we're pretty sure that Thomas Hobbes was right and that some form of government is necessary to keep life from being nasty, brutish, and short. Hobbes said that in the absence of a government (a.k.a. "**the state of nature**") it was every man for himself; you could (and would) do whatever it took to survive. That would essentially mean a war of all against all (*bellum omnium contra omnes*) and that any survival tactic would be allowable. (Think *The Purge*. No rules. No constraints.) Hobbes said governments need to exist in order to protect us from one another.

The "**state of nature**" is a thought experiment used by many philosophers and fiction writers to justify the existence and extent of government. William Golding's famous *The Lord of the Flies* is a classic state-of-nature story, a kind of allegory of why we need government at all (in his view, to keep us from brutal animalism). Other thinkers have disagreed on how humans would act in the absence of government. Basically, people's thoughts on whether we would descend into chaos in the absence of government seem to correlate strongly with their optimism (or lack thereof) about innate human nature. In fiction, we see both a pure state-of-nature setting in some works; others (like Kevin Costner's movie *The Postman*, from 1997) show a *failed state*, where state-of-nature elements begin to creep in once a government can no longer maintain law and order.

At the other extreme, we have Jean-Jacques Rousseau, who proposed that in the state of nature, people were completely free and lived blissfully uncorrupted by others since they basically avoided one another: no contact, no conflict. This peaceful (if lonely) existence then got all screwed up by the accumulation of private property, and the poor were tricked by the rich into accepting coercive government. He argued that it would be better to have a direct democracy wherein each citizen weighs in on what is best for the society, thus arriving at the "general will" of the people. This would be a "good" government, where all of the citizens have security and freedom—and they all work together to preserve the society.

Now, do we think Thoreau, Hobbes, or Rousseau is exactly right? No. But we lean a bit more toward Hobbes, particularly after we look at the states that political scientists would call failed states—ungoverned or ungovernable. States like the Democratic Republic of the Congo,[18] South Sudan, and Somalia have often seemed pretty close to a Hobbesian state of nature. But, unlike Hobbes, who thought that a strong sovereign was necessary to keep people in line, we're big fans of democracy. We like voting.

That's why we're not big fans of Locke, who thought only property-owning men should vote.[19] We're more with Montesquieu, who struck a kind of compromise on human nature.[20]

Montesquieu figured people were neither solely virtuous nor completely evil; they mostly just banded together into societies so that they would have enough food to survive. Only after they band together do people really mess things up and start fighting. But Montesquieu thought people could be kept in line under a reasonably good government. His version of good government is one with executive, legislative, and judicial branches of government, each of which could check the power of the others. This will sound familiar to American readers: the framers of the U.S. Constitution drew heavily on Montesquieu's writings.

To be clear: Montesquieu's vision wouldn't have been what we would call a democracy—it was more of a liberal aristocracy with many of the elements we now associate with democracy. (He also thought that most everyone should be able to vote but that rich people should get more votes than poor people. No one's perfect.) But he planted the seeds. We'll come back to democracy in a bit, but first we want to talk about why anyone would choose *not* to live in a democracy. Because some do choose that—and not as infrequently as you might think.

AUTHORITARIANISM RULES!

There's a story-within-a-story in Dostoevsky's *The Brothers Karamazov* called "The Grand Inquisitor." In the story, Jesus returns to earth after a long time away to find those he had freed back in chains. He yells at the Grand Inquisitor, asking why his people are chained up. The Grand Inquisitor sagely explains that they chained themselves in exchange for safety and food. People, the moral goes, will trade liberty for security.

Dostoevsky wasn't wrong. Some people choose oppression over freedom because democracy is scary. It requires citizens to have a certain level of comfort with uncertainty. Democracy, with its regular crazy elections and frequently changing personnel, feels unstable. Not only that, but democracy is inefficient by design. The leader can't just lay down the law. The political process requires negotiation and compromise. No one seems to have a firm hand on the wheel. Some people can't handle the instability, and they'll take a little oppression as a tradeoff for the happiness that stability brings.

Simply put: if comfort with authoritarianism were put on a scale, these people would be on the high end.[21] Note that there really *is* a scale (figure 1.1): 0–0.25 is the nonauthoritarian end; 0.26–0.74 is the midrange; and 1 is the highly authoritarian end.

The American archetype of the authoritarian citizen (the guy that maxes out the scale) sees life in black and white. Order and stability are obviously

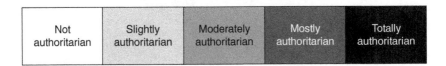

Not authoritarian	Slightly authoritarian	Moderately authoritarian	Mostly authoritarian	Totally authoritarian

Figure 1.1 Authoritarianism scale.
Source: Graphic by the authors.

good; chaos and confusion are clearly bad. A person who scores high on the authoritarian scale is going to be predisposed to obey leaders who display that type of black-and-white thinking, with its promise of a well-ordered society. Authoritarian citizens would consider that type of leader a *legitimate* authority and capable of providing order.[22]

We want to stress that these are *not* necessarily bad traits. We'd be very surprised if no one in your life thinks this way; political science research indicates that between 42 and 49 percent of Americans score a 0.75 or higher on the 0-to-1 authoritarianism scale. In contrast, people on the very low end of the scale (0.25 and below) make up only 23 to 34 percent of the population (see figure 1.2).[23] That means that a whole lot more people are authoritarian at heart than nonauthoritarian, with quite a few who don't mind some authoritarianism.

Even people who score highly on the authoritarian scale aren't always fine with authoritarian governing tactics; they become more comfortable with authoritarianism when they perceive a threat to the established social order. That's why exaggerating the terror threat, hyping the dangers of immigration, and demonizing the LGBTQ community are great ways to

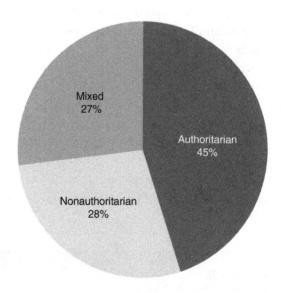

Figure 1.2 Authoritarianism preference among U.S. citizens.

Source: Graphic by the authors, based on data from Mark J. Hetherington and Jonathan D. Weiler, *Authoritarianism and Polarization in American Politics* (New York: Cambridge University Press, 2009), averaged estimates.

get authoritarian citizens to vote for you—in a highly authoritarian citizen's worldview, all of these things feel like threats.[24]

America doesn't come close to having the monopoly on highly authoritarian citizens. Post-Soviet Russia is a great example. Back in the early 1990s, just after communism fell, many observers were optimistic about democracy's fortunes in the former Soviet Union. Russia, they thought, would transition into a modern liberal democracy, and its people would bask in the glow of freedom. But that didn't happen. After a brief flirtation with mostly free and fair elections and an attempt at promoting civil liberties, the Russian people voted themselves into a more authoritarian state. Vladimir Putin didn't stage a coup and take over; he was elected. (So was Hitler.) Then between 2000 and 2003 he pushed sweeping changes that dismantled democratic institutions and tamped down on free expression, and the Russians voted him into office *again*.[25]

Think it can't happen in other places? In 2017, Turkey's president, Recep Erdoğan, and his party amended the Turkish Constitution to give the president sweeping new powers, which he has used to govern Turkey in ever-more authoritarian ways. He has engineered increasingly harsh crackdowns on opposition parties and journalists, implemented restrictions on civil liberties (like freedom of association or expression), weakened the rule of law, and censored the internet. The "reforms" he and his party engineered also give him the potential to stay in power, depending on election timing, until at least 2029 and possibly 2032. It helps that members of his party have bought up Turkish media companies and essentially turned them into government media outlets.

Many of us, likely even those of us that fall more toward the high end of the authoritarianism scale, cannot understand why people would vote to curtail their own freedoms. In the Russian case, and in others, we underestimated the lure of authoritarianism. Russia's new democracy was unstable. Its first president, Boris Yeltsin, wasn't particularly effective, and people got scared. They wanted a return to order, which is exactly what Putin gave them. Even as Putin was demolishing democracy, 60 percent of young Russians, the demographic that theoretically should be the most open to democracy, thought authoritarian governments were better at providing order, and 66 percent were fine with at least some level of authoritarianism in their government.[26]

This question about security versus liberty pervades the writings of the framers of the U.S. Constitution—this was a major and recurring debate between Thomas Jefferson's and Alexander Hamilton's factions. The framers could all agree on wanting freedom from Great Britain, but it turned out that forming their own functional government was harder than perhaps they had initially thought. Did they want a strong, centralized national government, with a powerful executive authority (à la Hamilton)? Or a rather weak national government, with a very weak president, but a relatively strong Congress and strong state governments (à la Jefferson)? They just couldn't agree. Ultimately, at least at the time, Jefferson kind of won—Article I is all about Congress, not the president, after all. But over time, both the national government (vis-à-vis the states) and the presidency (vis-à-vis Congress) have grown in power in response to crises. This is not unusual; as you will see, consolidation of power in the national executive branch is often how democracies die.

DEMOCRACY IS THE WORST

To paraphrase Winston Churchill, **democracy** is the worst form of government—except for all the others. We've said it before, and we'll say it again: democracy is slow, inefficient, and difficult to live with. That said, democracy gives people a whole lot more of a say in their lives than any other form of government that has been attempted in human history, so we're going to stick with it.

We've already mentioned that we're big fans of democracy. We like voting. We like accountability. We like free speech and a free press. And we love that the basis of democratic government is compromise.[27] In a democracy, it's rare that anyone gets exactly what they wanted. A policy *proposal* may be someone's ideal policy, but policy *outcomes* are the result of extensive negotiation and backroom dealing. Someone is always seriously unhappy with the resulting legislation, and even the people who mostly like a bill can point to sections they don't like. When legislation is terrible or policies fail, there's all manner of blame to go around because so many people had a hand in creating the final product. You never get the ideal, which means you always have to settle for second rate (at best). The bottom line is that if all dystopias start as someone's ideal society, then democratic compromise is the cure for dystopia.

As Ben Franklin once cautioned, getting a democracy is one thing, but keeping it is another. Franklin was echoing the warnings of the Greek philosopher Aristotle. Over two thousand years ago, Aristotle made some pretty solid predictions about the potential ills of democracy. To be fair, he liked democracy a great deal, mostly because it brings more voices into governing. "A feast to which all contribute," he famously wrote in the *Politics*, "is better than a feast out of a single purse." But he predicted that democracy could be dangerous if the people got scared or angry and elected a dictator—and he wasn't wrong. It's as if Aristotle foresaw Weimar Germany and the rise of Adolf Hitler. Given the poor economic conditions in Weimar Germany in the1920s and 1930s, it isn't hard to see why electing Hitler appealed to people. Aristotle's belief that people would vote in a dictator is the basis for the theory of regime cycling—democracies devolve into dictatorships, but then eventually the people get sick of a dictator, overthrow him, and try to return to democracy.

People turn to someone like Hitler because maintaining a democracy is hard work. The society has to share and perpetuate the values that make democracy function: freedom, moderation, tolerance, cooperation, and healthy skepticism of government, to name a few. The people have to believe in participation, both in government and in civil society. First, it's helpful if people believe that voting isn't just their right but their duty. Second, it's also pretty important that people believe that their vote counts and that their participation in elections matters. Third, they also have to see that participation in civil society—the organizations outside the control of government—allows citizens to work together for their own benefit and allows them to be another check on the power of government.[28] But the hard work doesn't stop there.

Citizens in a democracy have to embrace some instability. They have to be okay with their preferred party, candidate, or policy losing. They have to accept that other people have different and competing interests and opinions. In a democracy, you cannot use the coercive

"But the United States (or France) is a *republic*. And the United Kingdom (or Japan) is a *constitutional monarchy*."

In political science, we call any government that has regular free and fair elections, nonviolent turnover of power, rule of law, and protection of civil rights/liberties a **democracy**. We do this because it is simpler. And we do this even though Aristotle differentiated "republic" (one of the best forms of government) from "democracy" (one of the worst—"mob rule"). Here's why:

- There are different forms of democracy (republics, constitutional monarchies, and possibly even direct democracies, though this last type is rare outside of New England or ancient Athens).
- There are also different democratic operating systems (presidential, parliamentary, the French semi-presidential system, and God only knows what the Swiss system is).
- There are even different democratic decision-making philosophies (consensus, majoritarian/ pluralistic).

But no matter what combination of these things states choose, those that have free and fair elections, regular nonviolent transitions of power, rule of law, and protection of civil rights/ liberties all fall in the "democratic" rather than "nondemocratic" category, hence, "democracies."

power of the state to shut your enemies up; you actually have to deal with them and figure out how to resolve those differences peacefully. In addition, when the government tries to use its coercive power to shut down dissent, citizens have to push back to protect their own rights. All of this hard and often uncomfortable work is why Aristotle thought people would probably get angry or scared and vote a dictator into power, and it's why America's founders were so concerned about democracy sliding back into tyranny (we call this "authoritarian backsliding").

They had good reason to be afraid. New democracies are often little better than the nondemocratic states they replaced.[29] They're democracy "lite," with all of the elections and none of the freedoms.[30] We'll discuss these not-so-democratic democracies more fully in chapter 8, when we discuss how democracy is prone to authoritarian backsliding. The reason for introducing them here is to point out that full-on democracy, with constraints on government power and legal transparency, isn't exactly second nature to humanity.[31] People don't naturally tend to share power; instead, they hoard it and work hard to keep it for themselves.[32] Dr. Martin Luther King Jr. put it best in his "Letter from a Birmingham Jail": "We know through painful experience that freedom is never voluntarily given by the oppressor. It must be demanded by the oppressed."[33]

THE BORG ARE WRONG: RESISTANCE IS NOT FUTILE

A year from now, ten, they'll swing back to the belief that they can make people . . . better. And I do not hold to that. So no more running. I aim to misbehave.

—Captain Mal Reynolds, *Serenity*

Dystopian governments do hate the misbehavers, but the misbehavers are always the heroes of the story, whether it's Tally in the Uglies series, Mal in *Firefly/Serenity*, Katniss in *The Hunger Games*, or even Emmet, the plucky construction-worker hero of *The LEGO Movie*. Most of these heroes are ultimately provoked into violent resistance against their oppressive governments, but we're going to spend two full chapters cautioning against that. Dystopian governments *want* to provoke violence—then they have a solid reason to break out the big guns and demolish the resistance.[34] Given that it's a pretty good bet that the state has both more *and* bigger guns than the

Figure 1.3 Anonymous #StandingMan posters.
Source: Public domain.

resistance, engaging the state on its terms is not usually a good idea. In real life, David almost never beats Goliath. That's not to say that people shouldn't resist—just that they should resist on their own terms, not the government's. A 2013 protest from Turkey provides an excellent example.

In 2013 there were massive antigovernment protests in Turkey. Many turned violent, so the government began a brutal crackdown—beating protesters, targeting medics who were treating the wounded, and even revoking the licenses of medical personnel who treated protesters. In response to this brutality, a protester named Erdem Gunduz stood his ground. Literally. He just stood. For hours. Police prodded him. They tried to provoke him. He just stood, passively resisting. With this simple, still, and silent protest, Gunduz did something that no one else had been able to do: he stopped the government in its tracks. The *Guardian* nailed the government's dilemma: "Gunduz's protest was both an affront and a question for the authorities: beat him? Why? He's just standing there. Leave him alone? Then he wins, doesn't he?"[35]

Once the image of Turkey's #StandingMan (*#duranadam*) went viral, people all over Turkey began to emulate him. In the nonviolent-resistance arsenal, silence "is a method . . . for expressing moral condemnation."[36] This became evident when #StandingMan protests were staged at the sites of government brutality. While the standing protests did not bring down the government, they showed the government that although the protests were silent, the *protesters* would not be silenced.[37]

We will go into more detail on methods of resistance in a few chapters, but for now remember: everyday acts of nonviolent resistance *can* and *do* work. Nonviolent resistance has brought down governments in Africa, Asia, South America, and Europe. Nonviolent techniques like the #StandingMan protests have been used successfully from Argentina to Thailand. During Argentina's "Dirty War" (1976–1983), the government "disappeared" tens of thousands of people. In response, the mothers of the disappeared protested in the Plaza de Mayo outside the presidential palace. The Mothers of the Plaza de Mayo faced government ridicule, and when that failed to cow them, the government turned to brutality. Some of the Mothers were even disappeared. *Nevertheless, they persisted.* When the regime was on its last legs, the Mothers ramped up their protests, inspired others to protest, and made it impossible for the regime to keep the issue of the disappeared out of the public eye during the transition to democracy.[38]

In the Thai case, Thailand's military staged a coup d'état in 1991, ostensibly to curb government corruption and push through constitutional changes. But, inspired by the scholar Gene Sharp's writings on nonviolent action,[39] Thai civil society refused to allow the military to go unchallenged. NGOs, democratic politicians, and student groups used standard tactics such as protests, demonstrations, and even a hunger strike—but they also resisted by pulling money out of the Thai military bank and refusing to do business with known soldiers. It worked: the military relinquished control in 1992, and a new constitution—one with a guaranteed right to nonviolent protest—was passed.[40]

All governments rely on the support of the people—when enough people withdraw their support, a dystopian state *will* fall.[41] The basic idea here is rooted in **social-contract** theory. In the absence of protest, a dystopian government can claim legitimacy and "authorization" from the people it represents. Violent protestors can be dismissed as hooligans or lawbreakers. But a nonviolent protest removes the assumption of consent without giving the government justification to repress it—it cleverly breaks the underlying social contract in a visible and effective way.

Social contract: During the Enlightenment era, Hobbes, Locke, and Rousseau explicated the theory that government is the result of a "compact" or "contract" either among citizens or between citizens and rulers. The idea, however, is even older; we trace its origins back to the Magna Carta ("Great Charter") of 1215, when a group of nobles forced King John of England to sign a document limiting the supposed "divine right" of kings. Translation: John could no longer do whatever he damn well pleased. He became (somewhat) accountable to the nobles.

FINAL THOUGHTS

The future is always a dystopia in movies.
—Alex Cox, writer and film director

Despite what the movies tell you, dystopian futures are *not* inevitable, and present-day dystopias are not permanent. When you're living in a real-life dystopia, though, it can *feel* like there's no way to bring it down. Keep in mind that authoritarian regimes go to great lengths to make you feel that way; if you feel like the regime is impervious to resistance, then you won't resist. In the next chapter, we discuss the hallmarks of dystopian states—and much of what we discuss is related to making you feel that the regime is all-powerful. Don't believe it.

2

Defining Dystopia

The point at which you know you're under totalitarianism is when a peaceful protest crowd is fired upon. You're getting close to it when that happens just a little. But when you have a full-out shutdown, then there aren't any more protests because people know what will happen.

—Margaret Atwood

The easiest way to know you're in a dystopian state is when you find that there are no civil liberties to speak of. We will explore what we mean by "civil liberties"—and the complexities of that concept—in this book. But first we will identify what we might call the "hallmarks" of dystopian government. This does not mean that all dystopian states will be (or do) all of these things—far from it. In fact and fiction, dystopian governments are surprisingly agile and inventive in their creative mixing of various governmental forms, institutions, ideologies, and strategies of control.

These hallmarks are therefore only a partial catalogue. Not all dictatorial dystopian governments will manifest these traits, and not all of these traits will be used by any particular government. But they are worth listing and exploring, if only because so many of these hallmarks come up again and again, to the point that we can sometimes use them to classify a regime as "dystopian."

So let's get into it. What are the hallmarks of a dictatorial dystopian government, in fiction and in real life?

WHATEVER IT TAKES

The most famous dystopian governments, like that of Big Brother in Orwell's *1984*, tend to be totalitarian. Totalitarian states are those that seek to change and control every aspect of society. Typically, they are one-party states driven by an extremist ideology. The political scientist James Scott explains how authoritarian governments use extreme ideologies to remake the state:

> [This ideology] is best conceived as a strong, one might even say muscle-bound, version of the self-confidence about scientific and technical progress, the expansion of production, the growing satisfaction of human needs, the mastery of nature (including human nature), and, above all, the rational design of social order commensurate with the scientific understanding of natural laws.[1]

The danger is that an authoritarian government has no problem doing *whatever it takes* to make its vision of society a reality.[2] In both fiction and fact, some of these states are more totalitarian than others. In this section, we're mostly going to talk about the most totalitarian governments—the ones most willing to exercise the power of the state in pursuit of *full* control.

In the "most totalitarian" category, you have the fictional states found in *We*, *1984*, *The Handmaid's Tale*, and so on, wherein the state controls almost every aspect of life. The state tells you what to think, how to feel, how to act, how to dress—how to *be*. It even dictates when to eat, when to sleep, when (and with whom) to have sex. In *The Handmaid's Tale*, the state even dictates a specific, symbolic, and highly uncomfortable sexual position for the Commander, his Wife, and their Handmaid. Examples of totalitarian states are everywhere in dystopian literature because they capture the imagination; they clearly show what we don't want. The most famous work in this class is probably Orwell's *1984*.

Novels like *1984* don't come out of thin air. Orwell was particularly obsessed with Stalin and Stalinist tactics (see also *Animal Farm*), but it's also clear that Hitler and the Nazi regime in Germany, Franco in Spain, and others of that ilk were not far from his mind.[3] In particular, he was worried about a state that could claim without serious opposition that "two and two were five," as his Big Brother can do in *1984*. Big Brother is your classic dictator type—he even has a mustache, for full effect. He is the personification of the state, omniscient and omnipresent, making all of the decisions for the state of Oceania and its people.[4]

While some might think that the extreme control exercised by Big Brother can only happen in fiction, they'd be wrong. The historian Mary R.

Beard makes that point plain in her description of the power of the Nazi Women's Bureau (Frauenwerk) and its leader, Reichsfrauenführerin Gertrud Scholtz-Klink:

> [She] rules the lives of women in all things. She tells them how many children they must have, and when; what they shall wear, what they shall cook and how. What they shall say, laughing to their husbands and sons marching to war. How they shall behave, smiling, when their men are killed. Here is the responsibility for the home spirit, the core of national morale.[5]

This type of control is at the heart of every totalitarian state, and leaders will go to extreme lengths in order to get and keep control over their citizens. This includes not just the overt force used to coerce compliance but also the social and educational indoctrination that shapes citizens into obedient followers.

FATHER KNOWS BEST

Fictional dystopian states tend to be not just totalitarian but also paternalistic. And we mean that literally—they "raise" their citizens to share the state's ideology, values, and morals. They mold their citizens the way parents mold children. We see this in *1984*, where Big Brother expects Party members to be vigorous, healthy, and, if possible, rugged and outdoorsy (sport is encouraged as a form of state-sponsored play). The ideal citizen is young, healthy, attractive, but asexual (although once married, heterosexual pairs may "do their service to the Party" to produce little Party members). Winston Smith, the main character, in no way measures up. He is middle-aged, unfit, lustful—and not for his wife (with whom he has failed to produce a little Party member).

Similarly, in Zamyatin's *We*, the One State (so named because the entire world is ruled by this one state) delineates the perfect citizen—or in their case, "cypher." A good cypher is rational, unemotional, and wholly committed to the One State. A good cypher has no imagination, nor a pesky soul to interfere with the cypher's rational and orderly mind. Indeed, when our protagonist, D-503 (cyphers don't get names), develops a soul, his doctor tells him that the soul is incurable. After D-503's new soul leads him to love and his love leads him to rebellion, the One State surgically excises his soul in order to return him to the perfect state of soulless cypherdom.

In the Uglies series, by Scott Westerfeld, the government uses surgery both to sculpt uniformly beautiful people ("Pretties") and to create brain lesions that make all of the Pretties less intelligent and more compliant. Westerfeld gives new meaning to the phrase "It's okay. You're pretty." The ideal young citizen is pretty and *bubbly*—the Pretties' word to describe things that are cool and exciting. In middle age, citizens undergo additional surgery that transforms them into Middle Pretties, who are a calm and reassuring presence, helping maintain order in the Pretty universe. In older age, citizens are transformed into Late Pretties (a.k.a. "Crumblies"), who are far removed from the goings on of the young and bubbly set. At all stages of prettification, though, obedient beauty is the duty of the perfect citizen, and disobedient citizens will likely be given a few more brain lesions to induce compliance.

YOU'LL FEEL LIKE A NEW MAN

Just like their fictional counterparts, real-world totalitarian states are paternalistic. They work hard to implant the state's belief system into each citizen.[6] Both the Soviets and the Nazis indoctrinated citizens with their ideologies and expected those citizens to behave as standard-bearers of the state—model citizens, or "new men," if you will.[7] Each of the regimes, Nazi and Soviet, had its own conceptions of the model citizen, but both discussed the model citizen using the term the "New Man," *Mensch* and *Chelovek*, respectively. Although the two were polar opposites in ideology, their concepts of the New Man were similar in that they meant "man" in the "humanity" sense of the word. Each regime wanted to remake its men *and* women into a new type of citizen, turning Germans into Nazis and Russians into Soviets.

In the Nazi case, Hitler and his henchmen wanted his people to be the best Aryans they could be, within explicitly defined gender roles. As the historian Claudia Koontz puts it, "Men in the Nazi state would direct politics, the economy, and the military; women would breed 'absolutely healthy bodies.'"[8] The ideal Nazi citizen (male or female)—portrayed beautifully in Philip K. Dick's book *The Man in the High Castle*—was obedient, blonde, blue eyed, racially pure, and in excellent health. The ideal Nazi man was a warrior and defender of the Aryan race. As such, he should be an exceptional physical specimen, possessed of uncommon valor, and willing to "fight stubbornly and die laughing."[9]

The ideal Nazi woman was, according to the Frauenwerk, "brave, German, and pure."[10] She should be an excellent wife and mother, and she should bear as many children as she could for the Fatherland. These children were her contribution to the success of the Reich, so women who had large broods received a fancy medal called the Cross of Honor of the German Mother, on which the inscription read "The Child Ennobles the Mother."[11] A woman with four living children received the bronze, eight living children the silver, and ten living children the gold. To be fair, the French gave a similar medal—but French mothers didn't get a bronze until they got to five living children. Also, when you birthed number 5, you could name a Nazi leader as the godfather of the baby—"but when Hindenburg proved more popular than Hitler...the program was suspended."[12] Men and women who were not racially pure or who were deemed unfit for procreation were often sterilized and prevented from marrying.[13]

In building *their* New Man, the Soviets had zero interest in racial purity. Their interest was in producing citizens (and lots of them) who exemplified and extolled the Soviet goal of the universal liberation of humanity through socialism. The ideal Soviet man, particularly in Stalin's time, was an intellectually brilliant and physically strong exemplar of the proletariat. He was the working man's working man.[14] Early on, the ideal Soviet woman was an "equal" comrade—a working woman, freed (by the state) from childrearing.[15] That didn't last long, given the Soviets' perceived concerns about falling birthrates.[16] By the 1930s, the ideal Soviet woman was a robust working woman *and* the mother of the nation. Like the Nazis, the Soviets were big on medals for women who bore a lot of children. The medals came with snazzy titles: five to six kids got you the "Motherhood Medal" (second and first class, respectively), seven to nine kids got you the "Order of Motherhood Glory" (third to first class, respectively), and ten or more got you the title of "Mother Heroine," complete with a certificate from the Supreme Soviet.[17]

In both the Soviet and Nazi cases, the New Man sacrificed all for the good of the state and was disciplined, focused, and supremely loyal to it. Few Nazis or Soviets lived up to this ideal, but that didn't stop other

Figure 2.1 Propaganda posters of Nazi and Soviet families.
Source: Public domain.

totalitarian states from attempting to build their own New Men. In China, Chairman Mao envisioned the ideal Chinese citizen, the *duomianshou*, as an "omnicompetent ideal person."[18] The *duomianshou* would be "the jack-of-all-trades, whose life would combine in equal measure the responsibilities of the worker, the peasant, the soldier, and the student."[19] And the Kim dynasty in North Korea also seems to have been aiming for the "ideal communist 'new man,' an altruistic citizen dedicated to the welfare of his countrymen."[20] Of course, it takes a strong commitment to the state's ideology to maintain a totalitarian level of paternalism, so most authoritarian states in real life are far less paternalistic than their fictional totalitarian counterparts.

In the "less paternalistic" category, we would put the Alliance, from Joss Whedon's *Firefly*, and the overly bureaucratic government of Terry Gilliam's film *Brazil*. These governments, while authoritarian, are mostly content to let people live their lives, provided they don't challenge the powers that be. In real life these would be the Saddam Husseins (Iraq) and Robert Mugabes (Zimbabwe) of the world. They weren't trying to change every aspect of their societies; they just wanted to keep and exploit their power, usually for reasons of personal gain and/or ego. We don't see as many of these in fiction because they aren't as extreme—they generally don't make for good copy. We'll be talking a lot about them later, though, because these nontotalitarian authoritarian regimes are *everywhere* in the real world.

A PLACE FOR EVERYTHING AND EVERYTHING IN ITS PLACE

In the past the man has been first; in the future the system must be first.
—Frederick W. Taylor

Dictatorial dystopian states tend to be rule based, orderly, clean, rational, and efficient—in fact, this is often their raison d'etre. Rules make the game more fun for everyone, as any good coach will tell you. Aldous Huxley's *Brave New World* is a masterwork in this tradition; scientific efficiency is at the heart of Huxley's created world. But Margaret Atwood's *The Handmaid's Tale*, Ray Bradbury's *Fahrenheit 451*, George Miller's recent film *Mad Max: Fury Road*, Ally Condie's Matched series, and a host of other key works in this genre demonstrate the state's concern with rules, particularly about who does what and who gets what.

THE IRON FIST OF FICTIONAL EFFICIENCY

Scientific efficiency is also at the heart of some of the most iconic early-twentieth-century dystopian visions, like Zamyatin's *We* or even Fritz Lang's long-lost but recently reconstructed film *Metropolis*. Like *Brave New World*, both *We* and *Metropolis* imagine a rule-bound, conveyor-belt society where the factory-style principles of division of labor and efficiency underlie the structure of work, certainly, but also play, religion, marriage, and other aspects of life. Advanced technology, whatever form that took at the time the work was written, figures prominently in these futuristic visions and mostly serves to distance people from their emotions or their capacity for connection with other humans (and such connection often becomes a large part of the story of resistance in these worlds).

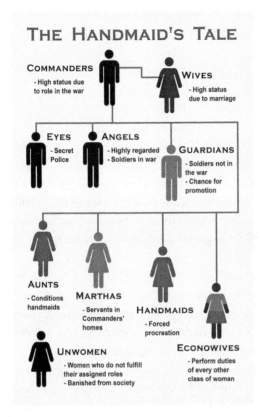

Figure 2.2 Societal hierarchy, Republic of Gilead.

Source: Emily Adair (used with permission).

Often, though, dystopian governments don't need technology to inhibit people's connections. The Republic of Gilead in *The Handmaid's Tale* provides an excellent example. The government is a theocracy, and the rules are nominally religious. (This later turns out to be a front, but everyone pretends it is true.) In this world, everyone fits into some rule-bound and class-conscious category. The hierarchy looks something like figure 2.2. The story centers on a Handmaid named Offred ("Of Fred"—Fred is her "Commander" and head of her household). Handmaids are domestic slaves whose job is supposed to be child bearing. In the book, we don't see much of the outside world, since Handmaids are mostly confined to household activities, but Offred spends a lot of time thinking about the rules that define her entire existence. How she explains these rules and sometimes tries to get around them (like worrying about sneaking a butter pat from her dinner plate into her slipper to use later as contraband face lotion) gives us insight into how strict the Republic of Gilead is and how careful its citizens are about even the smallest-seeming things.

THE NOT-SO-IRON FIST OF REAL
WORLD *IN*EFFICIENCY

In real life, few states are powerful enough to make and enforce rules like the ones in our fictional examples. Many, like Singapore, are unbelievably strict about what may seem like small things—chewing gum comes to mind.[21] But few states have the ability to dictate people's lives to the extent these fictional examples do. Modern China, for instance, is an authoritarian oligarchy, but the state's ability to get things done (its "state capacity") is far from absolute.

The central state (in Beijing) has transferred some power to local governments, including responsibility for suppressing some forms of dissent and for implementing some economic policies. On one hand, this is good for Beijing, since it can now blame local leaders for the mistreatment of local protesters or for the failure of the government's economic policies.[22] On the other hand, decentralization is bad for Beijing because it has compromised the power of the central state. As the political scientist Yang Zhong notes, "Central government [economic] policies are often ignored . . . and the central government is losing fiscal control."[23] And although an authoritarian state is usually good at tamping down resisters, Beijing is plagued by resistance on many fronts.

First, given the comparative ease of transnational communication, the Chinese government is now dealing with a growing cadre of homegrown and high-profile dissenters. For example, the prodemocracy activist Hu Jia won the European Union's prestigious Sakharov Prize for Freedom of Thought in 2008, the dissident and human rights activist Liu Xiaobo won the Nobel Prize in 2010, and the artist/dissident Ai WeiWei was awarded the Václav Havel Prize for Creative Dissent in 2012 *and* the Amnesty International Ambassador of Conscience Award in 2015.

Next, Beijing is facing a relatively nonviolent separatist movement in Tibet and a substantially more violent separatist movement in Xinjiang from its Uyghur ("*wee-gur*") Muslim minority. And although we don't have enough space to fully address the pressure Beijing is under as a result of quasi-autonomous/quasi-democratic Taiwan and Hong Kong, suffice it to say that China's "one country, two systems" approach—in which the mainland remains autocratic and both Taiwan and Hong Kong remain relatively democratic—has not fully quelled anti-China sentiment and rhetoric in either Taiwan or Hong Kong. Finally, Beijing has a middle-class problem. Political science professors can go on ad nauseam about the role of the middle class in bringing about democracy, but we'll keep it short: a growing/educated middle class tends to organize (often with the working class) to demand political reforms—after all, if you're paying the bulk of the taxes, you want a say in how they're spent.[24]

Would the governments in *1984*, *We*, or *The Handmaid's Tale* allow anything like this to happen in their worlds? No. But China is no Big Brother, One State, or Republic of Gilead. Although our fictional dystopias have total control over their people, China simply doesn't have enough state capacity to rule with an iron fist over every aspect of society. Fictional governments have the advantage in that books tend to have a small cast of characters, and the author can ensure that the characters' actions fit the storyline. In reality, it is almost impossible to fully regulate all human behaviors.

YOU WILL BE ASSIMILATED

Consider the Borg, a dystopian sci-fi alien race introduced in *Star Trek: The Next Generation* and near the top of the list of the "nastiest villains of all time," according to *TV Guide*.[25] The Borg are cybernetic organisms—part flesh, part machine—and have a hive-mind society; there is no "I" in Borg. The Borg Queen does the thinking for all of them, and they obey without question, increasing their ranks by "assimilating" any other species they come across. "Resistance is futile" is their motto, and up until they come across the *Enterprise*, it works for them.

In dictatorial dystopias, people exist to serve the state, not the other way around. So it is best if people are standardized—scientifically, if possible. Much dystopian fiction centers on this fear, that the state is trying to make "we, the people" into some faceless, conforming mass, to take away not just our rights but our individuality, the qualities we think make us "us." In many fictional dystopian states, individualism is frowned upon. In the Uglies series, this is quite literal; everyone gets surgery at age sixteen to become "pretty" (in a highly standardized and Eurocentric way)—and while they're at it, the doctors remove key brain functions too, to prevent the kind of individual creative thinking that might lead to questions that would be awkward for the state.

In real life, this desire to reduce individuality may be true of totalitarian states, but it is less true of other forms of dictatorship. Not untrue, just less so—authoritarian states have no respect for individual rights, civil liberties, etc., but they also may not feel a need to be totally controlling (which, let's face it, takes a lot of work). It depends on how ideological the ruler or rulers are. Some dystopian fiction reimagines this, so the danger is not as clearly state oppression of the individual, but that is in the background. In *Brave New World*, for example, there is no Borg hive-think. And there doesn't need to be. The individual has choices about how to live and work and relate to other people, but only to a point—there is still no marriage, no real thinking, and no real human connection; those are the things that can get you into trouble. But, hey, sleep with who you want! ("Everybody belongs to everybody else," the citizens are taught from an embryonic age.)

WHAT FRESH HELL IS THIS?
CLASSIFYING DYSTOPIAS

Although we are trying to keep things entertaining here, dystopian governments are no joke. Even the fictional ones are terrifying. So far, we have tended to talk about horrible governments as if they are all alike. This is not strictly accurate. As the political scientist Barbara Geddes put it:

Different kinds of authoritarianism differ from each other as much as they differ from democracy. They draw on different groups to staff government offices and different segments of society for support. They have different procedures for making decisions, different ways of handling the choice of leaders and succession, and different ways of responding to society and opponents.[26]

We often lump dystopias together because it is a useful way to explain the things they have in common, and this way we don't have to explain stuff over and over. It is useful, though, for you to understand that there are different types of nondemocratic states. Because this is political science, there's not a ton of agreement on how we should classify all of the different types of nondemocratic regimes. The debate comes from the fact that dictators have come up with a wide variety of ways to control their societies and, while nondemocratic regimes have a lot in common, it's hard to categorize some of them. But we'll try.

The first important distinction is totalitarian versus authoritarian.[27] We talked about totalitarian states extensively in this chapter, so you already know that the classic fictional totalitarian states are Big Brother in *1984* and the One State in *We* and that the archetypes in real life are Nazi Germany, Soviet Russia, and the Kim family's North Korea. What all of these states have in common is that the state controls every aspect of society—to the point that the line between state and society is blurred. The *totalitarian* state has a particular ideological bent (fascism in Nazi Germany, communism in Soviet Russia, and *Juche* in North Korea),[28] and seeks to superimpose that ideology on society by co-opting not just the institutions of government but also social structures (clubs, social organizations, the church, etc.), turning them into extensions of the state.

Authoritarian states, on the other hand, aren't really into imposing an ideology on the people, and they don't co-opt your social organizations in order to better control you. In fact, limited **pluralism** is a defining characteristic of authoritarian regimes (versus totalitarian regimes, in which no pluralism is allowed at all). Authoritarians don't care what you believe so long as you obey, so they leave control of the population up to the security apparatus (the military and police). The authoritarian category is where we get a lot of variation in how the government is set up, how decisions are made, and so on. Box 2.1 provides a handy cheat sheet of the most commonly discussed types.

Pluralism is the idea of representation of groups in the governing structure. This is based on the idea that power should not be concentrated in the hands of the few. Different groups (religious, civil, ethnic, etc.) should have a say in how they are governed. Policy, then, would be a result of competition among these groups. Full pluralism would be dangerous to a dictator, but limited pluralism could be possible in a dictatorship because only a few groups would be allowed to operate, and their participation in politics would be tightly controlled.

BOX 2.1: VARIETIES OF AUTHORITARIANISM

MONARCHY: A royal family controls the state, and power is passed from one member of the family to the next.[29]

Fictional example: Red Queen (Aveyard)   *Real examples:* Bahrain, Eswatini

---

PERSONALIST: A single dictator personally controls policies and officials. The dictator likely has the support of the security apparatus, but the security apparatus doesn't have the ability to control or limit the dictator's actions.[30]

Fictional examples: President Business   *Real examples:* Vladimir Putin in
in *The LEGO Movie*, Lord Voldemort in   Russia, Saddam Hussein in Iraq
the Harry Potter series

SINGLE-PARTY: Access to power is controlled by a single party; that party exercises influence over the chief executive.[31]

Fictional examples: It Can't Happen   *Real examples:* Communist Party of
Here (Lewis)   China, Revolutionary Party of Tanzania

MILITARY: This one can get complicated because of the variety within the category (and because bureaucratic-authoritarian states tend to be military led), but we're keeping it simple: rule by the military, usually a group of senior officers. Their rule can be out in the open, or they can be pulling the strings behind the scenes.[32]

Fictional example: Cardassian Central   *Real examples:* Myanmar (1962–2011),
Command, *Star Trek: Deep Space 9*   Nigeria (1966–1998)[33]

BUREAUCRATIC-AUTHORITARIAN: Control of the government by an elite group, often—but not always—military men. These elites found their (often brutal) govern-ments on the idea that economic progress and social stability require a strong technocratic (rule by experts) hand. The leadership typically originates from the highest levels of the military or public bureaucracy—or even the corporate bureaucracy.[34]

Fictional example: Manhã Cinzenta   *Real examples:* Argentina (1966–1973),
(Grey morning)[35]   Chile (1973–1990)

HYBRID/SEMI-AUTHORITARIAN: There are multiple types of hybrid regimes—most types of authoritarian systems aren't mutually exclusive, so you can have combinations of different institutions from different types of nondemocratic states.[36] You can also have elements of both democracy (e.g., competitive elections) and authoritarianism (e.g., disregard for civil rights/civil liberties).[37]

Fictional example: Feed (Anderson)[38]   *Real example:* Venezuela (1998–present),
    Pakistan (2008–present)[39]

THEOCRACY: Rule by religion—either religious authorities are in charge, or the entire system is based on religious principles or law.

Fictional example: The Handmaid's   *Real example:* The Holy See (Vatican
Tale (Atwood)   City)[40]

There are two types of dystopias you won't find in box 2.1. The first is the *capitocracy*, and it's not here because—despite the mass of modern dystopian capitocratic fiction—no capitocracies actually exist. Modern dystopians would argue that a capitocracy just doesn't exist *yet*; they would point to the rise of laissez-faire (low government involvement) capitalism as a sign that we're headed toward capitocracy. The second one that's not here is the *failed state* dystopia. The failed state isn't in box 2.1 because there's no functional government in a failed state, and if there's no real government, it can't be authoritarian. Failed states often give rise to other bad forms of government, like when warlords arise to fill the power vacuum (nature abhors a vacuum, so someone *always* fills the void) and then turn into personalist dictators. We'll be discussing capitocracies in the next chapter and failed states throughout the book, so you might want to make a note of them.

FINAL THOUGHTS

Dystopian fiction gives us some good stories, sure, but also some great political science and philosophy to chew on. Dystopian governments, as we hope you are seeing, are fascinating, endlessly inventive, and important to study and understand. They can be totalitarian or not, but they tend to be authoritarian in some form. They will want to dictate (hence, "dictator") your actions, and some also want to control your thoughts. The fiction telling us about these states does not come out of thin air; in fact, the reality of terrible government usually comes first, and then artists and authors respond to it.

Having introduced you to some basic defining characteristics of dystopian government and some of the classics of dystopian fiction, we next turn to some new trends in the fiction (which, of course, mirror recent happenings in real life). The next chapter looks at how the trends in the modern global economy and environment have inspired a tremendous amount of new capitocratic dystopian fiction and what that means for how we understand the role one of the most important factors in government—the economy.

3

The Invisible Hand Strikes Again

The beauty of dystopia is that it lets us vicariously experience
future worlds—but we still have the power to change our own.

—Ally Condie, author of the dystopian novel *Matched*

For more than a century, dystopian fiction has given its creators a useful and artistic vehicle for hard-hitting social commentary. It magnifies contemporary patterns or trends to warn us about what could result from them in the future. Such fiction, then, is closely linked to the times—and especially the politics—of its creation. It is no surprise, then, that for much of the twentieth century, the great evil was seen as overbearing government. What George Orwell, Aldous Huxley, Sinclair Lewis, and Ray Bradbury were afraid of most was totalitarianism—and with good reason, considering what they witnessed. Think about Orwell's *1984* in the context of the looming specter of Soviet communism or about Lewis's *It Can't Happen Here* as a reaction against the ease with which fascism took root in some European states in the 1920s and 1930s. Oppressive government and how it stifled individuality and the human spirit were at the center of dystopian fiction from World War I to the Cold War.

Many modern dystopian works feature not communist or fascist governments but "capitocratic" governments, meaning rule by capitalism/market forces. This major shift in the focus of dystopian fiction really gained steam in the mid-1980s, with the "power of the authoritarian state giv[ing] way to the more pervasive tyranny of the corporation," as the dystopia scholar Tom Moylan puts it.[1] Moylan points out a feature of all dystopian fiction is that people's lives are controlled by the state. The difference in capitocratic dystopias is that people's lives are also exploited and *commodified* by the state, meaning that people's lives are treated as commodities that can be bought and sold.

In your basic capitocracy, business has "captured" government—meaning the state serves business interests rather than citizens' interests. These are often tales of the market run amok—where everything and anything has been commodified. Some of the most famous fictional capitocracies are Margaret Atwood's 2003 book *Oryx and Crake* (and its sequels), Marge Piercy's 1991 book *He, She, and It*, Neal Stephenson's cult classic *Snow Crash* from 1992, and Octavia Butler's 1993 *The Parable of the Sower*. In these, the government fails to protect its citizens from the ravages of unrestrained capitalism and/or the climate change capitalism has caused. Less well-known examples include the "Oxygen" episode of the TV series *Doctor Who*, where everyone on a space station must pay for the air they breathe (see also Frederik Pohl's 1977 book *Gateway)*; Gregory Scott Katsoulis's novel *All Rights Reserved®*, where you have to pay rights holders for any words you speak; and the musical comedy *Urinetown*, where you have to pay someone each time you pee. In all of these examples, the majority of people are poor and live a precarious existence without enough food, water, jobs, or security. The lucky ones who can escape live in "company towns," in Butler's parlance (called "enclaves" in Stephenson's work, or "compounds" in Atwoodian parlance), where the company provides for their employees' needs.

In a more specialized form of capitocracy, the *corporatocracy*, the government has been completely taken over by a megacorporation. Three great

Figure 3.1 Adbusters' United States of Corporations Flag.
Source: Public domain, via Wikimedia Commons.

COMPARING DYSTOPIAS THE REDUCTIO AD ABSURDUM OF INTELLECTUAL
PROPERTY LAWS

Country: United States of America, present day

Freedom House Score: 89 (free)

Background: Article 1, Section 8, Clause 8 of the U.S. Constitution is the Patent and Copyright Clause. Yes: copyrights and patents were so important that the Founding Fathers put them in the Constitution.

The intent of this clause was to balance a work's economic value to its creator versus the societal benefits of free use of the work.[3] In keeping with the founders' idea that patents and copyrights be in place for a limited time, intellectual property rights historically expired after thirty-two years. After the copyright or patent expires, the work enters the *public domain*, meaning anyone is free to use it without first obtaining permission from the (former) rights holder. The U.S. Congress, responding to pressure from corporations like the Walt Disney Company, has now extended that to nearly one hundred years and will likely extend it again in 2019. Corporations want to profit from a work for as long as they can . . . but if we privilege *corporate* interests over *public* interests, then we inhibit the free exchange of ideas that helps stimulate creativity and invention. Arguably, keeping Disney's *Steamboat Willie*[4] out of the public domain doesn't harm any sort of societal progress. However, the fact that corporations have patented things like DNA sequences really *can* harm our scientific progress and perhaps our individual human rights.

Current U.S. law allows trademarking of common words/phrases. For example, the scholar Kembrew McLeod trademarked "freedom of expression,"[5] and the socialite Paris Hilton trademarked "That's hot." This does not restrict *all* uses of the phrase, just uses for commercial purposes. Also, the rights are not held in perpetuity; they must be renewed.

Sharing of not just music files but all sorts of uses of music have been increasingly restricted by ever-more-stringent copyright law. Traditional songs like "Happy Birthday to You," "This Land Is Your Land," and "God Bless America," were all copyrighted and their commercial use was constrained, though the rights holders could decide what was and was not allowed. For example, the American Society of Composers, Authors, and Publishers (ASCAP) attempted to force the Girl Scouts of America (GSA) to purchase a license in order to use the latter two songs at Girl Scout summer camps, threatening the GSA with fines and *jail time* for unauthorized performances. Public outcry forced ASCAP to back down, but the GSA has to pay a symbolic $1/year for use of the songs.[6]

---

examples are the Tyrell Corporation in *Blade Runner*, which seems to control what the government does and does not do; the "Buy-n-Large" corporation in *Wall-E*, whose CEO is also the U.S. president; and *The LEGO Movie*, where our hero Emmet tells us that President Business is "president of Octan Company . . . and the world."

Modern fears about hypercapitalism are both about its effects on us as people (as workers and citizens but also on our desires and our souls) and its effects on our planet. As scientific data about environmental

COMPARING DYSTOPIAS THE REDUCTIO AD ABSURDUM OF INTELLECTUAL PROPERTY LAWS

Country: America* in *All Rights Reserved (ARR)*

Freedom House Score: 5 (not free)

Background: *ARR* is set in a future America* where speech is no longer free—rights holders own every word and gesture. After the age of fifteen, people have to pay the rights holders for every word they speak and every gesture they make. Communication is monitored by a cuff that's permanently affixed to a person's wrist (the government also makes everyone get corneal implants so that people's eyes can be shocked every time they use words they can't pay for). Since paper cannot easily be monitored, people aren't allowed to have it. In America*, the premise of economic benefit from intellectual property has completely overridden the societal benefits of free expression. People don't write books, and since every note is copyrighted, no one can write music. People, particularly poor people, lead a relatively empty existence because it's expensive to develop relationships. (This is grade-A atomization—make it expensive to talk *and* monitor what they say at all times.) *All Rights Reserved* is the reductio ad absurdum of current intellectual property laws in the United States—it's about what *could* happen if we continue to go down the ever-more restrictive, ever-more-corporation-friendly path we're currently on. Here, we contrast current U.S. laws with the laws presented in *ARR*. The parallels are, as *ARR*'s author likely intended, seriously freaky.

In America*, all words are copyrighted, trademarked, registered, or restricted. Words are paid for at Word$ Market™ prices each day ("Sorry" is a fixed $10 charge). Rights holders own the words in perpetuity. Individual rights holders can pass ownership down to their heirs. Music—of all types—is never free in America*. The Musical Rights Association of America* (MRAA) has locked down not just all written music but every combination of notes that could ever possibly be written. Writing new songs incurs massive fines from the MRAA, as does playing music without first securing a license. The Historical Reparations Agency can dredge up intellectual property crimes (like illegal downloads) committed by a person's ancestor; that person is then responsible for paying centuries' worth of royalties for that ancestral download. Adults who cannot pay are taken into Collections to work off their debt. Their children are made wards of the state.

---

degradation has mounted in the past few decades, authors have responded with dystopias set in worlds ruined by climate change, like Paolo Bacigalupi's novels *Ship Breaker* and *The Drowned Cities*. Recent films also depict dystopias: the movies *Snowpiercer* and *The Day After Tomorrow* both envision a world trapped in a new ice age, with few humans surviving.

Rampant consumerism and unchecked capitalism, these works are saying, pose grave threats to both humanity and the environment. We still fear too-powerful governments (and we should), but modern dystopian authors are warning us that a lack of strong government (particularly government capable of reining in business excess) can be equally disastrous.

Good government needs to strike a balance; it should be neither the fascism of *1984* nor the tyranny of the market in capitocratic dystopias. The economist John Kenneth Galbraith, writing in 1952, clearly saw that businesses needed some "countervailing power," like trade unions or the state,[2] to prevent large corporations from engaging in harmful, unethical, and coercive behavior, like exploiting workers, setting prices, and engaging in monopoly. Our preferred form of a countervailing force to business power is good government. If democracy is the cure for dystopia, a democracy with a solid social safety net—a **social welfare system**—is the cure for capitocracy.

> A **social welfare system** provides programs that prevent citizens from being destitute in the event of a crisis—like unemployment, illness, or disability. These programs often attempt to reduce poverty, particularly among vulnerable groups like children and the elderly.

Today's capitocratic dystopias are the reductio ad absurdum of current political and economic trends. That is, they take some current trend and exaggerate it, extrapolating what the future might look like if that current thing is allowed to continue. To put the current capitocratic and environmental themes in dystopian fiction into context, this chapter examines some key history and the capitalist ideology that has become the dominant force in modern politics.

A good governing system is the first step, and, as we've stated many times, democratic governance is the best way to prevent dystopia. Unfortunately, democratic government can easily be undermined by hypercapitalist pressures, which hurt citizens and put the state at risk of environmental catastrophe. The good news from history (yes, there is some) is that things can change. In particular, workers and consumers can be protected from the worst effects of capitalism—but only with activism and good government.

THE CAPITALIST UTOPIAN IDEAL

If you've ever taken an economics class, chances are you've heard the phrase "the invisible hand" of the market. The phrase was popularized in Adam Smith's classic 1776 tome *The Wealth of Nations*.[7] The premise is that the market—a collection of individuals pursuing their own self-interests—will benefit society even when public good isn't the goal. In Smith's conception, **economic liberalism** is the best mechanism for social improvement.

In Smith's ideal world, the market will be largely self-regulating *and* self-correcting—market forces would (a) police the behavior of market participants and (b) fix most of the problems market participants might create (like unfair wages or poor working conditions).[8] As the scholar David Harvey put it, Adam Smith's was a "utopianism in which individual desires, avarice, greed, drives, creativity and the like could be mobilized through the hidden hand of the perfected market to the social benefit of all."[9]

> **Economic liberalism**
> (a.k.a. "classical liberalism")
> is the idea that people are
> the best judges of their own
> needs, the market is the best
> mechanism for the allocation
> of resources in society, the
> government should not
> interfere in the market, and
> barriers to free trade are bad
> for the economy.

In other words, in a capitalist utopia, an individual's selfish and greedy impulses aren't necessarily bad, since the invisible hand of the market will aggregate everyone's selfish and greedy impulses into a net positive for all of society.

THE CAPITALIST DYSTOPIAN REALITY

Is the condition of the English working people wrong; so wrong that rational working men cannot, will not, and even should not rest under it?
—Thomas Carlyle

The Wealth of Nations was written during the early stages of the Industrial Revolution, and it might not yet have been clear how unrestrained capitalism would affect the workers.[10] It was a time of intense social change, rapid innovation, and scientific progress, all of which likely influenced Smith. The Swedish social scientist Gunnar Myrdal pegged it when he said, "a sunny optimism radiates from Smith's writing."[11] As the world became more industrial, it became clear that Smith's optimism about a self-regulating and self-correcting market that benefits everyone was unwarranted.

If you've read any of Charles Dickens's novels, you probably have a sense of the poverty and squalor that were the lot of most working people in Victorian-era England.[12] Although Thomas Hobbes wrote the phrase "nasty, brutish, and short" to refer to life in a state of nature, the phrase also applied to life in English factories and mines of the eighteenth and nineteenth centuries.[13]

The jobs involved long hours, intense physical labor, and such low wages that poverty was "not so much the special experiences of a particular group

Figure 3.2 *Midnight at the Glassworks*, Lewis W. Hine, 1908.
Source: Public domain, via Wikimedia Commons.

in the labor force as a regular feature of the life of almost *all* working families."[14] Families with young children or elderly members were particularly disadvantaged; children typically couldn't be put to work until they were five or six, and the elderly could no longer keep up with the brutal pace required of factory workers. (In fact, given the working conditions and grinding poverty, many people didn't live to see their forty-second birthday.)[15] Poverty, malnutrition, and overwork resulted in death rates in industrial areas that were more than double the death rates in the rest of England, with women's death rates in some areas being *triple* the national rate. Infant mortality, too, was appallingly high—15 to 20 percent of all babies died in infancy. To put this in context: the country with the world's highest infant mortality rate in the modern era, the Central African Republic, was 89 of every 1,000 births (8.9 percent) in 2016.[16]

Working conditions were horrific. Factories were built to economize on space, meaning they were cramped, with low ceilings and few windows. They were dark, dirty, and unsafe, just like the mines of the time. In cotton mills, the lint in the air caused lung disease; in coal mines, deaths from explosions or collapse overshadowed the chronic respiratory illnesses that more often caused miners' deaths. Cramped and unhygienic factories, plus the overcrowded slum housing in which laborers lived, were ideal breeding grounds for infectious diseases—and the combination of infectious diseases and malnutrition was a recipe for death.[17]

On top of all of this, the factory and mine owners had complete control over their businesses; there was no oversight to ensure decent treatment of workers. If wages could be cut to maximize profits, they were cut. If forcing each worker to work longer hours maximized profits, workers were forced to work longer hours. If physical abuse induced workers to work harder, physical abuse was used. Employers took no responsibility for workers injured on the job—workers were owed wages, and that was all. The demand for labor was such that orphanages sold children into indentured servitude by the hundreds; children are easy to control, so they made

Figure 3.3 *Child Laborer Supporting the Robber Barons* (author unknown, c. 1874).
Source: Public domain, via Wikimedia Commons.

ideal workers. Once in the mills, the children were typically abused and underfed.[18] There are accounts of children as young as three (!) working sixteen-to-eighteen-hour days.[19] We've picked on England here, but conditions were similar in all of the industrializing countries of Europe and North America. It's hard to overstate just how bad it was to be a factory worker or miner in *any* country in the eighteenth and nineteenth centuries.

WORKERS OF THE WORLD, UNITE!

Let the ruling classes tremble at a Communist revolution. The proletarians have nothing to lose but their chains. They have a world to win.
—Karl Marx and Friedrich Engels

It was the hellish landscape of the industrial labor market that inspired Karl Marx to theorize about the likely long-term outcomes of unregulated capitalism. Marx discussed wealth as "the formation of capital, and the reckless exploitation and impoverishing of the mass of the people."[20] He called this mass the "proletariat," from which Orwell drew his term for the poor, "proles." Marx predicted that if the capitalist class didn't stop their ruthless exploitation of the workers, a revolution would ensue: the workers would fight back against the elite.[21]

Since Marx isn't well regarded in today's capitalism-driven world, you can be forgiven if you laughed at his revolutionary fervor—but you have to understand that the leaders of industrializing countries weren't laughing.[22] They had serious concerns that Marx and Engels might actually be right.

It just so happens that, as industrialization continued, Marx's predictions started coming true—the workers started to get fed up, and then they started to organize. Then, in 1871, one of the biggest events in labor history blew up: the Paris Commune. Working-class Parisians united, declared their opposition to the French government's plans to restore the monarchy, elected a leftist city council (called the Paris Commune, which lent its name to the whole event), declared that the French state must recognize the rights of the city of Paris, and—the kicker—to do all of this, they had the audacity to *take up arms* against the French government.[23]

As one historian put it: "The ambitions of the communards were boundless, and their belief in the possibility of social justice, equality, and international solidarity was intense. A new form of government based on mass active democracy was generated—the first workers' state."[24] Even though the Commune was short-lived, conservative leaders in Austria and Denmark were shaken by the events in Paris. In particular, the German chancellor Otto von Bismarck was determined that nothing like that would happen in his newly unified Germany.[25] A shrewd politician, Bismarck quickly implemented a basic social safety net (pension, sickness insurance, and worker's compensation)—not through any love for the working class, mind you.[26] This was a classic divide-and-conquer strategy: he undermined the unity of the working class by giving different benefits to different segments of the populace, in effect creating *multiple* working classes.[27] By undermining their unity, he made it less likely that the working classes would organize against the ruling elite.[28]

The strategy was deemed such a success in preventing a revolution of the proletariat that other states (like Austria and Denmark) quickly adopted Bismarck's reforms. Although Bismarck gave the workers no *say* in the reforms, a highly organized working class led to elites' fear of working-class violence. In turn, elites implemented constraints on capitalism so as to prevent Marx's predicted revolution.[29] Of course, we have no way of knowing if the limited social safety net really *did* prevent a worker revolt; the important thing is that elites believed it would.

Efforts to prevent a workers' revolution were not limited to Europe; in the United States, Teddy Roosevelt saw that workers were the big losers of the Gilded Age. Roosevelt wasn't hostile to industry, but he became hostile toward industry's control of American society. He understood that the public's concerns about the abuses by big business had to be addressed— the people needed to see that the rich and powerful were being held accountable for unfair business practices. Roosevelt became increasingly convinced that, unless workers got a "square deal," the country was headed for a violent revolution.[30] Because of this, he grew increasingly concerned with workers' rights and, in a 1911 editorial, called for government action to "put a stop to the iniquities done in the name of business."[31]

And inequities there were. If you want to understand today's world, especially in the United States, you need to understand the Gilded Age—the period of rapid economic expansion and mass inequality between the mid-1860s and the early 1900s. The term comes from Mark Twain's 1873 satire of the economic and political corruption of the era. This is the era of the "robber barons," the super-rich tycoons who made their fortunes through unfair and exploitative business practices, and government was complicit.

It is no coincidence that one of the very first modern dystopian novels,[32] Jack London's *The Iron Heel* (1908), emerged in this era. Like Roosevelt, London was deeply troubled by massive economic inequality and the growing power of business relative to government. London feared that the Gilded Age was the precursor to a vast oligarchic corporatocracy. The narrator of the book is a twenty-seventh-century academic who reflects on the U.S. Gilded Age:

> Following upon Capitalism, it was held, even by such intellectual and antagonistic giants as Herbert Spencer, that Socialism would come. Out of the decay of self-seeking capitalism, it was held, would arise that flower of the ages, the Brotherhood of Man. Instead of which, appalling to the likes of us who look back and those who lived at the time, capitalism, rotten-ripe, sent forth that monstrous offshoot, the Oligarchy.[33]

Concerns about the treatment of workers were also put front and center by the first dystopian movie, Fritz Lang's *Metropolis*, a German silent black-and-white film from 1927. The protagonist, Freder, is an oblivious rich playboy until he meets and falls in love with Maria, a labor organizer; she shows him the exploitative factories hidden under his city. The life of leisure and beauty enjoyed by the super-rich is only made possible by oppressing workers, Freder learns, and he rebels against his captain-of-industry father.

Figure 3.4 Promotional poster for *Metropolis*, a 1927 film by Fritz Lang.
Source: Public domain via WikiMedia commons.

BOX 3.1: DOWN WITH CAPITALISM! (NOT.)

Okay. We've given you lots of negatives about *unregulated* (or poorly regulated) capitalism. But you know by now that we're deeply skeptical of anyone's utopian claims—and none of the twentieth century's so-called communist states give us faith that communism would go according to Marx and Engels's overly optimistic plan. Although Lenin and his fellow Bolshevik revolutionaries based the Russian Revolution on the ideas of Marx and Engels, the "withering away of the state" Engels wrote about certainly never happened in the Soviet Union (or in any other nominally communist state). Nor did Marx's prediction about the equalization of production and consumption—meaning that in the communist utopia, there would be enough goods to meet everyone's needs—come to pass. Instead, Soviet citizens wound up with the opposite: extreme totalitarian government and a centralized economy that couldn't produce enough of the right goods at the right time.[35]

Over the course of the book, we'll be giving you *a lot* of examples of the dystopian nature of totalitarian Soviet-style governments, but here's one that's of particular interest to fiction lovers: Stalin—because only *he* had the ability to envision the great Soviet future—performed what the literary scholar Erika Gottlieb calls "Stalin's 'fantasectomy,' his banning of works of speculative literature after 1929." Translation: no futuristic novels and no sci-fi(!). At the same time, he gave the power over all literary fiction to the Russian Association of Proletarian Writers, and in 1934 he dictated the rules for writing Soviet fiction in his "Guidelines to Socialist Realism."[36] The rules boiled down to this: all fiction must glorify the utopian Soviet socialist system; anything that criticizes the system is dystopian. We sincerely doubt that Stalin saw the irony of his actions . . . but it wasn't lost on Gottlieb, who points out that Stalin did to Soviet fiction what the One State did to D-503 in Zamyatin's *We*: he excised its soul.

Many Soviet authors worked to subvert Stalin's "Guidelines," delivering pointed criticisms of the Soviet state while technically staying within the rules.[37] A great example comes from Vladimir Dudintsev's 1956 novel *Not by Bread Alone*,[38] in which our main protagonist (Dmitrii Lopatikin) is a model working-class man whose selfless devotion to true Soviet socialism earns him the love of not just one but two women. In true Soviet-hero fashion, Lopatkin invents a machine to increase industrial production. Sadly, he is undermined by rival inventors and jailed at the hands of a corrupt bureaucracy that stifles invention. He is then set free once the truth is revealed and continues his noble fight against the enemies of socialism.[39]

Despite its seeming adherence to the "Guidelines," this is not your average Soviet production novel. Although Dudintsev denied that writing *Not by Bread Alone* was "washing dirty linen in public," the publisher's note at the beginning of the English-language translation reports that "Soviet readers discussing Dudintsev's book . . . used one word more than any other: 'truthful.'"[40] To the Soviet authorities, telling the truth about the flaws in the socialist system was, in fact, airing dirty laundry. The wildly popular book spurred a far-ranging public conversation not only about the issues Dudintsev identified but also about a host of other economic and social problems facing the Soviet Union. Dudintsev was blacklisted, no one would publish his work, and his family ended up impoverished.[41] The government also fired the editor who gave the book the go-ahead and "recommended" he take up voluntary exile in Tashkent, Uzbekistan.[42] Slightly happy ending: Dudintsev made a literary comeback in the 1980s under more moderate Soviet leadership, and he ended up outliving the Soviet state.[43]

Just two short years after *Metropolis* was released, the U.S. stock market crashed, American banks collapsed, and the Great Depression ensued. The crisis wasn't contained to the United States—up to one-third of workers around the world lost their livelihoods. At the same time, governments' attempts to fix their economies worsened the plights of workers—and workers were not willing to take that lying down. They organized and protested, once again terrifying their governments about the possibility of a worker revolt and causing them to scrap economic policies that had made life worse for the working class.[34]

In the United States, it took the Great Depression to set up the right conditions for Teddy Roosevelt's cousin, Franklin Delano Roosevelt, to pass the minimum social protections adopted in Europe decades before—minimum wage, restrictions on working hours, and an old-age pension (Social Security). These were FDR's attempts to promote European-style **social democracy**.

> **Social democracy** is a political ideology that promotes the use of democratic mechanisms to achieve the traditional socialist goals of "equality, justice, freedom, and solidarity" for all. Social democrats promote a strong social safety net to ensure that people are protected from the worst inequalities of the market.

IN THE LONG RUN, WE'RE ALL DEAD

Economists can (and do) debate what brought the Great Depression to an end, but the increase in manufacturing and return to full employment during World War II was likely a factor.[44] The prosperity that followed World War II brought about a boom in pro-labor welfare policies throughout Europe and North America—between 1945 and the mid-1970s, states dramatically expanded worker protections and social welfare benefits.[45]

The memory of the Great Depression was still fresh, so governments sought to insulate workers from the harshest outcomes of the capitalist system. The economic philosophy driving state efforts came from the British economist John Maynard Keynes. Keynesian economics, in a nutshell, is the idea that unregulated market capitalism is *not* self-regulating or self-correcting. Instead, government has a role to play in reducing income inequality, regulating capitalism, and maintaining market stability.[46]

Keynes's position was that massive income inequality is bad for society and that government should intercede, when necessary, to correct grave inequality. He argued that government regulation is important on three grounds:[47]

1. Economic: income inequality means that large numbers of people don't have money to spend, so demand decreases; in turn, manufacturing (supply) slows, and workers are laid off.
2. Moral: the unregulated market doesn't distribute wealth fairly—it rewards people who already have money.
3. Political: the perception of injustice that comes with significant income disparity could lead to political turmoil and ultimately destroy capitalist society.[48]

The picture you should be getting here is that Keynes was a fan of the market but not the *unregulated* market. Governments took this to heart. The system that evolved during the Keynesian era is one of *embedded liberalism*, meaning a market-based system around which the government has built a system of regulations and controls in order to create a buffer between citizens and the often harsh outcomes of capitalism. Each country determined the strength of its buffer—the buffers in the social-democratic Nordic countries were far stronger than the buffers built by the Anglo-American countries—but all Western states pursued full employment and economic growth while also looking out for the basic welfare of their citizens (education, health care, unemployment benefits, etc.).[49]

In the Keynesian era, being a *citizen* meant having not just civil and political rights (that is, equality before the law and voting rights) but also social rights—a guarantee of basic economic security.[50] (Keep in mind that minority groups often did not get the same guarantee.) A *good* government ensured citizens have not just freedom of speech or religion but also freedom from *want*. As Franklin Delano Roosevelt said in his 1944 State of the Union address, "We have come to a clear realization of the fact that true individual freedom cannot exist without economic security and independence. Necessitous men are not free men. People who are hungry and out of a job are the stuff of which dictatorships are made."[51]

Once again, a strong social safety net was considered a smart way to prevent political unrest. Negative consequences were treated as a *collective* problem with a *collective* (government) solution. Indeed, there was general agreement that governments should use policy interventions to correct market problems rather than waiting for the market to correct itself in the long run—as Keynes famously said, "In the long run, we are all dead."[52]

THE MARKET KNOWS BEST

In the early twentieth century, the great threats portrayed in dystopian fiction were states that were too powerful, not those that were too weak. In particular, the emergence of fascism in Italy in the 1920s under Mussolini and in Germany in the 1930s under Hitler, and their support for the military dictator Franco in Spain, terrified artists, intellectuals, and anyone else who prized democracy. Especially horrifying were the barbaric methods used by fascist governments to achieve control and spread fear, such as air raids against civilian targets in Guernica (memorialized in Picasso's haunting painting of that name), to say nothing of the Holocaust.

After London's (1909) *Iron Heel*, where the great fear is oligopoly (appropriate to the U.S. Gilded Age), the next two decades' most influential books in the genre were Zamyatin's *We* (1921) and Huxley's *Brave New World* (1932). In both, the motivating fear is totalitarian government imposing human conformity based on scientific rationality. Both authors portrayed a state that would create its own version of "happiness" for the people, at the expense of their freedom—a theme that reappears in Ray Bradbury's *Fahrenheit 451* (1953). By the end of World War II, Orwell had seen Hitler's rise and fall and had his eye on Stalin in Russia, using both as inspiration for the totalitarian "Big Brother" government in *1984*.

BREAKING UP WITH KEYNES

Politically, except for the communist dictatorships of Eastern Europe, democracy had been on the upswing after World War II, with a retreat from fascism in Western Europe and a wave of decolonization in the Global South. As we've noted, the post–World War II economy was going pretty well, too. But things had changed again by the 1970s. Several Latin American and African states had returned to authoritarian governance, and economically, the Keynesian "Golden Age" came crashing to a halt. Inflation soared and unemployment skyrocketed—and nothing Keynes (who died in 1946) had ever written addressed the high inflation/high unemployment combination of economic events (a.k.a. "stagflation") that characterized the 1970s.[53] Governments abandoned Keynesian policies aimed at low unemployment and, particularly in the United States and the United Kingdom, embraced a then-obscure economic ideology called neoliberalism.[54]

Neoliberalism starts with Adam Smith's original idea that in the absence of government interference and regulation (but with strong government protection of private property), free markets and free trade would create prosperity; it then adds the idea that the state must actively create an environment in which the market can work.

In the 1980s, the two most famous proponents of neoliberalism were President Ronald Reagan of the United States and Prime Minister Margaret Thatcher of the United Kingdom, both of whom steered their states toward increasingly market-oriented policies in pursuit of the new capitalist utopia—one even more far-reaching than Adam Smith's. The 1980s neoliberal utopia was much closer to Ayn Rand's depiction of a free-market utopia in *Atlas Shrugged*,[55] in which she champions drastic action to confront the crises brought about by government interference in the market.[56]

In the neoliberal utopia, as the economist David Harvey puts it:

> The role of the state is to create and preserve an institutional framework appropriate to [market] practices. The state has to guarantee, for example, the quality and integrity of money. It must also set up those military, defence, police, and legal structures and functions required to secure private property rights and to guarantee, by force if need be, the proper functioning of markets. Furthermore, if markets do not exist (in areas such as land, water, education, health care, social security, or environmental pollution) then they must be created, by state action if necessary.

In the wake of the Keynesian era, setting up the neoliberals' optimal environment meant rolling back much of the economic policy of the preceding three decades: cutting the taxes used to pay for the social safety net, deregulating financial markets, and generally reducing as much regulation on business as was politically possible.[57]

Neoliberalism redefined *good* government as market-based government.[58] If government operated like industry, neoliberals argued, government would be more efficient and provide better outcomes for society—which is why rolling back the Keynesian era also included privatizing public industries, selling off government assets, and outsourcing many government functions to the private sector.[59]

In the neoliberal ideology, any attempt to limit the market or the ability of individuals/industry to make a profit becomes an attempt to limit *freedom*—because as the political scientist Lester K. Spence writes, "[Neoliberal] ideas also radically change what it means to be free—freedom is redefined as the ability to participate in the market unfettered."[60] This redefines *citizen* as *consumer* and *unemployment* or *poverty* as *individual problems* brought about by individuals' bad choices rather than as collective problems with collective solutions. This means that the solutions are individual, as well—individuals must make better choices if they want to succeed in the market.

AROUND THE WORLD IN NEOLIBERAL WAYS

In the more economically developed countries, neoliberalism took root quasi-organically, with states adopting neoliberal policies out of true belief (United States, United Kingdom) or simply to put themselves in a better position in the global market (France, China).[61] But in the 1980s, many developing countries found themselves in dire financial straits. They turned to the international community, in the form of the International Monetary Fund (IMF) and the World Bank (WB), for help.

Prompted primarily by the United States, the IMF and WB adopted what came to be known as the **Washington Consensus**, which made international assistance conditional upon the developing states' adoption of neoliberal policies. Since so many states needed IMF/WB bailouts, neoliberalism spread quickly and accelerated *globalization*, the "flow of technology, economy, knowledge, people, values, and ideas . . . across borders."[62]

Dystopian fiction at times shows great uneasiness with the way rich nations pressure poorer ones economically. In George Saunders's "The Semplica-Girl Diaries,"[63] young women from developing countries are paid to be live lawn ornaments for rich people. The Semplica-Girls are labor migrants who *choose* to do this demeaning and possibly dangerous

The **Washington Consensus**, so called because the policies it promoted were developed by agencies and think tanks based in Washington, DC, promoted neoliberalism as the key to economic development in poor countries. The policy prescription included market liberalization/ removal of barriers to trade, reduced government spending, and privatization of state-owned assets. (Deregulate, downsize, privatize, economize!)

"work" (a justification our narrator uses to feel better about displaying them on his lawn). But how much of a choice did they have if the alternative was poverty or starvation in their home countries? As Saunders demonstrates, the ultimate blindness of neoliberal capitalism is the way massive inequality and overbearing consumerism structure the choices (and morality) of both sellers and buyers. To paraphrase Nelson Mandela, the South African freedom fighter, former president, and Nobel laureate, both the oppressor and the oppressed must be liberated. Enacting oppression, he said (even slowly and in little bits), takes away one's humanity.

DO MARKETS *REALLY* KNOW BEST?

We know what ultimately happened to the unregulated capitalism of the Industrial Revolution and Gilded Age: mass profits for owners, worker exploitation, massive income inequality, and (eventually) a worldwide depression. But what has happened in the era of the neoliberal technological revolution?

EVERYTHING'S POSSIBLE WITH MODERATION

In the 1990s, the end of a period known to economists as the Great Moderation (because it seemed that neoliberalism had erased the booms and busts of the business cycle),[64] things looked good in the larger economy. The stock market—largely on the strength of internet technology—was booming, international trade and capital were flowing freely, and profits were excellent. But at the end of the 1990s, and the so-called dotcom boom turned to a massive bust in 2000. But, thanks to loose **monetary policy,** the American financial sector never really felt the effects of that bust (dotcom companies and IT workers certainly did, but not the financiers who made the boom/bust possible).[65]

That same loose monetary policy (which encouraged low interest rates) then intersected with innovations in the largely deregulated banking sector,

Monetary policy is how central banks (like the US Federal Reserve or the European Central Bank) change the supply of money in the economy. Want more money flowing? Loosen policy: encourage lower interest rates, so more people will borrow. Want to cool down an overheated economy by getting money out of circulation? Tighten policy: encourage high interest rates, so that fewer people borrow. Don't confuse *monetary* policy with *fiscal* policy—which is what we call government policies related to taxation and spending.

resulting in the US housing bubble of the 2000s. Long story short: easy-to-get credit allowed people to overextend themselves, and the drive for profits gave lenders incentives to give dodgy (usually variable-rate) mortgages to nearly anyone, regardless of creditworthiness or ability to pay (a.k.a. subprime borrowers); this coincided with rising home prices. Investors assumed that real estate values would continue to rise and that any devaluation would be local, not nationwide, which led to widespread real estate speculation (risky real estate purchases made in the hope of selling at high profits later).

Along with all of this, investment banks developed increasingly complex and speculative mortgage-backed securities (essentially, investors buy a large pool of mortgages so as to profit from the interest generated by those loans) that now contained many subprime mortgages. By 2006, global investors had invested trillions of dollars in these speculative investment packages. The profits, on paper at least, looked fantastic.

In 2007, the housing bubble started leaking as housing prices began to fall and borrowers began to default on their mortgages. By 2008, the bubble wasn't just leaking: it had burst, and a financial meltdown—the largest since the Great Depression—ensued, bringing us into the Great Recession. Given the interconnectedness of the global economy, America's financial meltdown triggered a global recession. It's hard to say exactly how much the Great Recession has cost, but in 2013 the US Government Accountability Office, a nonpartisan federal agency that works for the US Congress, estimated that from 2007 to 2009 in the United States alone there was an estimated $13 *trillion* loss in economic output and another $9.1 trillion lost in home equity.[66] For perspective: the 2006 gross domestic product (the value of all goods and services produced in the United States) was about $14 trillion.

What all of that would indicate is that from a macro-level perspective, neoliberalism and deregulated markets are problematic—resting as they do on the ideas that the market knows best, that it is self-correcting and self-regulating. The Great Recession, and to a lesser extent the dotcom bubble, undermined the fundamental assumptions of neoliberalism. During the 2000s, it became clear that the market was terrible at assessing the value of investments (bubbles, by definition, mean that value has been seriously overstated) and that it didn't correct itself (or at least not in a timely enough fashion to avoid the bust). Plus, it utterly failed to regulate itself— once the U.S. government lightened banking regulations, the "light touch" regulation system relied on assessments made by the banks themselves(!).[67] Even Chair of the Board of Governors of the Federal Reserve System Alan Greenspan (a member of Ayn Rand's inner circle, a champion of neoliberal ideology, and a proponent of deregulation) was forced, in sworn congressional testimony, to admit that ideology had blinded him to the fact that markets *don't* adequately self-regulate, saying "I made a mistake in presuming that the self-interests of organizations, specifically banks and others, were such as that they were best capable of protecting their own shareholders and their equity in the firms."

But what about from a micro level—what about how individuals have fared under neoliberal policy? The Great Moderation looked pretty good for individuals, too: the 1990s saw income improvements across the board, strong stock market performance produced big gains for the wealthy, and house prices started to rise. This was all good! Except that it masked what the Yale political economist Jacob S. Hacker calls *The Great Risk Shift*.[68]

RISK WITHOUT REWARD

The neoliberal revolution weakened or fully reversed much of the policy adopted under the post-World War II "security for all" paradigm. This was the Great Risk Shift, transferring the risk back to the individual, which—in the context of the stability of the Great Moderation—meant that if you lost a job, you should be able to find another one. If you couldn't, it was a personal failure, not a failure of the market.[69] The Great Risk Shift also meant that job security was no longer something workers could count on, since cutting workers became a common mechanism for maximizing short-term profit—so, when "faced with the ever-present risk of job loss, employees accepted a faster pace of work and reduced working conditions as the price of continued employment."[70]

Margaret Atwood, our modern "prophet of dystopia,"[71] has turned her sights on the insecurity of the neoliberal capitalist workplace in her 2015 book *The Heart Goes Last*. In the story, Stan and Charmaine have lost their jobs after an economic collapse (bigger than 2008's) results in widespread unemployment and the inability of the government to provide security. They live in their car, trying to avoid violent roving gangs and drugged-up crazies. They're so desperate that Charmaine is toying with the idea of turning the occasional trick in the sleazy bar where she works. Then it appears:

a single option for safety and economic security, in the form of an offer to live and work in Consilience. It's basically a prison-industrial complex with an elaborate timesharing system (half the time they are prison employees, the other half they become the prisoners—the company motto is "Consilience = Cons + Resilience. Do Time Now, Buy Time for Our Future."). What does capitalist oppression look like, Atwood asks? Like the complete absence of good choices that allow you to live with dignity.

OLD FEARS ARE NEW AGAIN

Capitalist production, therefore, develops technology, and the combining together of various processes into a social whole, only by sapping the original sources of all wealth—the soil and the labourer.

—Karl Marx

All this history about the rampant growth, midcentury checking, and eventual growth again of pro-free-market forces and ideology shows a few key things: (1) unregulated capitalism is really bad at restraining itself; (2) trade unions are a good start (though in decline today), but it usually takes governments to be an effective counterweight to the power of the market; and (3) the great mass of real people are better off in a well-regulated capitalist system. Regulation is important both to protect people (as workers and consumers) and the environment.

The instability of an individual's position in the neoliberal world order, combined with deregulation, particularly environmental deregulation, has sparked many people's fears about where we're headed as a society. Those fears are being expressed in such diverse works of capitocratic dystopian fiction as *Wall-E* and *The Parable of the Sower.* As the quote that starts this section demonstrates, Marx wrote the basic plot line for modern capitocratic dystopian fiction: unrestrained capitalism destroys the worker and the environment.[72] Even Keynes was concerned that the drive to maximize profits would result in massive income inequality and a lack of "protection for the countryside from exploitation."[73]

Although the fears about inequality and the environment are old, they used to be rooted in the *refusal* of government to regulate the market. Now, however, they're rooted in the potential *inability* of the government to regulate the market—a fear that governments are being intentionally weakened until they become unable to resist capture by corporate interests that don't have the public interest or the environment at heart.

THE YAWNING CHASM BETWEEN THE HAVES
AND THE HAVE-NOTS

While economists debate whether neoliberalism is the *cause* of rising income inequality, no one questions that the gap between rich and poor is growing. Real wages have been falling for decades, even as the rich have gotten increasingly richer over the past three decades, especially in the United States (but elsewhere, too).

The Organization for Economic Cooperation and Development (OECD—basically, the rich countries' club) estimates that in the wake of the Great Recession, the level of income inequality (the gap between rich and poor) hit its highest levels since the end of the Keynesian Era. The OECD's estimates indicate that the top 10 percent of earners now make nearly ten times more than the poorest 10 percent. And in the wealthiest OECD countries, the top 1 percent earn more than 10 percent of the total pretax income in those countries (in the United States, it's over 20 percent).[74]

The pace at which income inequality is increasing shows no signs of slowing any time soon—and that has a lot of people very concerned about what happens when the have-nots get fed up with their shrinking sliver of the economic pie.

BUY YOUR HEART OUT

This is especially true in consumerist societies in which the have-nots go into debt to buy all of the things society tells them they need in order to be considered successful. Along with the growing gap between the super-rich and the regular people, we have seen massively rising expectations about what counts as baseline middle-class levels of education, possessions, vacations, and living practices.[75] All around the developed world, the economic gains since the "bad old days" of stagflation in the 1970s have largely been driven by increased consumerism. Particularly in the United States, all of this conspicuous consumption is based on rising levels of consumer debt (since real wages have remained stagnant for a long, long time—meaning that people's paychecks don't buy as much as they used to). A driving force behind this increased consumerism is a whole lot of advertising—this is why so many modern visions of the future (*Wall-E*, *Blade Runner*, *Oryx and Crake*) depict a world awash in ads and the language of consumerism.

PAY-TO-PLAY

Because governments seem to be shrinking the social safety net and leaving the have-nots increasingly vulnerable to market fluctuations, modern dystopian fiction often centers on what happens to the have-nots in a world where the market reigns supreme and government is unconcerned about the fate of the poor. These works of fiction are dramatic warnings of what could happen if we continue along our current economic path. Books like Paolo Bacigalupi's *Ship Breaker* show us a vision of a future that looks a lot like the early industrial past: the poor are left to fend for themselves, child labor is rampant, and life is Hobbesian again—nasty, brutish, and short. Similarly, Octavia Butler's *Parable of the Sower* is a strong warning about the harms of neoliberalism on regular (nonrich) people. There's so much packed into that book that we're only going to talk about one of the sub-themes: the effect on society when government is so focused on cutting budgets that it abdicates its responsibility to provide security for anyone who can't pay for it.

Parable is set in a future America suffering from environmental degradation and economic ruin (at least for the poor). Our heroine, Lauren Olamina, and her family live in the fictional town of Robledo, California. The Olaminas and their neighbors have gated their not-quite-completely-impoverished neighborhood to keep out gang violence, thieves, and rapists; they have to patrol it themselves because of cuts in government funding to public services. The police and fire department will come only if you pay them, and Lauren's neighborhood doesn't have that kind of money. Since they couldn't pay, no one even bothers to call for help when the gangs finally break in, murder Lauren's family (and most of her neighbors), and destroy the community.

Pay for fire or police services? No government would go so far as to make police and fire service *pay-to-play*, would it? Of course it would—if it has so little in the public budget that it can't afford to cover everyone. In fact,

---

BOX 3.2: PRIVATE PRISONS, PUBLIC PROBLEMS

A good example of the dangers of privatization comes from private prisons. There is a central tension between the goals of a business (make a profit) and the goal of a government (produce justice and the public good). Are human rights abuses in the public interest? And, if the coercive power of the state is transferred to a private entity and the government fails to prevent abuse of that power through sufficient oversight, capitocracy wins.

The private prison industry has exploded in the United States; from 2000 to 2015, the population of private prisons increased by 45 percent, despite the fact that the overall prison population only increased by 10 percent. Several states have increasingly turned to privatization in an attempt to cut costs and handle larger volumes of prisoners more efficiently. The problem is that efficiency can be dehumanizing; in the prison system, it means stripping services to the bare minimum, like substandard food and health-care services.[76] It also means human rights abuses, such as an overuse of solitary confinement, abuse of prisoners, and inmate deaths.[77] Fundamentally, the incentives are wrong if the goal is profit driven but human beings are the commodity at stake. There is also the even more frightening backward incentive to get more people locked up, as more prisoners mean more profits. For example, in 2010, Arizona passed a law (SB 1070) that drastically increased arrests of suspected illegal immigrants; it turned out private prisons were behind the push for this legislation and stood to benefit enormously from the resulting arrest boom.[78]

A 2016 report from the U.S. Justice Department found that not only were there no real cost savings from private prisons but that there were more safety and security issues at private prisons than at those operated by the Federal Bureau of Prisons. The deficiencies were such that the Justice Department announced it would be eliminating or reducing its use of private prisons, saying that they "simply do not provide the same level of correctional services, programs, and resources; they do not save substantially on costs; and as noted in a recent report by the Department's Office of Inspector General, they do not maintain the same level of safety and security."[79] Citing concerns about safety of both inmates and staff, as well as a lack of cost savings, since 2000, six states have eliminated private prisons completely; six more have significantly reduced their reliance on private prisons.[80]

---

this is a solution actively promoted by hardcore neoliberals to reduce the tax burden, shrink government, and make services more *efficient*. And some cash-strapped localities are indeed trying it, either turning their fire services into subscription-based services or fully privatizing them. In rural Tennessee in 2010, firefighters literally stood and watched a home burn to the ground because the homeowners hadn't paid for fire service—but when the fire spread to a neighbor's home, the firefighters sprang into action. The neighbors, of course, had paid the subscription fee. And that's not an isolated incident. In theory, this solution could be fine, provided that services are provided at an affordable rate, with subsidies for the poor, and provided that there is strong oversight to ensure that services are both of high quality and provided equitably. Unfortunately, privatization of government services is a dangerous game—and one in which oversight is often lacking and corporations' focus on profit shortchanges taxpayers (and can exacerbate inequality).

IF THE ENVIRONMENT WERE A BANK . . .

We would already have saved it. Or so the internet meme goes, the implication being that society has chosen profit over the environment. Environmental deregulation (or lack of regulation to begin with) has effects on air and water quality, as well as the extreme weather events associate with climate change (bigger hurricanes, worse heat waves, more polar vortices). We know some of you don't believe in climate change—we also know we won't change your minds. But it's hard to deny the effects of pollution on air quality when, for example, in New Delhi in 2017 pollution reached more than thirty times the levels recommended by the World Health Organization, international news organizations labeled the city a "gas chamber," and

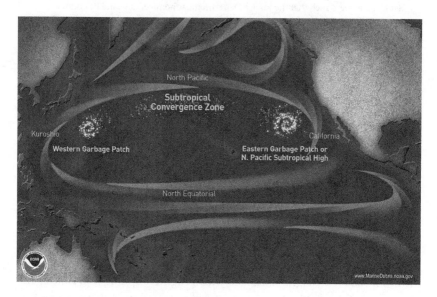

Figure 3.5 Garbage patches in the Pacific Ocean.
Source: Graphic by NOAA, public domain, via Wikimedia Commons.

parents' groups on WhatsApp were seriously debating the best gas masks for their children.[81] It's also hard to deny what pollution is doing to the oceans; see figure 3.5 on the great Pacific garbage patch (one of the spots around Earth where debris collects because of the way currents work). There are hypoxic dead zones all over the world, in lakes and rivers as well as oceans, caused by pollutants that reduce oxygen levels in the water to such low levels that marine life suffocates.[82] All of this means that authors, film-makers, and other artists (musicians, video-game designers, and more) have no shortage of fears about environmental destruction, likely caused by environmental exploitation (pollution, overfarming, overfishing, etc.), to address in their work.

For instance, environmental destruction from deregulation features prominently in Marge Piercy's *He, She, and It* (1991), a kind of cybercapi-tocracy. In this world, decimated by climate change, government seems to have vanished almost entirely; giant global corporations rule their own megacompounds, and the area outside of these ("the Glop") is pretty much a lawless failed state. Food and water are scarce in the Glop, which leads to desperation and violence. There are similar versions of environmentally decimated futures in Pixar's *Wall-E*, Atwood's MaddAddam series (which includes *Oryx and Crake*), Bacigalupi's *The Drowned Cities*, Bong's *Snowpiercer*, and many other modern dystopias.

Our shared environment is what we call a public good—something that we all share and can take from equally. Except someone always has to cheat, and then others cheat, and then the public good is destroyed (political science calls this the "**tragedy of the com-mons**"). In this case, "cheating" is using more than your fair share of the environment by dumping tox-ins in the air and water, overfishing, etc.

Resistance to either hypercapitalism or environ-mental degradation means collective action, which is when a group undertakes an effort that could not be completed by one person working alone (more on this in chapter 6). It is to everyone's advantage to live in a better world, but no individual has enough incentive

The **tragedy of the commons** starts with the premise that people will always try to get the most benefit possible out of a common resource. The tragedy is that the resource will be depleted to the point of no return because once one person starts taking more than their fair share, everyone else—concerned that now they won't get theirs—starts consuming the resource at a faster pace. The resource eventually hits the point where it can no longer recover. The classic example is the public grazing lands held in "common," where all the shepherds can graze some of their sheep. The shepherds will add more and more sheep to the land until it is so overgrazed that it can no longer grow back. Individuals can't prevent the tragedy—for that you need coercive power, like a state.

or power to get it done alone. We need to work together, and it turns out that that is the hardest thing, *ever*.[83]

FINAL THOUGHTS

In chapter 2, we introduced you to the basics of dystopian government, and in this chapter, we've looked at how some of the concerns dystopian authors have brought forward about the potentially dystopian outcomes of unrestrained capitalism speak to the integral role of the economy in a functioning government and society. Next, we turn to the strategies dystopian states adopt in order to fulfill two overarching goals of governance:

1. Control the country and all the people in it
2. Prevent a revolution (a.k.a. total loss of control)

Authoritarians and totalitarians differ on how *much* control they want over the population—obviously, totalitarians want control of *everything*, but your garden-variety dictator just wants people to do what they're told, and this latter group sometimes masks their ambitions with pseudodemocratic language. Regardless, both authoritarians and totalitarians often use similar tactics to achieve their goals, and those tactics are the focus of chapter 4.

4

Strategies and Tactics of
Dystopian Governments

There will come a time when it isn't "They're spying on me through my phone" anymore. Eventually, it will be "My phone is spying on me."

—Philip K. Dick

S o much for what a dictatorial dystopian government *is*. Now we want to know what it *does*. In this chapter we will explore the repertoire of strategies and tactics that dictators use to accomplish their dastardly deeds and remain in power. People often confuse strategies and tactics—but they're different, albeit connected, things. An English comedian, Frank Muir, once said, "Strategy is buying a bottle of fine wine when you take a lady out for dinner. Tactics is getting her to drink it." While we don't endorse the sleaze factor inherent in the quote, it's helpful for understanding the difference: Strategy is about defining your goal. Tactics are about how you achieve that goal.

In a dystopian state, the ultimate goal is control of the country and its citizens. That doesn't just magically happen—a dystopian leader needs a strategy that lists not just the short- and midrange goals that they'll need to achieve in order to gain control but also the tactics they can use. We've helpfully compiled such information here—if you see any of this in action, you might be heading toward a dystopian future—or even living in one.

STRATEGY 1: CONSOLIDATE POWER

Every dictator, tyrant, or one-party state has to come to power somehow. We don't really care how they do—it could be the result of a catastrophic near-annihilation of the human race (*Uglies*), world domination after widespread war (*We*), environmental crisis (*The Handmaid's Tale*), or election in the midst of economic depression (*It Can't Happen Here*). Once in power, the ruler must act to quickly consolidate (a.k.a. *institutionalize*) their power. This includes eliminating the opposition and terrorizing the populace so that they don't push back before the regime has all of its tactics of oppression in place.

TACTIC: ELIMINATE ALL OPPOSITION

If "Father knows best," then any kind of opposition will get in the way and muck up all the good Father is trying to do. Different political parties, competing sources of influence (religion), critics of the government, and even those who *might* be critical (like newspapers) are all dangerous distractions from the real work the state is trying to do and must be eliminated as threats.

One common approach is to bring critics into the fold; if people will accept state control, then they will be allowed to live, but they must follow orders. If they fail to submit, as the other political parties did when the Nazi regime came to power, they can simply be banned. In Germany in 1933, the Nazi Party, which didn't even hold a majority of seats in the Reichstag (parliament), simply outlawed the opposing parties. First they outlawed the Communist Party, then they took down the Social Democratic Party, both of which had been voting against Nazi proposals. This was not done without opposition; the leader of the Social Democrats at the time, Otto Wels, bravely stood against the "Enabling Act." He famously said, "You can take our lives and our freedom, but you cannot take our honor. We are defenseless but not honorless."[1] With the competing political parties out of the way, the Nazis handily passed a series of legal measures collectively called the *Gleichschaltung*, meaning "synchronization, bringing into line, coordination."

If the government bans the opposition but pesky rebels are still resisting, violence often follows. Protestors can be tear-gassed and arrested. That usually at least slows them down. The threat of secret police torture chambers is handy here, too. And opposition leaders can simply be killed off, if need be. In *1984*, not long after the revolution that puts him in charge, Big Brother develops suspicions about the collaborators who helped him into power. They are then arrested, tortured, and forced to "confess" that they betrayed the state and that Big Brother is wonderful. Even doing this did not save their lives; as Stalin once said, "Death is the solution to all problems. No man—no problem."[2]

Generally the type of control that dictators want is not attainable without massive amounts of threat and force. Dystopian leaders think that they just have to force you to do what they *know* is right for you. Hannah Arendt draws an interesting distinction between power and violence: true power doesn't need violence to prop it up, but dictatorial power certainly does.[3]

TACTIC: THE EYE OF SAURON / BIG BROTHER IS WATCHING

Authoritarian leaders need the people to fear them. Without a healthy dose of abject terror, people might start to think they don't have to obey their leaders. On this subject, there is no better authority than the man, the myth, the legend: Niccolo Machiavelli. In *The Prince*, Machiavelli discusses fear at length:

> From this a dispute arises whether it is better to be loved than feared, or the reverse. The response is that one would want to be both; but because it is difficult to put them together, *it is much safer to be feared than loved*, if one has to lack one of the two. For one can say this generally of men: that they are ungrateful, fickle, pretenders and dissemblers, evaders of danger, eager for gain . . . . And men have less hesitation to offend one who makes himself loved than one who makes himself feared; for love is held by a chain of obligation, which, because men are wicked, is broken at every opportunity for their own utility, *but fear is held by a dread of punishment that never forsakes you.*[4]

This is where total surveillance and pitiless punishment come in. The state is omnipresent in dictatorial dystopian states. They use a concept called the "**panopticon**" to consolidate and maintain power. The panopticon was originally just a theoretical prison, designed by the mad genius (and possible psychopath) Jeremy Bentham.[5]

Think of the Panopticon a little like the Eye of Sauron, from Peter Jackson's film version of Tolkien's Lord of the Rings series. The defining characteristic is the sense of a total lack of privacy; the danger to the

The principle is simple: in a **panopticon**, you might be being watched at any and all times; you just never know for sure when. But you *feel certain* that if you *are* being watched and they catch you breaking the rules, the punishment will be swift and harsh.

prisoner is that the guard (or Sauron) could theoretically see what any prisoner is doing at any time and can punish them for *any* infraction.

Surprisingly, Bentham didn't appreciate the real genius of his design. It took about two hundred years and a French philosopher named Michel Foucault to figure out the deeper implications of such a model not just for prisoners but for citizens more generally: *the concept of the panopticon is why citizens obey the state.*[6] The cliché example is traffic cops: you never know where one will be, and the speeding ticket will be expensive, so most of us at least *try* not to speed.

The key mechanisms of panoptic control are, first, simply the people's *feeling* of being watched and, second, the certainty of punishment for wrongdoing. People will often behave properly without any additional prompting merely if they think they are being watched (thus a fake surveillance camera often does the trick). As long as you have a visible guard tower (preferably with mirrored windows), *there does not even need to be a guard in the tower.* This makes the panopticon design even more effective than the Eye of Sauron, which could only see what it was turned toward. The 360-degree guard tower, however, can make prisoners *think* they are being watched, even if they are not. This can certainly save money and effort in policing, which is why many real-life prisons were later made based in full or in part on this model.

The classic panopticon in dystopian fiction is epitomized by the famous slogan in Orwell's *1984*: "BIG BROTHER IS WATCHING YOU." Throughout Orwell's novel, we see how true this is. When our protagonist, poor Winston Smith, isn't trying hard enough one morning in the compulsory "physical jerks" routine, the instructor speaks directly to him through his "telescreen," urging him to reach farther and touch his toes. Turning off the screen is forbidden, so there's no escape from Big Brother's watchful eye.

But technology like the telescreen isn't necessary for the simplest of panoptic controls: *peer policing* (meaning the state gets people to report on one another). In Atwood's *The Handmaid's Tale*, Handmaids have to shop in pairs so they can spy on each other and report disloyalty to the regime. Everyone knows that the other Handmaids, the rest of the members of the household, and even perfect strangers are watching at all times and could report infractions.

Think about how useful this is to the state. First, how great is it to have people policing themselves ahead of time? Saves time! Prevents crime before it starts! Second, this structure of a surveillance state also does something

Figure 4.1 Tower of Doom: photograph of the Central Jail at Junagadh in Gujarat, India, by F. Nelson (1890s).
Source: British Library website, public domain, via Wikimedia Commons.

far more insidious: it gives each person the equivalent of a loaded gun that they can use on anyone else. Suddenly each and every player in any relationship holds a trump card over all the others: any accusation of disloyalty, whether true or not, can amount to either a literal or figurative assassination.

Any discussion of panoptic surveillance states must include East Germany, which adopted a Soviet-style communist state married with ruthless efficiency. The East Germans had the most extreme surveillance state in the world, portrayed to perfection in the German film *Das Leben der Anderen* (*The Lives of Others*). The historian Catherine Epstein gives a good picture of the massive size and scope of the Stasi's reach:

> One hundred seventy-eight kilometers of archival material. Personal files on six million individuals. Forty million index cards. One million pictures and negatives. Thousands of human scents stored in glass jars, 91,015 full-time employees, 174,000 "unofficial" informants. The highest

surveillance rate (agents to population) in history. Husbands spying on wives. Colleagues snitching on co-workers. Informants posing as dissidents. State officials harboring Red Army Faction terrorists. "Romeo" agents preying on hapless secretaries. Commandos kidnapping alleged traitors from West Germany. Agent provocateurs infiltrating literary groups and church circles.[7]

The playbook of the East German state security apparatus, the Stasi (the not-so-secret police), could have come directly out of *1984*. Like any effective secret police, the Stasi used brutal repression, imprisonment, and torture in their attempts to achieve total control. Unsurprisingly, that failed to fully control the hearts and minds of the East German people. Thus, the Stasi developed an extensive network of informants/collaborators. Anyone who found himself in trouble with the law might also find himself pressed into service as a Stasi informant; one account indicates that rather than prosecuting a pedophile, the Stasi coerced him into informing. The Stasi even forced prisoners to spy on prison guards.[8] And many informants weren't overtly coerced—they spontaneously informed on friends, neighbors, coworkers, and even family members either because they were true believers or because they feared what might happen if they were caught *not* informing.

The Stasi used a number of other surveillance techniques, too. These included your standard wiretaps and bugs, of course, but they also got creative. They had multiple models of spy kits that allowed people to blend in, dressed as technicians or business people. They invented a machine that could open and reseal mail, ostensibly without leaving a trace. Our favorite, though, is that they collected the scents of suspected dissidents so that, if necessary, dogs could track down the suspects. (This last tactic is also used by the Mechanical Hound in Bradbury's *Fahrenheit 451*. We're not sure if the Stasi got it from Bradbury or if Bradbury got it from the Stasi.)

TACTIC: THE BEATINGS WILL CONTINUE
UNTIL MORALE IMPROVES

In all honesty, no one in a dystopian government really cares about morale. It's the beatings that matter, because swift, harsh punishment is a key element of panoptic control. If a government is going to get people to self-police, it has to give them a good reason. If a dictator is worth his salt, that reason is to avoid pain (one's own or that of loved ones).

For a classic fictional work about state-sponsored torture and "re-education," we could do no better than point you to Stanley Kubrick's classic film *A Clockwork Orange* (1971), based on Anthony Burgess's 1962 novel of the same name. The story does little to endear you to its main character, Alex, who is a sadist, a rapist, a murderer, and apparently a psychopath—but the state-enforced experimental psychiatric "rehabilitation" he undergoes (the "Ludovico technique") is also horrific in its own right.

Generally, though, fictional works tend to favor drama, and therefore it is the pain of others (and not of oneself) that is most effective. In *The Empire Strikes Back*, for example, Han Solo is tortured by the Empire's forces—not to get anything from him but to lure Luke Skywalker out of hiding (he foolishly complies). Similarly, in the Hunger Games trilogy, although Katniss has long hated President Snow and his reign, she only becomes downright vicious after her little sister is killed.

Not to disparage our fabulous fiction authors, but their imaginations don't hold a candle to what *real* dystopian governments do to dissidents and rebels. The examples are legion, so we're going to narrow our focus and discuss some dictatorships that we've not delved into too deeply thus far: the military governments of Latin America (late 1960s–early 1980s, mostly). For an overview of which Latin American states had military governments and when, see figure 4.2. *Much of this section deals with brutality and sexual violence; it is disturbing, so proceed with caution.* We'll start with a little background and then move into accounts of the atrocities committed by these military dictatorships.

The nutshell version of the background is this: during the Cold War, the United States feared the spread of Soviet-led communism. Latin American elites feared that peasants and industrial workers would unite and threaten their power. Labor and peasant movements tended to be leftist, so the United States, fearing that the leftists would look to the USSR for support,[9] turned to Latin American militaries. The United States encouraged the generals to "turn their guns inward, against the 'internal enemies of freedom': revolutionary organizers in factories, poor neighborhoods, and universities."[10]

Militaries in Argentina, Chile, El Salvador, and Guatemala all enthusiastically complied.[11] In many cases, people were **disappeared**—to this day, their families have no confirmation of the whereabouts of their disappeared loved ones. There's no record of where or how tens of thousands of people

Disappearing people is a particularly sinister method of ridding the regime of its enemies. It is not unique to Latin America, nor is it an obsolete practice. The regime kidnaps, interrogates, tortures, and ultimately murders people who may be opponents of the regime. The kidnappers are usually plainclothes operatives; officially, the state denies any knowledge of the person, leaving their friends and family with no clue as to the disappeared person's whereabouts.

were killed or where their remains are. The states just made their captives vanish.

In Argentina and Chile, plainclothes military death squads kidnapped suspected dissidents.[12] In both Chile and Argentina, after the kidnapping, the victims were taken to secret facilities where they were tortured and interrogated until they gave up information on other so-called revolutionaries. In Chile, after an initial round of mass killings, the military also added long-term imprisonment—they didn't kill *everyone* they arrested.

In Argentina, many were not so lucky. The Argentine military was partial to "death flights," using

Country	Years of military rule
Argentina	1966–1973 1976–1983
Brazil	1964–1985
Bolivia	1964–1970 1971–1982
Chile	1973–1990
Ecuador	1963–1966 1972–1978
El Salvador	1948–1984
Guatemala	1963–1966 1969–1985
Honduras	1963–1966 1972–1982
Panama	1968–1989
Peru	1968–1980

Figure 4.2 Military Dictatorships in Latin America, 1964–1990.
Source: Created by the authors.

them to kill an estimated two thousand people. They would give prisoners a sedative, put them on a plane, and fly out over the ocean. The plane's crew would then throw the prisoners into the ocean alive.[13] It was an easy way of getting rid of the evidence. El Salvador and Guatemala both had death squads, as well—El Salvador's, for example, were prone to dumping dissidents' mutilated bodies in city streets. But the dirty wars in El Salvador and Guatemala centered more on widespread brutality in rural areas. In 1981, in the village of El Mozote, the Salvadoran army perpetrated one of the largest single atrocities in recent Latin American history, committing mass rape of the female population before slaughtering every man, woman, and child in the village.[14] A 2012 Inter-American Human Rights Court report indicated that there were 440 people *confirmed* killed in El Mozote but that the evidence indicates the death toll was far higher, by some reports closer to eight hundred (including those massacred in the surrounding area).[15]

El Mozote wasn't just a massacre. It was a warning of what the military would do to even *suspected* rebel sympathizers. El Mozote showed everyone in rebel territory that if the community supported the rebels, the army was very willing to make people suffer horribly before killing everyone in the community. Of course, the bitter irony is that the villagers weren't even rebel sympathizers, which makes the carnage of El Mozote even less comprehensible.

The Guatemalan government took a similar scorched-earth approach to eradicating suspected dissidents. That takes on a new meaning when you realize that the Guatemalan government classified the *entirety* of the Mayan population—men, women, children, infants—as "collective enemies of the state."[16] The effect of that pronouncement was nothing short of **genocide**—an attempt to wipe out the entire population of Maya in Guatemala. It's Maya women, though, who endured much of the horror of the genocide.

Genocides aren't just about killing—perpetrators can't be sure they'll get all of their targets. That's why rape is employed as a tool of genocide; genocidaires can dilute the gene pool while also terrifying and humiliating the target race. Rape is used to punish communities suspected of collaborating with the enemy, it is used to terrify the population, and it is often done publicly (or in front of husbands and fathers) to demonstrate just how powerless the people are against the regime's forces.

Genocide is an attempt to wipe a specific religious, ethnic, or racial group off the face of the earth. All genocides involve mass murder, but not all mass murders are genocides. Mass murder for political reasons, for example, is called *politicide*.

After the war in Guatemala ended in 1996, the UN-sponsored Commission for Historical Clarification (CEH) heard volumes of testimony regarding the military's atrocities, most of which are far too graphic and disturbing to be recounted here. In its report, the CEH deliberately pointed out the "special brutality directed against women, especially against Mayan women, who were tortured, raped, and murdered."[17] Indeed, the Guatemalan military leadership didn't just tell their soldiers that raping Maya women and girls was okay; the Guatemalan state "*trained* killers to rape, to mutilate, and to murder women during the war."[18] Testimony before the CEH revealed cases in which soldiers who refused to rape women were summarily executed.[19] The brutality of the Guatemalan military was legendary. The evidence against them is ample. But few people have been prosecuted for their roles in the genocide.

Sadly, the Latin American cases aren't unique in modern history. Authoritarian regimes the world over have found increasingly inventive, cruel, and inhumane methods of repression and murder. What is amazing, though, is that people continue to resist—even while aware of what horrors their governments might visit upon them. That continued resistance is what gives us hope for humanity.

TACTIC: DIVIDE AND CONQUER

We don't want the people talking. Next they'll start forming committees,
launching inquiries.
—The Master of Laketown (*The Hobbit*)

The dystopian state (in fiction and real life) views interpersonal relationships with deep distrust. If people are talking to one another and the state isn't involved, you might be discussing your dissatisfaction with the state. And if you're discussing your dissatisfaction, then you might decide to work together to fight back. And then you might recruit other people. And before the state knows it, it has a revolution on its hands. So, no. People cannot talk freely to one another. But people are social beings; we constantly make connections and bond with others . . . and the telescreens from *1984* don't seem to have been invented yet.[20] So, what's the state to do?

Well, all of the peer policing we talked about (earlier) serves yet another purpose for a dystopian state: it creates *atomization*. That's the fancy term for alienating people from their fellow citizens. When anyone can be a spy, no one can be trusted. Therefore, it's better all around for the dystopian state if no one engages deeply with anyone else. Rebellion plotting averted. Total win for the dystopian government.

Keeping people from trusting one another enough to share thoughts and questions is a solid first step in preventing rebellion, but sometimes those damn people bond anyway. And what about when people fall in love? That's an even more dangerous force. People will go to extreme lengths for the people they love. In *We*, love pushed D-503 to join the rebellion alongside his beloved, I-330. In *Serenity*, a brother (Simon) throws away his comfortable life to rescue his sister (River) from the clutches of the dictatorial intergalactic government, the Alliance. It seemed like madness to Alliance followers—but the operative assigned to track down Simon and River says, "Madness? Have you looked at his face? It's *love*. Something far more dangerous."

Another common tactic states use to prevent bonding is to target civil society, meaning all of the organizations outside of the state: nonprofits, social organizations/clubs (no model train collectors club for you!), even children's groups like the Scouts. The authoritarian state does not want people to have clubs and groups outside of the government; there can be *no* independently organized places to meet up where people could exchange unapproved ideas, share their dissatisfaction, or otherwise plant the seeds of revolution. To prevent such gatherings, a common tactic used by authoritarian governments is simply to ban civil society.

But people are social beings and want to congregate. The state to the rescue! Social organizations organized by the state are allowed and even encouraged, but only because they are controlled by the state. These include organizations like the fictional "Junior Anti-Sex League" in *1984* or real-life groups like the Hitler Youth (Hitlerjugend) and the Committee of Soviet Women (the Komitet Sovetskikh Zhenshchin).

STRATEGY 2: CREATE FALSE CONSCIOUSNESS

What the leadership wants here is not just to make the citizens believe that the state is doing what is best but actually to get the citizens to participate in their own oppression. For example, the state could pull a Hitler/Putin and get the people to vote for *more* oppression. Or a dystopian leader could stage massive nationalist spectacles that generate a patriotic frenzy. Even better, they could pick an enemy and rally the people in defense of the state—"*it may be cruel and oppressive, but it's ours and we will defend it!*"

TACTIC: USE YOUR ILLUSION

It is enough that the people know there was an election. The people who cast the votes decide nothing. The people who count the votes decide everything.

—Joseph Stalin

The dictatorial government may give the *illusion* of participation (for example, "elections" in the USSR), but true mass participation would lead to compromise, which would weaken the ideal. Father cannot have the family questioning his decisions. But Father also may not want to look like a total jerk. He may in fact listen, or at least pretend to listen, to what his charges say, if only to appease them and prevent outright rebellion. In real life, many authoritarian states hold elections, but they are usually not meaningful (as in Russia or North Korea) or meaningful only at the local/village level (as in China). Real elections that could put an end to the reign of a dictator or party must be avoided at all costs—just ask Chile's infamous Dirty War dictator, Augusto Pinochet, who allowed the election that ousted him.[21]

The real problem for dystopian governments is that, as Machiavelli says, people are selfish, ignorant, greedy, grasping, lying children and must be reined in. Left to their own devices, the people would lead themselves into oblivion! People also have all these ideas and thoughts of their own, which get in the way of the state's alleged work to keep everyone *happy*. In particular, citizens often think (wrongly, of course, in the mind of a dystopian leader) that they know better than the state about how to do something. And people with souls and consciences tend not to approve of the government's (brutal and deadly) methods for getting rid of the unhappy people and achieving state-sponsored happiness.

If the dystopian state wants stability, unhappiness is a real problem. Unhappiness could lead to thinking, resistance, or even rebellion. It is better for the state (and everyone involved, the state would argue) if everyone stops thinking and stays out of matters of governing. Offred, our

Handmaid, figured that out quickly: "Thinking can hurt your chances," she realizes, "and I intend to last."[22]

Also, too much *feeling* creates unhappiness . . . which is why everyone in *Brave New World* is always drugged up. Then there are books, as in Bradbury's classic *Fahrenheit 451*, which make people unhappy, so they must be stopped. And souls! Those are problematic, too. Remember when D-503 (in *We*) developed a soul? The One State surgically excised it. Extreme circumstances clearly call for extreme measures.

Sometimes the state just *has* to take these sorts of extraordinary measures in order to create its ideal society. This may involve a whole lot of carnage, but the state is taking a fairly utilitarian view here: the ends (societal happiness) justify the (brutal) means. *Some* people may end up being unhappy because of this authoritarianism. But this is not the state's fault, the dystopian leader would argue. The state, in the form of the dystopian leader, knows best. Therefore, that dystopian leader will conclude that the state's government *must* be authoritarian in order to impose its vision on the masses. People, he would argue, simply cannot be trusted to decide things for themselves because they will mess everything up.

TACTIC: STRUT YOUR STUFF

The use of spectacle is an important part of a dystopian government, both to distract people from the reality of the society *and* to reinforce the powerful image of the state. Even if you *were* thinking bad thoughts about the state, and even if the spectacle doesn't distract you from those bad thoughts, then the awesome power on display in said spectacle might dissuade you from trying to do anything about it. Hitler loved a spectacle, as did Stalin—both produced mass militaristic parades (Stalin put his nukes on parade, even). Such spectacle has both an internal and external purpose. Internally it is supposed to instill patriotic pride, even fervor, among the masses. Externally, it sends a strong "fuck with us at your own peril" message.

Along those lines, the theorist Achille Mbembe points particularly to the way postcolonial dictators use excess in speech and pomp. There is a sense, he notes, that they are playing a role, as demonstrated especially by their hyperbolic language. When they speak, or when the captive press speaks about them, everything must be "the most excellent," every meeting is the "most productive," and so forth.[23]

Trevor Noah, host of the "Daily Show" and a native South African, knows a little about the performative techniques of African faux-populist dictatorial leaders. Watching the U.S. 2016 election and reflecting on his own childhood and his memoir, *Born a Crime*,[24] Noah said that he thought the U.S. media too easily dismissed Donald Trump first as a potential presidential candidate and then as the Republican nominee. He has compared Trump to South Africa's then-president, Jacob Zuma: "when you look at Zuma and Trump, it seems like they're brothers from another mother." As if channeling Mbembe, Noah points out that Trump and Zuma govern in similar dramatic fashion—threats to the free press, high-visibility persecution of political rivals, and even installing their families in government jobs, all couched in excessive and often self-contradictory language.[25]

Such real-life pomp and hyperbole is reflected in some futuristic fiction, like the Hunger Games series, which deliberately evokes Roman Empire imagery and language. The fictional country (the Republic of Panem) takes its name from the Latin word for bread, evoking the classic Roman "bread and circuses" technique of keeping the masses happy (or at least quiet). The language of the Games is steeped in Roman history as well, for example, the word "tributes" (the children chosen to represent their districts in a fight to the death). The night before the Games begin, the tributes perform in a ritual parade, carried on horse-drawn Roman carriages through a giant ancient Greco-Roman inspired arena, in true Olympic style. And throughout the books and movies, we see the dystopian government, represented by President Snow, manipulating the optics and throwing lavish parties. In dystopian fiction, as in real life, the use of spectacle and over-the-top grandeur is meant to showcase the power of the state; the better the job the regime does at both distracting and intimidating the people, the less likely people are to think seriously about—or resist—the regime's repressive actions.

TACTIC: DIVISIVENESS IN PURSUIT OF UNITY

Dystopian governments suspect that, at heart, people are bloodthirsty animals who need to be restrained (thus the strict laws and brutal repression). But those homicidal impulses also need to be vented from time to time. And it is far better for the government if the people are given constructive ways to focus their anger and violence in a way that will help the state, rather than turning on the dictator. (Revolutions can be so messy.) So if a dystopian leader can manage it, it is great to have a war now and then, or at least some clear internal or external enemies on whom to fixate the minds of the masses. These conflicts create a lovely "rally round the flag" effect, with the flag, of course, really meaning the dictator.

Consider the "Two Minutes Hate," for example, from *1984*. Every morning, exactly on time, Winston and his fellow Party members in the Ministry must all gather in front of a large screen that broadcasts two minutes of video footage about the supposed enemies of the state (mostly Jewish intellectuals—sound familiar?). Even though initially resistant, by the end of the two minutes Winston always finds himself overcome with the emotion of those around him; people shout, gesticulate, and even throw things, winding one another up. This is a brilliant state strategy of controlled crowd violence that strengthens rather than undermines the dystopian government.

In real life, there are innumerable examples of scapegoating on the part of authoritarian governments and even by supposedly democratic governments. The Nazis, of course, are a classic example, carrying out the slaughter of six million Jewish civilians for the crime of being Jewish. (This was hardly the first time Jews were scapegoated. Jews have long been the victims of pogroms. Pogrom is the Russian word for "violent destruction"; the word has typically been applied to mass violence by non-Jewish populations on Jews.) It was Stalin, however, who took mass murder to the next level by scapegoating people as "Enemies of the State." Estimates of the number of his victims run a wide gamut (from as low as 3 million to as many as 60 million)—but the best estimates seem to hover in the area of 20 million.[26] As one observer wryly put it, "Dictators are, as you might imagine, not keen to record how many people they are killing."[27] There is huge debate, however, about whether victims of famines (many more millions) created by Stalin's agricultural policies should be added to that grim tally—but generally his extermination methodologies involved forced labor and a reign of terror based on far-ranging paranoia. All of that fits in well with scapegoating as a tactic.

TACTIC: BE AFRAID; BE VERY AFRAID

Leveraging fear of the other to stay in power is a classic tactic. Dystopian governments typically use extreme forms of nationalism to define "us" and "them" and then blame "them" for whatever problems "we" might have. In short, leaders use fear to maintain power because it works. When the people are sufficiently fired up about the dangers of "them," whoever "they" are, then the people can easily be convinced that the government, and only the government, can protect "us" from "them." In both fiction and fact, there are numerous examples of dictators leveraging ethnic, tribal, language, or other differences to divide and conquer and thus keep their hold on the reins of power.

In Orwell's *1984*, there is a war going on at all times—the thing is, the "enemy" seems to mysteriously shift overnight. So there is always the daily "Two Minutes Hate" exercise, but sometimes the enemy is Eurasia and other times Eastasia. In Terry Gilliam's film *Brazil* (1985), the government's use of fearmongering is even more pointed; there are constant "terrorism" attacks, but the suggestion is that the government might be planting these so-called terrorists to create fear and maintain its own power. In the Red Queen series, by Victoria Aveyard, the rulers of the warring states inflame their citizens against one another to fight a never-ending war. Eventually we learn that the war is a conspiracy between the leaders; the goal is population control so that the lower-class numbers don't explode and the elites can keep power.

Instilling and maintaining a fear of the other is an extremely popular tactic in the real world, too. During the Cold War, the United States was gripped by fears of the "Red Menace." The Soviets were dangerous and might strike at any time! Readers of a certain age might remember those ever-so-useful Cold War–era "duck and cover" drills—where children huddled under their desks in fear of a Soviet nuclear strike. But that wasn't the only thing to fear, because those commies were devious; they were trying to infiltrate American society and bring us down from the inside—or so the anti-Soviet propaganda of the day told us. Pressured by the U.S. government to prove they weren't harboring pinko commie sympathizers, film studios churned out a series of anticommunist propaganda films in the 1950s. Movies like *The Woman on Pier 13* (a.k.a. *I Married a Communist*), *I Was a Communist for the FBI*, and John Wayne's *Big Jim McClain* were designed to warn American viewers of "the nefarious activities of 'Communist fifth columns' and spotlight espionage and subversion."[28] While Hollywood propaganda films were relatively silly, the U.S. government's anticommunist foreign policy was anything but.

As we've already discussed, fear of communist infiltration drove the United States to encourage Latin American military governments to purge potential revolutionaries from their societies. This resulted in the rape, torture, murder, and disappearance of hundreds of thousands of people across the region. But the carnage wasn't confined to Latin America. The U.S. government spread its anticommunist message to militaries and military regimes around the world.

In Indonesia, the Johnson administration encouraged the military to overthrow the country's left-sympathizing President Sukarno and crush the Indonesian communist party, the PKI. Once the Indonesian army *did* move against Sukarno, U.S. officials were openly concerned that the army wouldn't go far enough against the PKI and those sympathetic to communism. U.S. diplomat George Ball told a journalist that the Indonesian army should "wipe up earth" with the PKI, and the only real question for the Johnson administration was "how best to encourage the army to such violence" without implicating the United States.[29] The answer was to use the CIA to strategize covertly with the army's leader, General Suharto. With U.S. help, the general led the military to overthrow President Sukarno and establish a military dictatorship. General Suharto, with U.S. backing, went about consolidating his power, eliminating all potential opposition. The result was a politicide of massive proportions; anyone even suspected of communist sympathies was slaughtered. The Indonesian government's official death toll at the time was an estimated 78,000, but no one outside of Indonesia believes that figure is realistic.[30] Expert observers have estimated that the real death toll is far higher, likely between 500,000 and two million people slaughtered between 1965 and 1966.[31]

And lest you think that scapegoating has to be religious or ideological, the result of this type of virulent nationalism has been genocidal "ethnic cleansing" in multiple conflicts in the modern era. The first took place in Rwanda in 1994, where the Hutu-majority government encouraged its people to slaughter ethnic Tutsis. The death toll is estimated at more than 800,000. Less than a year later, we saw similar carnage in the former Yugoslavia, where Serbs employed rape as a tool of genocide throughout Bosnia to dilute the Bosnian-Muslim (Bosniak) gene pool. Serbs slaughtered as many as eight thousand men and boys in the town of Srebrenica alone.[32]

STRATEGY 3: KEEP YOUR HANDS ON THE WHEEL AT ALL TIMES

What the dystopian leader can never do is become complacent about his control over the masses. The leader must have a firm grip on every level of society, he must prevent his citizens from shedding their false consciousness, and if all else fails, he will try to crush any resistance that rears its ugly head.

TACTIC: KEEP EVERYTHING IN ITS PLACE
(ESPECIALLY THE PROLES)

Class divisions are rife in technologized visions of a dystopian future. In some versions, it is the very technology—engineered by the upper classes, though—that creates the oppression. In *Metropolis*, a privileged rich playboy becomes shocked when he sees how the other half lives, working long, brutal hours in underground factories to make things for the light, airy, pretty world above the surface. He is moved by human-fellow-feeling (and the desire to impress a girl, of course) to take a worker's place on the assembly line, doing himself grievous bodily harm. *Metropolis* is literally the embodiment of Marx's description of unrestrained capitalism leading to a worker rebellion. In the film, the capitalists exploit the proletariat and live large on the backs of their labor. Ultimately the masses rebel, and the lovebirds mediate an agreement between the workers and the head capitalist, a hopeful ending rather rare in this genre.

Kurt Vonnegut's *Player Piano* is far less hopeful. True to its title, the book grapples with the idea of machines that can run themselves, putting most people out of work (no small concern as we head into an era of driverless cars). This, too, is a class-stratified society, but there is no easy resolution; the workers are left to languish in bars (there is no soma in this world, but alcohol takes its place), wishing for jobs, while the company owners, engineers, and managerial class go on fancy corporate retreats (sound familiar?).

Although this was written more than half a century ago (1952), its theme of machines displacing human work still feels current. The discontent of displaced workers is apparently something that modern-day Silicon Valley executives worry about. Writing in the *New Yorker* in 2016, Evan Osnos tells the tale of tech-firm giants who fear unrest and revolution enough to start planning for a coming social meltdown. Specifically, he quotes Max Levin (a PayPal founder), who speaks of the greatest fear of this group being "the pitchforks." Osnos goes on to note that the seriously wealthy (to some minds excessively wealthy) are "are buying airstrips and farms in places like New Zealand because they think they need a getaway."[33]

Thinking ahead to these kinds of class-based fears, smart dystopian states engineer solutions to class conflict in advance. This involves knowing a classic truth, articulated best perhaps by our old friend Machiavelli in *The Prince*, which was published after his death in 1532. Machiavelli wrote that there were two "humors" (in the sense of fluids) in every polity, the people and the nobles. The nobles, he thought, want to oppress the people; the people simply want not to be oppressed.[34]

One "solution" often seen in authoritarian (dystopian) governments is for the state to intentionally create a kind of workers' underclass. In *Brave New World*, babies are genetically engineered and grown in test tubes, designed from conception to be Alphas and Betas (the ruling classes) or Deltas and Epsilons, the workers. Epsilons are disproportionately non-white, apparently, and also have alcohol added to their test tubes to prevent their brains from forming fully, so that they won't be unhappy with their reduced lot in life. Deltas are not necessarily stunted intentionally, but they are given poorer-quality genetic material and educated only minimally, in a job-centric way. Deltas are denied individuality; they are mass produced to have large groups of twins, who appear to work all together in the same jobs. They are the ones who actually make the economy and society function, but they demand (and receive) little.

It's the same with the "proles" (proletariat, in Marx's word) in Orwell's *1984*. At one point in his musings on the Party, Orwell's protagonist Winston reflects:

> If there was hope, it MUST lie in the proles, because only there in those swarming disregarded masses, 85 per cent of the population of Oceania, could the force to destroy the Party ever be generated. . . . They needed only to rise up and shake themselves like a horse shaking off flies. If they chose they could blow the Party to pieces tomorrow morning. Surely sooner or later it must occur to them to do it? And yet—!

And yet, they don't. Why not rebel? Mostly, Winston tells us, they are satisfied with the meager crumbs of life they get:

> Left to themselves, like cattle turned loose upon the plains of Argentina, they had reverted to a style of life that appeared to be natural to them, a sort of ancestral pattern. They were born, they grew up in the gutters, they went to work at twelve, they passed through a brief

blossoming-period of beauty and sexual desire, they married at twenty, they were middle-aged at thirty, they died, for the most part, at sixty. Heavy physical work, the care of home and children, petty quarrels with neighbours, films, football, beer, and above all, gambling, filled up the horizon of their minds. To keep them in control was not difficult.[35]

The best real-life example of a deliberately engineered class system comes from the Spanish conquest of Latin America. Not long after they started settling in the region, the Spanish realized that as people intermixed, the "European" and "Other" categories weren't specific enough to exercise full control over the population of Europeans, Africans, and Indigenous peoples. As the groups comingled, those with at least some European heritage should, the Spanish thought, get advantages over the strictly indigenous. They started with six legal categories—the three just mentioned, plus Afro-European, Afro-Indigenous, and Indigenous-European. A person's category went on his baptismal record and determined his possibilities in life. A European, of course, had no restrictions. But the less European people were, the lower their caste, and "people of low caste were legally prevented from becoming priests, attending the university, wearing silk, owning weapons, and many other things."[36]

Then, of course, members of different groups started to intermarry and have children—and those children needed classifications, too. Their racial composition did, after all, determine their legal rights. The system ended up with at least sixteen categories, more in some places: Mexico had fifty-three racial categories. An additional complication was that the Spanish government would occasionally allow a well-to-do lower-caste person to buy a legal exemption—making them "legally white."[37] If a family were able to buy themselves white, they received all of the rights of the European caste.

Although the legal role of the caste system diminished in importance after independence from Spain, race still plays a large role in the hierarchies of most Latin American societies. The sociologist Edward Telles calls the societal structure in these states "pigmentocracies," saying "skin color is a central axis of social stratification in many Latin American countries, though it is often ignored."[38] The wealth is still concentrated largely in the hands of people of mainly European descent, and poverty is still concentrated in communities that are largely indigenous—as one researcher told us, "the browner the neighborhood, the poorer it is."[39] Sadly, this quote could describe a whole lot of places in the present-day United States, too.

TACTIC: PROTECT THE PEOPLE FROM REALITY

Dystopian governments attempt to control the flow of information in as many ways as they can. It's helpful to the regime if it can keep people from realizing that they're being oppressed and that there is something better out there. Censorship is strict, news outlets are government controlled, and there are only certain very limited channels through which ordinary citizens can offer feedback to their government. But censoring the news is child's play for some dystopian governments: truly masterful authoritarian governments don't just control the media; they control the very language.

Much of Orwell's *1984* is based on linguistic manipulation—Big Brother's key innovation, in addition to mass surveillance, is the creation of a brand-new language that only accommodates certain thoughts but also, crucially, the idea of "doublethink." This, to Orwell, is the essence of dictatorial power: "Doublethink means the power of holding two contradictory beliefs in one's mind simultaneously and accepting them both." Big Brother's Party slogans, inscribed on their respective Ministry buildings, exemplify this concept: "War is peace. Freedom is slavery. Ignorance is strength." Winston's colleague Syme is in charge of writing a new dictionary of Newspeak, the language being invented by Big Brother and his Party, the better to rule you with. Syme explains to Winston—and the reader—the true meaning of belief in the Party teachings: "Orthodoxy means not thinking—not needing to think. Orthodoxy is unconsciousness."[40]

A shrewd dystopian government will take extraordinary measures to curtail the kind of active thinking work that might lead people to think about democratic reform. The first thing to do is cut down on what information people can get. As the Chinese philosopher Lao-Tzu once said, "People are difficult to govern because they have too much knowledge." Less knowledge, more governable.

Schools are okay, as long as the state can control what they teach. And they *will* teach that everything the dystopian government does is good and that anyone rebelling against it is wrong to reject the benevolence of the state. A great example is from *Serenity*, which opens with a teacher telling her class about the Alliance's war against the savage Independent planets who wouldn't accept Alliance rule. She ends her lecture by saying that now that the Alliance has won, "everyone can enjoy the comfort and enlightenment of true civilization." Witness also the fanatical school teacher in the film *Snowpiercer*, who has absorbed her state-given lessons so well that she takes up arms against the attempted revolution.

While public schools are acceptable to dystopian governments, free libraries are sources of grave danger. If it provides libraries, dystopian government must control every book, magazine, newspaper, and film that is collected by them. After all, the dystopian state wants everyone to be thinking the same things. As the novelist Haruki Murakami tweeted in 2013, "If you only read the books that everyone else is reading, you can only think what everyone else is thinking." Murakami meant it as a criticism, but the typical dystopian government would probably use this as a motto.

As the U.S. general William Westmorland once said, "without censorship, things can get terribly confused in the public mind." He was talking about the uncensored footage of the Vietnam War that was being beamed into every American living room on the evening news—people got the full picture of that war, and that picture prompted many Americans to question U.S. actions in Vietnam. In the mind of a dystopian leader, the public must be protected from too much news, as this could lead to unhappiness and/or confusion.

State control of the media is a must, which is why you see it in nearly every dystopian film or novel—*The LEGO Movie*'s President Business keeps the news studio so close that he walks through it on his way to his office. Big Brother controls all of the screens in *1984*. The One State publishes the only newspaper in *We*. The president's people take over all of the newspapers in *It Can't Happen Here*. We noted earlier that one of Putin's first moves was to take control of Russian news outlets. Similarly, Venezuela's Hugo Chávez pushed through laws that put the entirety of the country's TV and radio stations under his control. As the political scientist Larry Diamond wrote, "In typical Orwellian fashion, [Chávez] hailed it as an instrument for the Venezuelan people to 'free themselves from . . . the dictatorship of the private media.'"[41]

Discrediting the independent news media is a common tactic of authoritarian-leaning leaders. Once the media is discredited, the people are more dependent on their leaders for information. This, in turn, makes the people easier to control. During (and after) the 2016 U.S. election, the term "fake news" was used quite a bit. Right-wing politicians termed anything they didn't agree with "fake news" and warned their supporters to be wary of the news media.

Interestingly, just after the election, Orwell's *1984*, a fifty-year-old novel, suddenly topped the Amazon best-seller list.[42] Perhaps this is in part because the main character, Winston, holds a job in the Ministry of Information, which is all about historical revisionism. Winston is supposed to go through old newspapers to update them when they contradict some "fact" Big Brother has just asserted. So if Big Brother says the chocolate ration was raised when in fact the new ration is lower than it was yesterday, it is Winston's job to revise any old news source that could contradict the leader's assertion. Thus anyone claiming that the chocolate ration had actually been lowered instead of raised could be accused of spreading "fake news" (to which Big Brother, aided by Winston, could immediately offer "alternative facts"). You might think Winston's job sounds ridiculous, but it really was someone's job during Stalin's reign of terror in the USSR. When Stalin had someone killed, he also had them airbrushed out of all official photos. An excellent book called *The Commissar Vanishes* shows how the official photos were doctored, removing Stalin's victims one by one.[43]

TACTIC: NUMBING THE PAIN

Many dystopian governments presume that it is probably easier to protect people from reality by messing with their minds. We're going to look at two techniques here: drugs and distractions.

In fiction, governments may provide drugs to make the citizens more compliant and easier to control. Earlier, we mentioned the Deltas—the underclass that does much of the work in *Brave New World*. They are kept numb and compliant (even apparently happy) with daily doses of a magic drug, soma, which has no adverse side effects. Soma is handed out at the end of each day's shift; the workers are literally working for drugs. The only time in Huxley's story that the Deltas show signs of unrest, discontentment, or anger is when their daily dose of soma is threatened by a main character trying (unsuccessfully) to stir them to rebel.

In real life, governments don't drug people. It's probably not that they haven't considered it but rather that the effects of mind-altering drugs are unpredictable. There are always side effects, unintended consequences, and in some portion of the population, there will be paradoxical reactions. A good illustration is in Joss Whedon's film *Serenity*.[44] In an attempt to protect a member of the crew, the ship and its occupants end up on a secret

planet called Miranda that the system's government—the Alliance—has
kept secret. Why was Miranda kept hidden? The Alliance had pumped a
drug, G23 Paxalon Hydrochloride (Pax), into Miranda's atmosphere to create a calm and obedient populace. Except it worked too well—the unintended side effect was that most people got so serene that they stopped doing
anything; they just lay down and died. A tiny fraction of the population
had the opposite reaction, which turned them into terrifying, hyperviolent,
sadistic cannibals known (and feared) throughout the system as "Reavers."

The unpredictability of people's reactions to drugs makes using them
risky; fortunately for dystopian leaders, drugs aren't the only way to pla-
cate a population. In the real world, authoritarian states often *buy* support
from their populations. They do things like provide free electricity and
health care, or they subsidize food and housing costs. By giving the citizens these perks, the state creates a tacit social contract: the government
will take care of you, and in response, you'll accept some oppression
(because where would you be without the generosity of the state?). According to an oppressor's logic, this is a win-win situation. Saudi Arabia has been
a leader in the free stuff and subsidies game, providing education and health
care to its people as well as heavy subsidies for food and petroleum.[45]

But the Saudis aren't alone. Almost all of the authoritarian states in the
Middle East have at least subsidized food and cooking oil. Many populist
authoritarians have done the same. For example, Venezuela's Hugo Chávez
subsidized state-owned food markets, put free medical clinics in poor
neighborhoods, and gave free food to school children.[46] These programs
won him the undying support of Venezuela's poor, and the programs were
continued by Chávez's successor, Nicolas Maduro. Yet the success of these
programs in alleviating poverty is questionable at best, and Venezuela's
economy is currently, to use the technical term, a massive train wreck.

Bribes aren't the only possible distractions—some states distract their
citizens with inexpensive entertainment, which has the added benefit of
allowing the state to build propaganda into the entertainment. The Soviets
and their satellite states all had state-sponsored entertainment bureaus, and
even the Nazis had a film industry. These served the state interest; people
were reminded of the rightness and power of the state while also being distracted from reality. In fiction, the Hunger Games weren't just a tool to
show the Districts how little power they had versus the Capitol; they were
also a form of entertainment aimed at distracting the people from examining the government too carefully. Different dystopian governments

Country: Saudi Arabia

Freedom House Score: 9 (not free)

Methods of control: Provide or heavily subsidize citizens' material needs—food, housing, energy, medical care, and education, all without taxing citizens (until 2017, when they introduced limited valued-added taxes). Of course, they also monitor behavior closely, and have morality police (the Haia) to regulate behavior. Plus, the Saudi monarchy is tight with the religious establishment, so it's not a surprise that the imams have issued Islamic legal pronouncements (fatwas) condemning all protest against the ruling family.

Distraction: Having all of your needs met at low or no cost is a pretty good distraction from the oppressive nature of your government. Historically, one major distraction issue in the Kingdom has been the lack of entertainment. Just as the government is cutting benefits, they've implemented the General Entertainment Authority—essentially, a "Ministry of Fun," which legalized . . . wait for it . . . movie theaters in late 2017. (What? You thought they were going to legalize booze and nightclubs?)

Does it work? The methods have worked so far. Government control of nearly everything has kept opposition movements relatively fragmented despite the widespread use of social media in the Kingdom. Saudi propaganda tells people that Iran backs all Shi'a opposition, helping divide Sunni and Shi'a opposition groups. But since the Saudi government is now rolling back food and energy subsidies, all bets are off. Cuts like those contributed to the Arab Spring—people felt their governments were no longer providing for them. It's doubtful that the General Entertainment Authority can provide enough fun to distract from the economic pain many Saudis are now feeling.

And when it doesn't work? There's always the secret police, the Mubahith, to tamp down on dissidents. Public lashings and executions are also used to deter protest.

Country: The City in the Uglies Series

Freedom House Score: 9 (not free)

Methods of control: Use surgery to make everyone "pretty" at age sixteen, and then move them from Uglyville into New Pretty Town (away from people who are still ugly). The surgery that makes everyone pretty also alters their brains to make them less intelligent and more compliant. The City provides all of their material needs—food, housing, clothing, education, and medical care. The rulers of the City also monitor exactly where people are at all times and have an extensive surveillance state.

Distraction: The City is a leisure environment for the Pretties, with nightly fancy-dress parties, plenty of alcohol-fueled fun, and convenient pleasure gardens for trysts with the other beautiful people. It's, like, totally bubbly. And if you seem to not be feeling bubbly, peer pressure and parties get you back on track in no time.

Does it work? On most people, yeah. First, all your needs are met, cradle to grave. Second, until you're prettified, you're termed an "ugly." There is massive social pressure to become pretty. Once you get to New Pretty Town, all of the beauty, glitz, and glamour distract you from even realizing that you've been stupefied, much less that the government manipulates you at every turn. So, unless you rebel before you get prettified, it's virtually impossible to see that there's anything to rebel against.

And when it doesn't work? There's always the secret police, Special Circumstances, to tamp down on dissidents. If a visit with them doesn't scare you straight, they can just tamper with your brain a bit more and wipe your memories. There's a chance that might kill you, but it's a risk they have no problem taking.

provide different distractions, but they all do something to keep the people from thinking too hard about the oppressive nature of the state.

TACTIC: ~~VIVE~~ SUPPRESS LA RÉSISTANCE

So let's say a dictator has eliminated organized opposition, and they've repressed the citizens through surveillance and the weakening of civil society, following strategy 1, but there are still pesky dissidents. These people are like ants for a dystopian leader; one has to get at the first ones quickly and brutally, or they will bring others.

We've already talked a lot about punishments, but not all of the punishments dished out by authoritarian regimes are physical. It isn't all torture, imprisonment, and disappearances. Some techniques are more insidious. The East German Stasi, for example, were masters of what they called *Zersetzung*, "disintegration," which meant nothing short of the complete destruction of someone's life. Essentially, if they suspected you were a dissident they destroyed your personal and professional life. They used rumors and lies to get you fired, to get your spouse to leave you, to have you ostracized by your neighborhood, and so on.[47] Imagine what the Stasi could do with today's information technology—it's terrifying.

If the resistance cannot be cowed or beaten into submission, the next most commonly used method is exile, either to another state or, most frequently, to some sort of prison or work camp. This removes them relatively nonviolently from the potential conflict area and also from the spotlight. (Note that this is harder in the internet age; Edward Snowden, for example, is effectively exiled from the United States but still regularly appears in webcasts and such.) In Atwood's *The Handmaid's Tale*, exile is no idle treat; in that world, noncompliant women are shipped off to work camps known as the Colonies, where they are treated brutally, mine plutonium, and die from toxic exposure and overwork.

Remote prison or labor camps are very popular ways to get rid of problem citizens. The Soviet system, made famous by Aleksandr Solzhenitsyn in *The Gulag Archipelago*, consisted mostly of a series of "corrective labor camps" (many in remote and miserable Siberia).[48] These were *corrective* labor camps rather than *forced*-labor camps, ostensibly because the "prisoners were being reeducated so that they could be good Soviets upon their rerelease into society."[49] Rerelease, that is, if they lived through their imprisonments; mortality rates were high.

Some people do end up exiled in other countries. They may be forced into exile by the state, or they may choose self-exile. Either way, exile doesn't always offer a lot of protection from vengeful dystopian governments. Leon Trotsky, one of Stalin's nemeses, was forced into exile in Mexico in 1929 but ended up dead at the hands of a Stalinist assassin in 1940.[50] Six decades later, Alexander Litvinenko—a former KGB officer living in exile in London—was poisoned with radioactive polonium while investigating the murder of the Russian journalist Anna Politskaya. There are allegations that both Litvinenko[51] and Politskaya were murdered by the Russian state.[52] Most recently, Kim Jong Nam—a half-brother and critic of North Korea's "Outstanding Leader" Kim Jong Un—was assassinated while traveling from Kuala Lumpur back to Macao, his home in exile. As the old saying goes: you can run, but you can't hide.

More extreme is to keep dissidents in complete isolation. Myanmar (formerly Burma), for example, kept the Nobel Peace Prize winner Aung San Su Kyi under strict house arrest without visitors for the better part of twenty years. If the dissident, however, is not protected (fame, family, and money can all be protections), it is easier simply to kill or disappear them. Winston Smith, in Orwell's *1984*, frequently reflects on the people who have just vanished because they did something Big Brother did not like.

Most extreme is the mass slaughter of even suspected dissidents—a topic so truly horrifying that even dystopian fiction usually avoids showing it. In real life, unfortunately, mass slaughter happens all too often—we've already discussed mass murders in Indonesia, Argentina, Guatemala, and El Salvador; another infamous example is the Cambodian genocide (1975–1979).

The Cambodian genocide was perpetrated by the then-rulers of Cambodia, the Khmer Rouge (Red Khmers—the communist party of "Kampuchea," as the communists called Cambodia). After taking power, the Khmer Rouge, under the leadership of the megalomaniacal sociopath Pol Pot, embarked on a massive social restructuring of the country—the goal of which was to return Cambodia to its precolonial, rural state.[53] Cities were emptied as the populace was forcibly resettled in the countryside, where they were all to be "reeducated," indoctrinated with the Khmer Rouge ideology. Families were separated and dissenters executed as the Khmer

Rouge essentially turned the entire country into a "prison camp state" in which "1.7 million of the inmates were worked, starved, and beaten to death."[54] While extreme, the Cambodian genocide shows the lengths to which dictatorial governments may go to control the citizenry, stamp out potential dissenters, and maintain power.

FINAL THOUGHTS

The tactics used by dystopian governments, both in fiction and in life, are what typically prompt people to push back in protest. For many people, there's a defining moment—the straw that breaks the camel's back, if you will—that pushes them over the edge.

In *All Rights Reserved*®, the fictional world where you have to pay for every word you say, our heroine—Speth Jime—is pushed to her silent protest by the death of her boyfriend, Beecher Stokes, who was about to be shipped off to a Collections debtor colony. Ultimately, Speth's silent protest spreads and touches off a series of events that bring down her city's government.

In real life, in Tunisia in 2010, a fruit vendor named Mohamed Bouazizi was pushed to protest as a result of the confiscation of his livelihood and public humiliation by the police. When the governor refused to take his complaint, Mr. Bouazizi set himself on fire in protest of the government's actions. His protest—and subsequent death—launched Tunisia's Jasmine Revolution, toppling Tunisia's Ben Ali regime. Ultimately, Mr. Bouazizi's sacrifice triggered the Arab Spring and the downfall of multiple long-time dictators in the Middle East.

Individuals have a role to play in any effort to resist a dystopian state, but they cannot typically disintegrate the state by themselves—that takes a movement. In chapter 5, we will discuss acts of individual resistance, and in chapter 6, we will move on to why collective (nonviolent) resistance movements work. Although this chapter has probably felt pretty bleak, take heart; the next few are more hopeful, we promise. Dictators—in fiction and reality—can seem infallible and unstoppable, but ultimately violent power is a weak method of control. Hang in there.

5

Individual Survival and Resistance

All I'm trying to do is survive and make good out of the dirty,
nasty, unbelievable lifestyle that they gave me.

—Tupac Shakur

So now you know a little about what types of dystopias there are and how and why they function. There is still the important question of how you should respond. Like it or not, you will be governed by whatever government exists where you live.

As the famous economist Albert O. Hirschman put it, we all have three basic options when it comes to responding to things we don't like: voice, loyalty, or exit.[1] (His theory started with reference to consumers and markets, but it also applies to states.) Voice means speaking up and trying to change things; loyalty means staying silent, which becomes consent; and exit is simply taking off. Each has its benefits and drawbacks. If your government gets bad enough, and you can't fix it, leaving entirely may be the best choice. But being a refugee is not an easy life, even if you are lucky enough to be taken in and perhaps even treated well by a new host country . . . and sometimes leaving is just not an option.

If you can't leave, the question of voice versus loyalty (silence) is a critical one, and which you choose will depend on your long-term goals. Surely, we hear you thinking, if the government is bad and I can't leave, I should resist. *Vive la Résistance!* Our response is a definite "maybe." If the government is bad enough and you, ultimately, want to survive, silence may be the best choice, at least for a strategic period while you work toward a more sustained and sustainable resistance (we'll talk more about how to do this in chapter 6). Those who choose the voice option, especially if they do so through violence, tend to lose their heads (literally as well as figuratively).

Since it is hard to resist and rebuild if you've lost your head, we suggest that most of the time your first job is just to survive, even if that means choking down the bile brought on by bad governance. Ultimately, we want you to resist dystopian government, but we want you to do it thoughtfully, effectively, nonviolently, and sustainably, not in a burst of passionate anger that may end up hurting rather than helping you and your cause. In this, as in so much of life, timing is everything.

Individual acts of bravery in resisting terrible government often get buried in the rubble of history (which is usually written by the victors), but we can all draw strength from the likelihood that no terrible government came to power completely unchallenged. And sometimes we do hear about the resisters, like the Nazi-era dissenter Otto Wels (from chapter 4), who stood up to Hitler, or the innumerable Germans, Poles, Danes, and others who helped hide Jews from his reign of terror.[2] But individual resistance has also been well documented in less severe cases.

WHEN TO RESIST VS. WHEN TO SIT DOWN AND SHUT UP

A functioning democracy has, by definition, certain safeguards that protect its citizens from government oppression (see our discussion of civil liberties back in chapter 1). Democracy-monitoring organizations like Polity or Freedom House designate the following as essential liberties: freedom of speech/expression, free assembly, education, freedom of religion, the right to due process, and free and fair elections. (Implied in all of these is the idea of the rule of law, "rules that are binding even on the most politically powerful actors in a given society.")[3] These organizations also measure how democratic a state is by looking at the presence or absence of certain key institutions. These institutions include an independent judiciary that ensures rule of law, free economic activity and equality of access to it, separation of powers across the executive and legislative branches, competitive parties (including a functional opposition to whichever party wins power), and limits on presidential power. Whether these safeguards and institutions exist—or, if they exist, what state they are in—are key determinants of whether resistance is safe for you.

This means that if you find yourself trapped in a dystopian state—or one slipping into dystopia—you have to give serious thought to whether you can

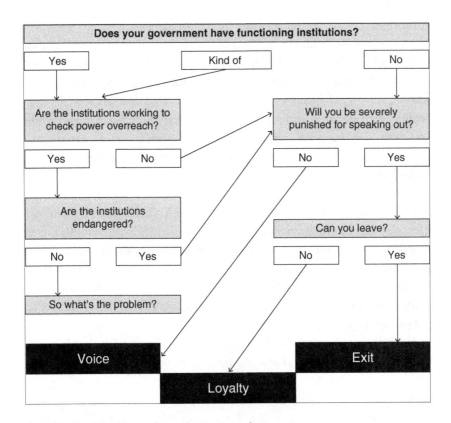

Figure 5.1 Decision tree under authoritarian rule.

Source: Graphic by the authors, based on Albert O. Hirschman, *Exit, Voice, and Loyalty: Responses to Decline in Firms, Organizations, and States* (Cambridge, MA: Harvard University Press, 1970).

resist safely. We get it: loud resistance is attractive and often important and useful. But depending on where your state is in the process of disintegration or authoritarian backsliding and how many people support the resistance efforts, speaking up could be hazardous to your health.

Passionate martyr-like action, where the human spirit bursts through, can serve a key role in getting a movement started, even (or, perhaps, especially) when such moments are carefully planned.[4] On December 1, 1955, Rosa Parks (a trained activist)[5] refused to give up her seat to a white man on the bus in Montgomery, Alabama, sparking a major insurgent phase in the black civil rights movement.[6] The Tiananmen Square "tank man," who was famously photographed in 1989 standing in front of and blocking a long line of tanks as part of the prodemocracy protests against the Chinese government, gave the world—and his movement—an image powerful beyond words.[7] Individual actors do not have to be well known, but the news of their actions must spread widely to be effective. Malala Yousafzai, shot in the head by the Taliban government in Afghanistan to stop her attending school and speaking out through a blog, survived and became a high-profile advocate worldwide for the education of girls. Such high-profile acts of protest break the intricate power arrangements of the panopticon and let others know that they are not alone in their opposition to the dystopian government.

Movies often glorify the idea that a single person can make all the difference, if they just believe in themselves enough. This is rarely true in real life; good resistance movements are built thoughtfully, slowly, and over time, and they come out of careful thinking, planning, and strategic intent, not individual passionate acts. As Anton Chekhov once said, "Any idiot can handle a crisis; it is this day-to-day living that wears you down." And while martyrs are sometimes useful for a movement, there are other ways to break the panopticon.

Ultimately, we recommend the slower, more frustrating, but in most cases infinitely more useful and sustainable strategy of joining with others

Figure 5.2 Tank Man, Tiananmen Square, 1989.
Source: Public domain via Wikimedia Commons.

in a movement for resistance; this is what chapter 6 will cover. But there are times when individual-level action for survival or resistance is not only necessary but your sole option. With that in mind, here are the strategies and tactics you might use.

STRATEGY 1: DON'T LET THE BASTARDS GRIND YOU DOWN

You're going to need survival tactics to stay alive and sane until you figure out what—if anything—you want to do about the dystopian nightmare you've found yourself in.[8] In the classic Hirschman "voice, loyalty, exit" formulation just described, you're going to use loyalty as a means of survival. Real loyalty is not needed, but you need to learn how to *look* loyal while also keeping yourself sane and alive.

One possibility, useful in the face of a horrible government, is simply outlasting the bad system. Truly terrible political leadership can get itself into trouble even without a movement against it (Bradbury suggests this in *Fahrenheit 451*, as does Atwood in *The Handmaid's Tale*); sometimes it pays just to watch it burn from the sidelines. The drawback, though, is that some very bad governments can last a long time—and hurt a lot of people—before failing.

Consider *The Handmaid's Tale*. In the fall of 2006 or thereabouts, one of us (Shauna) had the opportunity to attend a talk by its author, Margaret Atwood, about Atwood's dystopian capitocracy novel *Oryx and Crake*. At the end Atwood took questions, and Shauna asked, "Between this new vision and *The Handmaid's Tale*, which future do you find more frightening?" Atwood cocked her head to the side and said in a surprised tone of voice, "But I like to think of *The Handmaid's Tale* as a hopeful tale." No doubt noticing the highly confused look on Shauna's face, Atwood added, "Didn't you read the epilogue?"

The epilogue to *The Handmaid's Tale* ("Historical Notes") is an integral part of Atwood's larger argument. The book's fictional government, the Republic of Gilead, is a brutally repressive theocracy dedicated to perpetuating a particular status hierarchy through the strategic parceling out of fertile wombs (and the control over the women possessing them). The bulk of the story is a first-person narrative from one such woman, a Handmaid, who is forced into sexual and reproductive slavery to serve a rich, powerful

Commander and his wife. In the epilogue, however, the voice changes, and we are several hundred years in the future, the Republic of Gilead now merely a historical curiosity. The epilogue is mostly an academic's speech about the tapes that formed the basis (we are told) for the writing of the first-person text giving the Handmaid's story. Everything seems to have changed now; women are clearly scholars again, and there are jokes, humor, and fishing trips being discussed as part of the conference. The Republic of Gilead, we are left to deduce, as horrible and repressive and sexist as it was, did not last long. As Atwood finally put it to a confused Shauna back at that MIT talk, "All governments fail. Some fail faster than others." Gilead, it seems, failed fairly quickly.

On the other hand, for the Handmaid at the heart of Atwood's story, even a short-lived state lasted long enough to alter (and possibly destroy) her life in fundamental ways. Moral of the story: waiting it out isn't always an option. Whether you think you can outlast the government or you're biding your time until you can figure out how to resist, you're going to need some of the survival tactics we present here, at least until you can get to a place and time where you can safely resist.

TACTIC: PERFECT YOUR POKER FACE

Under a government that will not allow free speech, or even free thought, you must learn to be careful what you say, even when you're not saying anything at all. As the popular meme goes: "I can control my tongue; it's my face that needs deliverance." Orwell's Winston Smith is a good model for learning how not to show your real thoughts through facial expression. "He had set his features into the expression of quiet optimism which it was advisable to wear when facing the telescreen." Winston's beloved Julia is also a master of misleading. She has learned to participate vigorously in the daily "Two Minutes Hate" sessions, to the point of throwing things at the screen to show her enthusiasm, despite not believing a word of the Party's lies.[9]

In social science, this is called "preference falsification," as in making others (the government, in particular) believe something false about your preferences and interests. In particular, it is telling the government what it wants to hear—thereby ensuring a kind of "collective conservatism," with everyone clinging to the status quo. As Timur Kuran, a Duke University economist and political scientist, has put it, preference falsification happens when "because of group pressures, the policy preferences people express in public often differ from those they hold privately." This idea, Kuran explains, is not new. He quotes James Madison on the same concept: "The reason of man, like man himself, is timid and cautious when left alone, and acquires firmness and confidence in proportion to the number with which it is associated."[10]

Preference falsification is exactly what a dystopian government is trying to provoke in response to their panoptic measures of control and their attempts to atomize the population. As the character Dietrich (played by the immortal Stephen Fry) says in the 2005 movie *V for Vendetta*, "You wear a mask for so long you forget who you were beneath it." From the government's perspective, if you can never declare your true feelings, then you can never find people who agree with you. If you can't find the people who agree with you, then you can't band together and foment revolution. In these circumstances, we vote that you give 'em what they want, fly under the radar, and live to fight another day.

Preference falsification is pretty common in dystopian fiction. Katniss in Suzanne Collins's *The Hunger Games* learns to act helpless and play along with the media "spinning" of her story and not say what is truly on her mind. Tris, in *Divergent*, by Veronica Roth, knows that she fits into more than one government-mandated "faction" but carefully conceals this to avoid assassination. Mare, in Victoria Aveyard's *The Red Queen*, learns to imitate the cold, haughty demeanor of the "silvers" around her to maintain the pretense of being one of them. Surviving a dystopian government, these leading ladies know instinctively, often requires some heavy-duty acting skills.

TACTIC: STAVE OFF DESPAIR WITH SMALL VICTORIES

One of the greatest enemies in surviving a dystopian state is despair. Simply fighting the daily depression and anxiety that comes with living under such a regime is an achievement. We learn from dystopian fiction that we must do things to keep hope alive, to exercise the body and brain against the torpor of daily dystopia, and to create routines and projects that have meaning for us.

Unlike her predecessor Handmaid, whose misery led her to take her own life, Offred (the narrator in *The Handmaid's Tale*) refuses to give in to despair. Although she is denied any kind of true human connection or even personal comforts like hand cream, she learns to pilfer, hoard, and savor small luxuries quietly: "There's a pat of butter on the side of the plate. I tear off a corner of the paper napkin, wrap the butter in it, take it to the cupboard and slip it into the toe of my right shoe, from the extra pair, as I have done before. I crumple up the rest of the napkin; no one, surely, will bother to smooth it out, to check if any is missing. I will use the butter later tonight."[11]

Offred also carefully observes every detail of life around her, keeping track of tiny victories, like causing a teenage male guard to blush and avert his eyes when she walks by. She reads the misery in the face and actions of the Commander's wife, who has great power over her but is deeply unhappy. She keeps track of the seasons and savors even the plainest, simplest food or other pleasures, like feeling the sun's warmth. "But a chair, sunlight, flowers: these are not to be dismissed. I am alive, I live, I breathe, I put my hand out, unfolded, into the sunlight."[12]

TACTIC: KEEP HOPE—AND YOUR MIND—ALIVE

Offred is highly intelligent, but most of her life consists of boredom. "This is one of the things I wasn't prepared for," she tells us, "the amount of unfilled time, the long parentheses of nothing." She thinks back to her psychology classes in college, remembering what she learned about animal behavior, and uses it to try to understand her situation. "Somewhere in the eighties they invented pig balls, for pigs who were being fattened in pens. Pig balls were large colored balls; the pigs rolled them around with their snouts. The pig marketers said this improved their muscle tone; the pigs were curious, they liked to have something to think about."[13]

In lieu of a pig ball, she learns to keep her mind busy with silent wordplay: "I wait for the household to assemble. Household: that is what we are. The Commander is the head of the household. The house is what he holds. To have and to hold. Till death do us part. The hold of a ship. Hollow." And so on. Denied reading material, she stays sane by revisiting old memories, remembering discussions from college with her friend Moira, down to the last detail of Moira's jacket or the words Moira used to describe a term paper she was writing. She explores her room minutely, finding the "bastards" hidden message from a previous Handmaid etched in the closet, and draws strength and mental interest from every small thing that is out of place.

In these ways, Offred gets through her days without going mad. Becoming unhinged can get you killed. As she tells us at the book's start, "Thinking can hurt your chances, and I intend to last."[14]

In *The Postman*, a 1997 failed-state dystopian film directed by and starring Kevin Costner, a doggedly determined postman continues to deliver old U.S. mail. At first he does this to hide from his pursuers and to con people into believing the U.S. government still exists (and thus give him food). But then a strange thing happens: the con becomes real. Costner's character and the people around him begin to draw strength from the fiction of a functioning government and stand up to the warlord trying to take over their little town.

Such examples are not pure fictions, even if they are fictional. These examples feature the tools used in real tales of survival. In one of the most famous concentration camp survivor memoirs, Viktor Frankl (captured and imprisoned by the Nazis) wrote that for years he continued to converse in his mind with his wife, not knowing if she was alive or dead. Although both she and his parents had died, he did not know this, and he kept himself alive through sheer willpower thinking of them and his other family (some of whom had escaped) and by writing a book on slips of stolen paper. Perhaps because of his education (he studied philosophy and psychology as early as high school), he was able to keep himself alive by trying to understand his own experiences and derive from them lessons for others.[15] He explained:

> We who lived in concentration camps can remember the men who walked through the huts comforting others, giving away their last piece of bread. They may have been few in number, but they offer sufficient proof that everything can be taken from a man but one thing: the last of the human freedoms—to choose one's attitude in any given set of circumstances, to choose one's own way.

In 1945, Frankl was sick with typhoid fever and close to death when the camps were liberated by U.S. troops, but he survived, and his 1946 book, dictated from his scrawled prison notes, was later translated into English as *Man's Search for Meaning*, eventually selling over nine million copies.[16] Lasting can take the form of finding something to occupy your time that has meaning and resonance for you. As Frankl poignantly wrote, "Those who have a 'why' to live, can bear with almost any 'how.'"

STRATEGY 2: USING YOUR VOICE

Once you're pretty sure you're going to survive, you can start thinking about Hirschman's second option for responding to dystopian government: voice.

We've said it before: voice is dangerous. Witness Montag's friend, Clarisse, in Bradbury's *Fahrenheit 451*. Clarisse is a free spirit who asks interesting questions. Montag is fascinated by her, and they talk regularly; the government, however, is less entranced—particularly by her probing questions and nonconformist opinions. One day, Montag arrives home, and there's no Clarisse. His wife indifferently reports that Clarisse has died in a car accident. Montag does not believe it was an accident, nor does the reader; we all know that her critical thinking posed a danger to the government.

Government **legitimacy** simply means that people voluntarily accept the authority of the state.

Governments that lack **legitimacy** are dangerous because they rule through physically violent force rather than what the political scientist Jane Mansbridge calls "legitimate coercion."[17] All states use coercion of some form; indeed, this is how those in the know define what a state is—a "central authority that can exercise a monopoly of legitimate force over its territory to keep the peace and enforce the laws."[18] Mansbridge wants us to understand and appreciate that some coercion is legal and necessary and that not all coercion is violent or physical. We probably would not, for example, willingly pay enough in taxes to produce the roads, bridges, national defense, public education, and so forth that most of us seem to want for our society; we therefore coerce ourselves, through *law*, to make sure everyone pays so we can have these good things. Good government solves this kind of major problem to make life better for everyone.

Bad governments, governments that lack legitimacy, also use coercion, but in an illegitimate rather than legitimate way. This usually takes the form of state violence (force, threat, violence, jail, and other sanctions) because that government has lost the ability to rely on people's legitimate buy-in to state coercion. If a state needs to train its weapons on its citizens to maintain its own authority, it has already lost its legitimacy. As you may recall from chapter 2, reliance on physical force in the absence of legitimacy (particularly when the government starts shooting peaceful protesters) is what Atwood says is the best signal that we are in a dystopian government. Such a state still has force, and bad governments can survive on that for a while, but eventually force alone cannot substitute for genuine buy-in to its institutions from its citizens.

Violent coercion, the political philosopher Hannah Arendt theorized, may *feel* powerful because it achieves immediate results. An act of violence or the threat of it can exact what she calls "unquestioning obedience"—that is, "the obedience every criminal can count on when he snatches my pocketbook with the help of a knife or robs a bank with the help of a gun." But, she says,

> It is the support of the people that lends power to the institutions of a country, and this support is but the continuation of the consent which brought the laws into existence to begin with.... (Under conditions of representative government the people are supposed to rule those who govern them.) All political institutions are manifestations and materializations of power; they petrify and decay as soon as the living power of the people ceases to uphold them.[19]

Or, as William Penn (the founder of Pennsylvania) put it, "Governments, like clocks, go from the motion men give them."[20] In other words, force may give dictators the feeling that they are powerful, but legitimate power comes from the people. Dystopian states know this, and *that's* why they're terrified of people coming together. They work *so* hard to keep you from making connections with other people because if you make those connections you might figure out how powerful you could (collectively) be. As a result, standing up to such a state puts your own life (and probably the lives of those you love) at great risk. North Korea under the Kim family does not just arrest individuals who oppose (or even question) its rule; it arrests three generations of their families as well.[21]

Such is the choice faced by the individual lone actor deciding whether (and if so, how) to resist a dystopian state. Winston Smith, in *1984*, and perhaps (less consciously) Clarisse in *Fahrenheit 451*, made the calculus correctly; if you simply cannot live with yourself the way the state says you must live, the risk inherent in even small acts of resistance is preferable.

The assassination of Clarisse pushes Montag over the line from survival to resistance. Something clicks into place within him, and he decides his government is wrong. He begins, using Hirschman's tripartite formulation, to move from "loyalty" into "voice." What does that look like?

Individual-level resistance to a dystopian government can take multiple forms, ranging from the subtle and less risky (small, everyday acts like simple kindnesses to others or even quietly political art projects) to grand individual gestures like deliberately getting arrested or even martyrdom. Figure 5.3 gives a schema of the multiple forms of individual resistance we have catalogued from the fictional and real-life examples in this chapter. These forms of resistance fall on a continuum; although those on the far left, like the small-scale art project, may not seem as effective, they are part and parcel of the larger idea of resistance. And the smaller and more insidious forms help build the large mass movement that will ultimately be your best shot at overthrowing a dystopian government.

The rest of this section follows this idea of a continuum, starting with the smaller, everyday forms of individual-level resistance, like eye contact and empathy, and building up to the larger forms, like getting yourself arrested or a spontaneous protest. All of these actions, we think, are important, but ultimately we want you to join an intentional, long-term, nonviolent resistance movement. Winston, Montag, Mare, Katniss, and others give

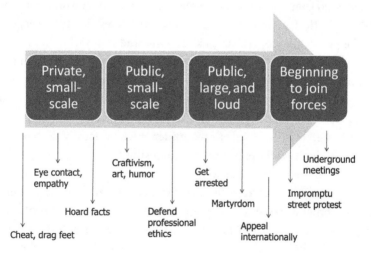

Figure 5.3 Varieties of voice: The spectrum of individual-level resistance.
Source: Graphic by the authors.

us good examples of individual resistance, but such individual lone actors cannot by themselves succeed in a rebellion. To overthrow a bad government, collective and nonviolent resistance is essential. It won't happen overnight, though, so you'll need tactics in the interim.

TACTIC: HOARD INFORMATION, COLLECT TRUTHS

In the last chapter, we discussed authoritarian regimes' tendencies to limit citizens' access to information. The Soviets built radios that could only be tuned to specific stations. The Chinese have built the "Great Firewall" to block access to the unrestricted internet. The North Koreans simply don't let people leave (or have internet or cell phones). All of this is done to prevent citizens from acquiring information that might be unfavorable to the regime (and foment dissent). Plus, depriving the people of good information is a great way of shutting down questions.[22] One of our favorite examples of this is from *All Rights Reserved*, where the government has forbidden the broadcast of negative information about the state and has made it legal to own a book only if you have a permit—free access to information is such a dim memory that people don't even know what a library is. (Speth's father explains to her that there used to be places called "liberties that would let you read any book, and all you'd have to do is show them a card.")[23]

Timothy Snyder, a Yale historian who has studied oppressive governments, writes, "Believe in truth. To abandon facts is to abandon freedom. If nothing is true, then no one can criticize power because there is no basis upon which to do so. If nothing is true, then all is spectacle. The biggest wallet pays for the most blinding lights."[24] For Orwell's character Winston, one of the worst things the government can do is treat facts as malleable. Good, doublethinking citizens should be able to believe that two plus two equals five if Big Brother tells them so. But Winston (alone, it seems to him) clings to facts. "Freedom," he decides, "is the freedom to say that two plus two make four. If that is granted, all else follows."[25]

Winston knows that most of the government-spread propaganda-infused news is false, but he rarely has information with which to counter it. He at one point had come across a photograph that directly contradicted one of Big Brother's pronouncements; although he had to destroy the photograph as part of his job in the Ministry of Truth (which spreads disinformation),

COMPARING DYSTOPIAS WINSTON SMITH VS. ALEKSANDR SOLZHENITSYN

Figure 5.4
Aleksandr Solzhenitsyn, 1994.
Source: Photo by Mikhail Evstafiev, Creative Commons BY-SA 3.0, via Wikimedia Commons.

Name: Aleksandr Solzhenitsyn (1918–2008)

State: The Union of Soviet Socialist Republics (USSR)

Freedom House Score: 4 (not free)[27]

> Occupation: Writer.
>
> Writings: *One Day in the Life of Ivan Denisovich* (1962), *Cancer Ward* (1968), *August 1914* (1971), *The Gulag Archipelago* (1973).
>
> Reason for writing: To stay alive, to stay sane, to remember, to share the Soviet government's terrible actions with the wider world.
>
> Government repression: Solzhenitsyn survived years of imprisonment in Soviet labor camps, cancer that went untreated for years while he was enslaved, multiple KGB investigations and smear campaigns,[28] and a 1971 poisoning (which failed to kill him).[29]
>
> Quote: "If only it were all so simple! If only there were evil people somewhere insidiously committing evil deeds, and it were necessary only to separate them from the rest of us and destroy them. But the line dividing good and evil cuts through the heart of every human being. And who is willing to destroy a piece of his own heart?"

Winston holds tight to the memory of that one true fact, using it as a touchstone to remind himself what is and is not true. His first major act of rebellion is to begin to write in a diary (thoughtcrime!); it allows him to stay sane and try to get down on paper his scattered memories. Our history, after all, is a large part of who we are. In so writing, Winston risks death but preserves his humanity and his memories. "If the Party could thrust its hand into the past and say of this or that event, *it never happened*—that, surely, was more terrifying than mere torture and death."[26]

COMPARING DYSTOPIAS WINSTON SMITH VS. ALEKSANDR SOLZHENITSYN

Figure 5.5 Big Brother.
Source: Sstrobeck23, Creative Commons BY-SA 4.0.

Name: Winston Smith, from *1984*

State: Oceania

Freedom House Score: 4 (Not Free)

Occupation: Bureaucrat in the Ministry of Truth (which concocts and disseminates government propaganda).

Writings: Invented biographies for the Party's purposes; short memos; historical reconstructions; and (secretly) a diary, which is forbidden.

Reason for writing: To stay alive, to stay sane, to remember, to share government's terrible actions with the wider world.

Government repression: Winston is captured, tortured, and broken by the Party that rules Oceania according to the precepts of Ingsoc and in Big Brother's name.

Famous quotes/insights: Truth matters: "Freedom is the freedom to say that two plus two makes four. If that is granted, all else follows."

A real-life version of Winston (albeit a far braver, cleverer, talented one) is the Russian writer and historian Aleksandr Solzhenitsyn, who could teach Winston a thing or two about withstanding torture and writing down truth. We compare the two in this chapter's "Comparing Dystopias" box.

Documenting the truth, Solzhenitsyn and Smith teach us, is not only an important part of what makes us human; it also can be a way to stay human even if your government is dystopian. Even if you can only write in your mind (as Solzhenitsyn did for years in the Soviet gulag), even if nobody can read it, writing is resistance.

TACTIC: MAKE HUMAN CONNECTIONS IN SPITE OF THE RISKS

Think back to the original panoptic prison design we talked about in chapter 4. The government creates an environment in which you may be being watched at all times . . . and if you're caught breaking the law, the punishment is swift and harsh. Remember: the point of panoptic measures of control is that when people are prevented from making connections with one another, it makes rebellion impossible. And the possibility of constant surveillance makes people police themselves, even in the absence of a guard actually watching from the tower.

Individualized, small-scale resistance under these governments, then, can be the simple but profound act of building real human connections with those around you. If the repression is built on separation and violence, those cannot be the root of your resistance; start instead from respect, empathy, and compassion. If the government is trying to divide you and make you fear one another, and especially if it is inciting based on differences (for example, ethnicity, language, class, race, education levels, and so on), then simply refuse to be divided. Find ways to connect across these differences and, where possible, speak up for others.[30]

Refusing to be divided and taking small steps toward connection can also show you who you can (and cannot) trust, information that might come in handy later. Timothy Snyder writes, "Make eye contact and small talk. This is not just polite. It is a way to stay in touch with your surroundings, break down unnecessary social barriers, and come to understand whom you should and should not trust. If we enter a culture of denunciation, you will want to know the psychological landscape of your daily life."[31]

Think about it this way: if you're going to need other people's help to survive, making real connections is vital. The idea of empathy—understanding/sharing other peoples' feelings—is so important to resisting dystopian government that Octavia Butler endows Lauren—the heroine in Butler's novel *Parable of the Sower*—with what she calls "hyperempathy," meaning that Lauren feels others' pains and pleasures as her own. She spontaneously starts to bleed when she witnesses someone else bleeding, even a stranger. Lauren lives in a failed-state dystopia, where climate change and corporate greed have caused a catastrophic social collapse. Forced to flee her home after her family is murdered, Lauren is a teenage girl on her own, but instead of increasing her vulnerability, her hyperempathic feelings save her by allowing her to connect with other good folks on the road going north. Together they are able to build a stable, protective community that keeps both hunger and the violent drug addicts at bay, things she could never have done alone. (Later in the series, in Butler's *Parable of the Talents*, Lauren's hyperempathy becomes more problematic, as it makes her a vicious killer—she learns to kill swiftly to spare herself further pain. We don't recommend hyperempathy, really. But regular empathy can be useful in connecting to others.)

TACTIC: RESIST OTHERING (AND BEING OTHERED)

Dystopian governments must shut down a real human instinct among their citizens toward empathy and connection; a divided populace is easier to control. Dictatorships must simplify and turn people against one another, often by **dehumanizing** one or more groups.[32] This plays into our nature, too; Simone de Beauvoir wrote in 1949, "Otherness is a fundamental category of human thought."[33] If a government can get you fixated on who is *us* (good) and who is *them* (bad), it ensures its own power and stability.

Dictators often **dehumanize** a group of people by referring to the group in nonhuman terms. For example, Hitler referred to Jews as "rats," and the Hutu leadership referred to Tutsis as "cockroaches" in the lead-up to the Rwandan genocide. When we dehumanize a group of people, it makes it easier to commit atrocities against them—you're not harming *people*, after all. You're eliminating *vermin*.

This is a classic and effective strategy for rising to and/or maintaining political power; it is a particularly devious and brilliant approach because it seems we already have an innate tendency to do just this. Social psychologists call this a tendency to "xenophobia," the fear of outsiders; it likely has evolutionary origins dating back thousands of years, when such fear conferred survival advantages. There are social-psych experiments that sort people into random groups (no ethnic/religious/linguistic/racial commonalities), and apparently people will still make it "us" against "them" (even when "us" is a random group of unrelated/unconnected people).[34]

Dystopian fiction gives us plentiful examples of deliberate government attempts to separate; Huxley's World State in *Brave New World* capitalizes on the human need for physical connection by encouraging meaningless sex, with free drugs to discourage feelings. In Atwood's *The Handmaid's*

Tale, members of each Commander's household are not only kept separated by rigid rules and a status hierarchy but also encouraged to spy on one another and report any potential misbehavior. As far as dividing people, take, for example, the five factions in Veronica Roth's 2011 novel *Divergent*, the districts in *The Hunger Games*, the uglies versus the pretties in the Uglies series, the proles versus the Party members in *1984*, the reds versus the silvers in Victoria Aveyard's novel *Red Queen*, the swanks versus the lice-biters in Paolo Bacigalupi's *Ship Breaker* . . . and more. Yet none of it works. Deep down, these authors are telling us, we as human beings need real connection. Hatred, cheap sex, drugs, or empty rituals will not do it.

Dystopian fiction gives us wonderful examples of resistance to attempts to divide and separate us. Wall-E, the plucky and hopelessly idealistic trash-compacting robot in Pixar's wonderful 2008 film of the same name, is arguably more human than the movie's human characters. Set five hundred years into a future where our earth has become uninhabitable and completely covered in trash, the animated movie is the unlikely love story between two robots who learn to trust their emotions and teach the emotionally stunted humans to do the same. Wall-E, who has followed his beloved Eve into space and aboard the remaining humans' ship (the capitocratic, corporate-controlled *Axiom*), shuts off the screens to which two of the human passengers had been glued in a consumerist frenzy. Freed from the seduction of commercial control, the two humans (John and Mary) look around as if for the first time. Mary exclaims, "I didn't know we had a pool!" She and John fall in love, all thanks to the emotional "awakening" instigated by little Wall-E.

George Saunders, through several short stories, tells us that we should listen to those nagging instincts like empathy and refuse to treat people like things. As discussed earlier, his story "The Semplica-Girl Diaries" tells of a world that seems not dissimilar from our own. We do not hear about the nature of its government, but we know it does nothing to prevent the employment (and surgical mutilation) of young impoverished women as lawn ornaments. The story's narrator is a hapless middle-class Everyman dreaming of wealth and trying to make his children happy, and he thinks that giving in to this new commercialist fad is the way to do this. But the proximity of such a human rights abuse in his front yard is too much for the burgeoning empathy and compassion of the narrator's eight-year-old daughter Eva, who finally frees the dangling Semplica Girls in the dead of night.

TACTIC: RESIST SIMPLIFICATION

Another dehumanizing effect of dystopian government arises from its attempts to simplify complex social realities, even beyond splitting people into groups. As the political scientist James Scott puts it, some of the worst things that governments have done derive from attempts to "improve the human condition." Specifically, the human "disasters" of which Scott writes (the Great Leap Forward in China, **collectivization** in Soviet Russia, and compulsory settlement in Tanzania, Mozambique, and Ethiopia) "are among the great human tragedies of the twentieth century, in terms of both lives lost and lives irretrievably disrupted."[35]

Collectivization was a Soviet (and later Maoist) practice of removing peasants from individual farms and forcing them to work together on large, state-run collective farms. Mass famine followed Stalin's initial push for collectivization.

States, Scott writes, have a great interest in creating and maintaining borders and, then, in oversimplifying the enormous complexity of the human life within, to make it "legible" (visible and taxable). Sometimes the motives behind these governmental schemes are good, as in attempts to help people and alleviate suffering, but the projects vastly simplify existing cultures—plus, they are narrow minded, dehumanizing, shortsighted, and often disastrous.[36]

Scott's solution is to resist such simplification and dehumanization. First, beware the arrogance of simplification; there are important limits on what the state can and should do, even in the name of helping people. Government is essential for our survival and the creation of our freedom, but "certain kinds of states, driven by utopian plans and an authoritarian disregard for the values, desires, and objections of their subjects, are indeed a mortal threat to human well-being."[37] Second, be on guard against state action that dehumanizes, treating human beings like cogs in a machine. Even when the state thinks it has a good reason for grand-scale social-reinvention projects, watch out. Ask questions.[38] It is often precisely the striving for someone's utopian ideal that plunges the rest of us into dystopia (Pol Pot and Hitler come to mind). As Sinclair Lewis wrote in his 1935 antifascist novel *It Can't Happen Here*:

> Is it just possible . . . that the most vigorous and boldest idealists have been the worst enemies of human progress instead of its greatest creators? Possible that plain men with the humble trait of minding their own

business will rank higher on the heavenly hierarchy than all the plumed souls who have shoved their way in among the masses and insisted on saving them?[39]

TACTIC: ART FEEDS THE SOUL

It may sound trivial—how can art bring down a dictator or keep the human spirit alive? But that is exactly what it does. Creativity is a fundamental part of being human. It brings us together, makes us think, makes us feel, breaks us open, and breaks down walls. Art as resistance is a time-honored strategy; it is another way to hold to truth and resist atomization—and don't forget that people find meaning and hope in art. See, for example, Emily St. John Mandel's *Station Eleven*—a failed-state dystopia where most people are just in survival mode. A few brave souls, among them the members of the "Traveling Symphony," go from town to town, bringing music and performing various Shakespeare plays. The symphony's motto, inscribed on the side of one of the traveling caravans, is "Survival is insufficient."

The words of Shakespeare, in fact, are frequently referenced in dystopian fiction, as an epitome (and reminder) of the best humanity has to offer. In *1984*, Winston, who is prohibited from using language other than "Newspeak," has dreams where he wakes with Shakespeare on his tongue. In *Fahrenheit 451*, Montag is drawn to (despite not understanding) the lines in books, including Shakespeare. And the collected works of Shakespeare form what is essentially a substitute Bible for John the "Savage," the protagonist of Huxley's *Brave New World*.

In the modern world, art-as-protest is a regular occurrence. A good resistance movement needs music (perhaps above all else!); one of the most prominent critics of Russia's Putin regime is a feminist punk band called Pussy Riot. With lyrics like "The head of the KGB, their chief saint / Leads protesters to prison under escort / Don't upset His Saintship, ladies / Stick to making love and babies" and a chorus that goes "Virgin Mary, Mother of God, banish Putin," Pussy Riot has become famous for pushing back against both Putin and the powerful Russian Orthodox Church. Beyond music, protest art runs the gamut from **craftivism** to high art and from literature to theater and dance.[40]

And artists can be more directly and vocally resistant, as in the case of the prominent Chinese dissident Ai WeiWei, who has achieved international renown for his artwork and both fame and repression for his outspoken criticism of the Chinese government. Now a "rootless exile who rarely leaves his studio in Berlin," WeiWei's political activism is inseparable from his art. After being beaten and jailed, he turned his post-beating medical treatment into an art project, further angering his government, and his latest project is on refugees. Ai has learned, better than most, the lessons on resisting division and extending empathy. "I am a refugee, every bit," he says. "Those people are me. That's my identity."[41]

> **Craftivism** is the idea of using craftwork as protest, like the pink "pussy hats" of the women's marches in 2016 and 2017. There is a worldwide craftivist movement; look up the "Social Justice Sewing Academy," for instance, or the "Craftivist Collective."

One of the most poignant examples of art as protest comes from *Never Let Me Go*. Its author, Kazuo Ishiguro, imagines a world in the not-too-distant future where the government initiates a cloning program so that privileged people have access to replacement organs when they need transplants. Clones are generally shunned by so-called polite society, treated as domestic animals or lepers. But some people see their humanity—like the headmistress of the clones' boarding school, who protests the ill-treatment of her students by emphasizing that they are indeed regular *human* children with feelings and abilities. Her evidence? The artwork they produce in drawing class.

TACTIC: KEEP A SENSE OF HUMOR, EVEN IN THE WORST OF TIMES

Dictators are prone to self-aggrandizement. They have people telling them how wonderful they are all the time, distorting their sense of reality. This also is a clever strategy; if you repeat something enough, people start believing it. We often mistake confidence for competence.

Reasonable argument rarely interrupts such confidence; sometimes you need ice to fight fire. Consider Charlie Chaplain in the controversial but hugely popular 1940 film *The Great Dictator*. Chaplain's brilliant satire of a fascist dictator probably did more to harm Hitler's reputation than all the newspaper denunciations. One scene in particular stands out, an odd duet described here by the film historian Jeffrey Vance:

> This scene, which stands with the very best set pieces of Chaplin's silent films, requires no words to convey its message. Accompanied by the

delicate, dreamy prelude to act 1 of Wagner's *Lohengrin* (Hitler's favorite Wagnerian opera), Hynkel (the dictator) performs a graceful, seductive ballet with a balloon globe, a wonderful symbol of his maniacal dream of possessing the world for his pleasure. Yet when he believes he has it within his grasp, the bubble literally bursts. This is Chaplin's symbolic comment on the futility of the dictator's aspirations and reflects his optimistic belief that dictators will never succeed.[42]

Mel Brooks, a brilliant writer, comedian, and film producer, has basically made a career out of making fun of Hitler (and other terrible people and human behaviors). "By using the medium of comedy," Brooks explains, "we can try to rob Hitler of his posthumous power and myths."[43]

The Serbian democracy activists Srdja Popovic and Mladen Joksic argue that humor forces bad governments into "lose-lose scenarios, undermining

Figure 5.6 Charlie Chaplin in *The Great Dictator*, 1940.
Source: Public domain, via Wikimedia Commons.

the credibility of a regime no matter how they respond. These acts move beyond mere pranks; they help corrode the very mortar that keeps most dictators in place: Fear."[44] They should know; as students in Serbia in the late 1990s, they helped pull a prank that interrupted the reign of fear of the dictator Slobodan Milosevic:

> We took an oil barrel, taped a picture of [Milosevic] to it, and set it up in the middle of Belgrade's largest shopping district. Next to it we placed a baseball bat. Then we [hid and] watched the fun unfold. Before long, dozens of shoppers lined the street, each waiting for a chance to *take a swing* at "Milosevic"—the man so many despised, but whom most were too afraid to criticize. About 30 minutes in, the police arrived. . . . They couldn't arrest shoppers—on what grounds? And they couldn't arrest the culprits—since we were [hidden]. So what did Milosevic's police do? The only thing they could: They arrested the barrel. . . . Milosevic and his cronies became the laughing stock of the nation.

Laughtivism is not a widely used strategy in dystopian fiction, but the "irreverent rebel" character often serves a vital role in breaking the panoptic hold, forging real human connections, and recruiting for the resistance.[45] Think of the errant, fly-by-night heating-duct engineer Harry Tuttle in Terry Gilliam's film *Brazil*. The premise is ridiculous—Tuttle (played by Robert de Niro) crisscrosses the city by zip line, fixing neglected heating and cooling ducts for beleaguered citizens whose maintenance has been held up by the foot-dragging bureaucracy. Harry's infectious irreverence, bonhomie, and sense of humor inspire Sam, our antihero protagonist, to resist. "Listen, kid, we're all in it together," Harry explains with smile and a wink.

Back in the real world, the 2011 Egyptian revolution is an excellent case study in the use of humor to depose a dictator. Bassem Youssef, known as the "Egyptian Jon Stewart," was a major player in the prodemocracy uprising and its aftermath, until it became too dangerous for him to remain in Cairo. The cost of speaking out, for Youssef, has been steep; he was forced to flee Egypt for his safety. But still, and despite the sorry state of his country, he says the Egyptian uprising stirred something important. "There are conversations in my part of the world that were not even imaginable 10 years ago," Youssef says. "People are speaking about religious freedom, gender

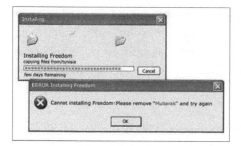

Figure 5.7 Humor vs. Mubarak.
Source: Widely shared internet meme
(2011).

roles. Freedom to do whatever you want. . . . It's a beginning."[46] Youssef
was in no small way a part of that change.

Using humor, Popovic and Joksic say, had multiple advantages in the
Egyptian case. For decades, Mubarak's Egypt was a country in which political opposition was stifled at the hands of state-sanctioned abuse, arrest,
and murder. In 2011, rather than shrinking away, activists successfully used
Mubarak's culture of fear against him. Humor quickly became a central
part of the anti-Mubarak communication strategy, using witty puns, bit-
ing caricatures, and snarky performances to make it "cool" to come to Tah-
rir Square and to be *seen* as politically active. Every day, larger crowds and
new faces joined the square's protests—not only because they wanted to oust
Mubarak but because they wanted to be a part of the "comic explosion."[47]

TACTIC: LEGALISTIC RESISTANCE AND UPHOLDING
PROFESSIONAL NORMS

*Recall professional ethics. When the leaders of state set a negative exam-
ple, professional commitments to just practice become much more important. It is hard to break a rule-of-law state without lawyers, and it is hard
to have show trials without judges.*

—Timothy Snyder, "20 Lessons from the 20th Century"

The Polish journalist Martin Mycielski recently wrote a fifteen-point guide
to surviving authoritarianism based on his own experiences in Poland,
which he shared publicly, adding "With love, your Eastern European
friends." He explained that one of the first moves by a clever dictatorship is
to attack the judicial system, which then removes the checks and balances

on the executive branch. He warns, "Preserve the independence of your courts at all cost; they are your safety valve, the safeguard of the rule of law and the democratic system."[48]

While the best resistance strategy is a widespread, nonviolent movement, there is always a place for individual acts of conscience and resistance, such as those based in professional ethics. Some of these forms of resistance might invite negative social or professional consequences, but doing these early on, as a dictatorship is trying to take root, can prevent many people dying later under that government's rule.

Consider the real-world example of the German (and one British) airplane pilots who have recently refused to deport Syrian refugees from their respective countries on the grounds of flight safety. "The decision not to carry a passenger, was ultimately down to the pilot on a 'case-by-case decision,' Lufthansa spokesman Michael Lamberty told the *Westdeutsche Allegeimeine Zeitung* newspaper which originally reported the story." According to the *Independent*, a British newspaper, "Pilots can face disciplinary measures if they refuse to fly on moral grounds." Instead, the pilots have cited their judgment and their professional standards to justify their refusal to transport deportees. If a potential deportee, when asked by the pilot whether they wanted to take the flight, answered "no," the pilot would refuse to fly with that person on board. "'We have to prevent anyone from being freaked out during the flight, and we have to protect the other passengers as well,' the pilot reportedly said."[49] In all, these pilots' actions have prevented more than two hundred planned deportations.

TACTIC: "WEAPONS OF THE WEAK"

When the great lord passes the wise peasant bows deeply and silently farts.
—Ethiopian proverb

The political scientist and anthropologist James Scott has made a career of studying, in the words of two of his book titles, the "weapons of the weak" and the "arts of resistance" to domination.[50] He delves deeply into the forms of resistance available to the poor—which, he tells us, do not look like those forms available to middle-class people and the intelligentsia. "Most subordinate classes throughout most of history have rarely been afforded the luxury of open, organized, political activity . . . such activity was dangerous, if not suicidal," he explains. "Since 'peasant' uprisings are both rare and doomed, he says, instead it's more important to look at 'everyday forms of resistance' that the common people use against those who seek to extract labor, food, taxes, rents, and interest from them."[51]

A phenomenal example of everyday resistance comes from Richard Wright, one of the foremost writers of the twentieth century. Wright, who is African American, grew up in the Jim Crow South, and he wrote powerfully about the individual acts of resistance that he used to survive and keep his spirit alive. In his early twenties, he moved from the Deep South to Memphis. He explained how his survival tactics changed in response to the different atmosphere:

> Here my Jim Crow education assumed quite a different form. It was no longer brutally cruel, but subtly cruel. Here I learned to lie, to steal, to dissemble. I learned to play that dual role which every Negro must play if he wants to eat and live. For example, it was almost impossible to get a book to read. It was assumed that after a Negro had imbibed what scanty schooling the state furnished he had no further need for books. . . . One day I mustered enough courage to ask one of the men to let me get books from the library in his name. . . . Armed with a library card, I obtained books. . . . I would write a note . . . saying: "Please let this nigger boy have the following books" . . . [signed] with the white man's name. When I went to the library, I would stand at the desk, hat in hand, looking as unbookish as possible. . . . If the books listed in the note happened to be out, I would sneak into the lobby and forge a new one. . . . No doubt if any of the white patrons had suspected that some of the volumes they enjoyed had been in the home of a Negro, they would not have tolerated it for an instant.

Wright's story illustrates the importance of Scott's emphasis on everyday resistance, such as "foot dragging, dissimulation, desertion, false compliance, pilfering, feigned ignorance, slander . . . and so on."[52] These are the forms of individual-level resistance that can, if enough individuals engage in them, start to undermine a dystopian state before it becomes vulnerable to full-scale revolution. Scott writes, "It is my guess that just such kinds of resistance are often the most significant and the most effective over the long run."[53]

Sometimes, in the face of terrible government, all you can do is cheat and betray (but be careful). In the 1997 film *Gattaca*, directed by Andrew Niccol, a genetically inferior "invalid" man (Vincent) assumes the identity of a genetic superior (Jerome), with both getting something from the illegal bargain. Although Vincent is a master of disguise, he is almost caught by the end of the story, but a sympathetic doctor (whose son is also "invalid") passes him as "valid," helping him achieve his dream of becoming an astronaut.

In *Pretties*, the second book of Westerfeld's Uglies trilogy, small, daily acts of resistance are the name of the game for Tally Youngblood and her friends.[54] In Tally's world, everyone starts out "ugly," but at age sixteen most people have the free cosmetic surgery offered by the government, turning them into "pretties"—but the surgery (cleverly) also produces brain lesions that impede critical thinking and make citizens far less likely to question the government. Even with no clear resistance plan, Tally and a few friends start to fight the incessant "bubbliness" that keeps them dumb and distracted, drinking black coffee to stay sharp and using pain to focus their minds and drown out the dullness. While we emphatically do *not* endorse self-harm, we do encourage resourcefulness in the face of a government that is out to do you harm.

TACTIC: GO DIRECTLY TO JAIL (DO NOT PASS GO)

In real life and in fiction, going to jail is a time-honored tradition for those taking a stand for some principle of importance. One of our favorite examples comes from Susan B. Anthony, a nineteenth-century American suffragist. Anthony was not one to take the denial of her rights lying down. On November 5, 1872, in Rochester, New York, she cast an illegal ballot in the presidential election. Ann Gordon, the editor of Anthony's papers, wrote, "The government charged her with the crime of voting without 'the legal right to vote in said election district'—she, in the words of the indictment, 'being then and there a person of the female sex.'" Anthony's lawyer did not deny it; it was a primary point for the defense. The denial of her voting rights because she was female was unconstitutional, he explained to the jury, adding, "I believe this is the first instance in which a woman has been arraigned in a criminal court, merely on account of her sex."[55]

The judge prohibited Anthony from testifying in her own defense, but she made a statement to the court after her conviction, when the judge (unwisely) asked if she had anything to say. She replied (in a speech that became instantly famous and widely published and reenacted):

> Yes, your honor, I have many things to say; for in your ordered verdict of guilty, you have trampled under foot every vital principle of our government. My natural rights, my civil rights, my political rights, my judicial rights, are all alike ignored. Robbed of the fundamental privilege of citizenship, I am degraded from the status of a citizen to that of a subject; and not only myself individually, but all of my sex, are, by your honor's verdict, doomed to political subjection under this, so-called, form of government. . . . Your denial of my citizen's right to vote, is the denial of my right of consent as one of the governed, the denial of my right of

Figure 5.8 Susan B. Anthony (c. 1880–1906).
Source: Public domain, via Wikimedia Commons.

representation as one of the taxed, the denial of my right to a trial by a jury of my peers as an offender against law, therefore, the denial of my sacred rights to life, liberty, property.[56]

In dystopian fiction, resisting oppression from one's government is a time-honored tradition, although it often does not end well for the protagonists (poor Winston). Many dystopian works have protagonists that join or help create resistance movements: Katniss in Collins's *The Hunger Games*, Madrone in Starhawk's *The Fifth Sacred Thing*, Montag in Bradbury's *Fahrenheit 451*, Selver in Ursula K. Le Guin's *The Word for World Is Forest*, Mal Reynolds in Joss Wheedon's *Firefly*, and more.

And then sometimes there are radicals who may not be part of a movement per se but live resistance through their very existence, inspiring others. Consider Moira, Offred's best friend from *The Handmaid's Tale*. The thought of Moira helps keep Offred going through the hard moments in the repressive Republic of Gilead. Moira is funny, irreverent, and irrepressible. These qualities continually get her in trouble in the new regime, where women are supposed to be seen, not heard. At the Red Center (the "retraining" facility for fertile women), Moira is severely beaten for resisting the Handmaid training. After recovering, she plots and then executes a daring escape, nearly making it across the border into Canada before she is caught. She ends up in Jezebel's, a prison (of sorts) for wayward women who won't conform. The place is fairly miserable, and Offred is shocked to see Moira working as a prostitute, but Moira prefers that life to being a Handmaid.

A real-life example of a woman who wouldn't conform is the Russian poet Natalya Gorbanevskaya, who in 1968 very publicly began to resist Soviet rule, at a time when those who did so often just disappeared. In 1969, she helped found a group to promote civil rights and was arrested by the end of that year. As a result, she was imprisoned until 1972 in a psychiatric hospital, having been diagnosed by Soviet doctors as having "continuous sluggish schizophrenia," whatever that means. To the singer-songwriter Joan Baez, Natalya Gorbanevskaya was perhaps the sanest person in the USSR. Baez famously said, "It is because of people like Natalya Gorbanevskaya, I am convinced, that you and I are still alive and walking around on the face of the earth."[57]

Writing from jail is another important tradition; imprisonment can be a megaphone. One of the most famous pieces written by an imprisoned dissident is Martin Luther King Jr.'s "Letter from a Birmingham Jail" (1963),

Figure 5.9 Natalya Gorbanevskaya.
Source: Public domain, via Wikimedia Commons.

penned after King was arrested for violating a court order prohibiting protests for black civil rights. King directly attacks a seeming contradiction; how can civil rights fighters, he asked, "diligently urge" the country to obey the Supreme Court decision in *Brown v. Board of Education*, which outlawed racial segregation in education (and which was angrily protested by whites), but deliberately break other laws? The answer, he says, drawing on St. Augustine, is that "An unjust law is no law at all."

Getting oneself arrested to make a point is, to be sure, a rather extreme form of voice, but as you can see, it has an excellent pedigree. Without a more robust movement behind you, your single arrest may not matter much, but hell, it can be a great start.

STRATEGY 3: SHOULD YOU STAY OR SHOULD YOU GO?

When life becomes intolerable in your dystopian state, it's time to exercise Hirschman's exit option. It's highly likely that you should go, particularly if the government has identified you as a troublemaker (recall our discussion of Bassem Youssef).

Exit has a somewhat interesting history. Some authoritarian regimes permitted—even promoted—the exit of possible dissenters, particularly in the late 1800s and early 1900s. As Hirschman put it, large-scale exit

> alleviated a number of problems, economic as well as political. . . . People who chose emigration were obviously dissatisfied in some way with the country and society they were leaving. With exit available . . . they were less likely to resort to voice: the ships carrying the migrants contained many actual or potential anarchists and socialists, reformers and revolutionaries.[58]

This has been less the case in the recent past, however. In the 1970s, Soviet premier Leonid Brezhnev allowed thousands of Soviet Jews (long the target of Soviet anti-Semitism) to exit the USSR.[59] In 1980, Cuba's Castro announced that any Cuban who wanted to go to America could do so—just board a ship at the Mariel port. About 125,000 Cubans did—it later turned out that about 2,300 of them were people Castro had released from prisons and/or mental hospitals and sent over—but the majority of the exiles from the "Mariel Boatlift" were simply people who wanted out of Cuba.[60] Other than those two notable exceptions, modern dictators (particularly of the highly ideological totalitarian variety) haven't been big on exit. After all, if you let a few people leave, the rest might get ideas . . . not to mention that if you allow dissidents to leave, they may bring unwanted outside attention to your regime once they are out of your control.

TACTIC: GET OUT IF YOU CAN

Fleeing is an extremely common individual response to a terrible government. Terrible governments know this, however, and some take great pains to prevent dissidents from exiting. Think of the Berlin Wall, which was built to prevent people from escaping Communist East Germany. That notwithstanding, East Germans attempted to flee to West Germany on a regular basis. If they made it, the West German government helped resettle them; if they didn't make it, the East German government imprisoned them. And, particularly toward the end of the Cold War, being imprisoned became a backdoor to freedom. Given that it was a nominally socialist government in a resoundingly capitalist world, East Germany was chronically short of hard currency (which you need for trade). So the West and East Germans worked out a secret deal: West Germany would buy East Germany's political prisoners. The prisoners were sent to freedom in West Germany, while East Germany got cold hard cash.[61] Win-win.

Protagonists in dystopian fiction often opt out of their governing systems by trying to flee (but usually not succeeding, as this genre is allergic to happy endings). A classic here is *Blade Runner* (the good version).[62] After years of unhappy resignation, Deckard has found love and is unable to put up any longer with working for the government and killing androids like Rachel. The film ends with the beleaguered bounty hunter Deckard escaping (perhaps) with his beloved, Rachel.

In *The Handmaid's Tale*, escape attempts bracket the entire story. At the beginning, our unnamed narrator ("Offred," eventually) and her husband are trying to escape the new Republic of Gilead by crossing the northern border into Canada when they are caught. At the very end, Offred is taken away in a black van belonging to the "Eyes," but there is the suggestion that it is actually a rescue. She suddenly stops narrating, and it seems that she did indeed manage to escape (maybe). As in *Blade Runner*, Atwood's ending here is deliberately vague, but it is clear that for these protagonists, exit eventually becomes the preferred (or only remaining) strategy.

STRATEGY 4: JOINING FORCES

At some point, likely when you start to feel that your individual resistance is not enough, you'll want to connect with other people. This can take the form of spontaneous protests, like the one in Ursula K. Le Guin's novel *The Dispossessed*, when the workers of A-Io protest their mistreatment (and then are slaughtered, but that's not the point here). You could also band together and go underground, as in *It Can't Happen Here*, when the editor of the local paper joins with those closest to him to print and distribute antigovernment materials. Either way, once you start working with others, you *could* be on your way to a movement.

TACTIC: SPONTANEOUS COMBUSTION

We don't mean literal combustion—explosions are bad. What we do mean is that a spontaneous protest is an excellent way to break the panopticon—it shows people that they aren't alone in their dissatisfaction with the dysto-pian regime. That's an important early spark to igniting a mass movement (see what we did there?). But even a huge demonstration is not the same thing as a sustained mass movement. A demonstration *can* turn into a movement, but not without a lot of effort (and good organization). Until you put in that effort, a mass demonstration is simply a collection of indi-vidual protests . . . and that is *highly* unlikely to bring down a regime. We've got three examples for you, one protest that turned into a movement, one that did not, and one that still might.

Our example of a success comes from a Chilean protest during the Pino-chet era. Prompted by a Chilean copper miners' union, people began a series of national days of protest. In one, they just slowed down, walking and driving at half-speed . . . and you can't really arrest people for driving at half-speed.[63] The democracy activist Srdja Popovic explains that "people were afraid to talk openly about despising Pinochet. . . . Watching the slow drivers and walkers . . . you could be certain that everyone hated the tyrant."[64] At prearranged times of day, people also banged pots and pans (a traditional form of protest in many countries), honked their horns, and flipped their lights on and off. Predictably, the government met these actions with arrests and violence, but the national days of protest continued.

Initially, these were essentially just displays of dissatisfaction. Of course, some people really thought these protests might bring down the Pinochet government, but without a clear goal (or plan), that was unlikely. Out of these protests, though, a broad coalition came together from across Chile's political spectrum. This group, called the Alianza Democratica, had a goal of using nonviolent means to promote a free and democratic society; it had a leadership team and local organizational support. It was, in short, *a move-ment*. The Alianza Democratica didn't break up the government, but it did succeed in gaining concessions from the regime, including an agreement that the government would allow some public political activity.

Our example of an unsuccessful attempt to form a movement comes from Belarus in 2011. At the time of this writing, Belarus is (still) ruled by Alexander Lukashenko—often called Europe's last dictator. After protests related to fraudulent elections and major economic problems, Lukashenko started a crackdown on protesters. In response, a Belarusian group used social networks to call for a flash mob to gather and simply clap. At the first one, a few hundred people showed up and, according to the *Atlantic*, "clapped with hesitation, looking over their shoulders to be sure they weren't acting alone." More and more people started showing up to these clapping flash mobs, which left the regime with a dilemma: people are challenging your authority . . . but can you really arrest them for *clapping?* Sadly, in the Belarus case, the answer was an emphatic *yes*—the government even arrested a one-armed man. For clapping.[65]

In the absence of strong leadership and a well-defined goal, the brutality of the repression, combined with an improvement in the economy, sent Belarus's clapping protesters back home. The economy is an important factor here, because it's part of Belarus's implicit "shot and a pork rind" social contract, meaning that there's a tacit agreement that as long as people have some economic stability (that is, food and drink), they won't protest.[66] In 2017, a serious economic downturn sent people back out into the streets to protest the state's economic policies. As of this writing, however, Lukashenko is still very much in power.

Last but certainly not least, we want to talk about the #MeToo protest that went viral in late 2017 and was (weirdly) named *Time*'s Person of the Year. The hashtag took off in October 2017, when the actress Alyssa Milano asked her Twitter followers to tweet #MeToo if they'd ever experienced sexual harassment or assault. Milano's tweet gave #MeToo visibility, but #MeToo was not her invention; it was started in 2006 by an African American activist named Tarana Burke in her efforts to help young women of color who were victims of sexual harassment and assault. In an interview with CNN, Burke, the program director of a New York–based organization called Girls for Gender Equality, describes #MeToo this way: "On one side, it's a bold declarative statement that 'I'm not ashamed' and 'I'm not alone.' On the other side, it's a statement from survivor to survivor that says 'I see you, I hear you, I understand you and I'm here for you or I get it.'"[67]

Just two days after Milano's tweet, the social media numbers were staggering: 825,000 posts on Twitter and more than 12 million posts, likes, and comments, representing 4.7 million people around the world, on Facebook.[68] Since then, #MeToo has been translated into a number of different languages and has spawned other hashtags, like #MeTooCongress (highlighting sexual harassment in the U.S. Congress). And information that has come out of this campaign, which involves individuals stepping forward relatively autonomously rather than in a coordinated, movement-structured way, has brought down the careers of many powerful men in Hollywood, politics, and beyond.

Despite the high-profile nature of the #MeToo protest, it's too early to say if it will become a well-defined, goal-oriented, widespread movement.

At the time of this writing, there's now a Hollywood commission—headed by Anita Hill, the lawyer who alleged, under oath, that now–Supreme Court justice Clarence Thomas had sexually harassed her—to tackle the culture of sexual abuse that pervades the film industry.[69] It's a good start, but what about women whose industries aren't so glamorous—like teachers and administrative assistants? What about women whose jobs are precarious—like domestic and retail workers? The point here is that, while we fervently hope that #MeToo will become a strong movement that crushes the patriarchy, it's not one yet.

TACTIC: GO UNDERGROUND AND FIND YOUR PEOPLE

As we'll caution you in chapter 6, secrecy is ultimately very detrimental to your efforts to unseat your dystopian government. However, in the early days, it is likely necessary if you're going to grow from a small group of protesters into a mass movement. For example, as a wave of laws criminalizing homosexuality has swept across parts of Africa, LGBT organizations have moved underground, fearing arrest or even death.[70] In Uganda, the leading LGBT activist group, Sexual Minorities Uganda (SMUG), was forced to hide its operations when Uganda passed a law criminalizing LGBT activity. One of SMUG's founders, in an interview with the *Guardian*, said, "We are an illegal organization. We are underground. We are essentially operating guerrilla warfare and could be raided by the police at any minute."[71] Although the anti-LGBT law was declared unconstitutional, well-known SMUG activists still regularly receive threats of violence and death, and anti-gay vigilante violence is common.[72]

Perhaps the most famous example of a quiet underground in futuristic fiction is the "Living Books" at the end of Ray Bradbury's *Fahrenheit 451*. By the end of the story, the city has been bombed to smithereens, but Montag and a few others escape and hide in the forest and start walking, following the streams. Each man (mostly former professors, apparently)[73] has been charged with remembering a text; these are the "Living Books." Their leader, Granger, introduces him to the circle: "I want you to meet Jonathan Swift, the author of that evil political book, *Gulliver's Travels*! And this other fellow is Charles Darwin, and this one is Schopenhauer, and this one is Einstein." There are thousands, Granger tells Montag, living on the edges of the corrupt society, biding their time. " 'All we want to do is keep the knowledge we think we will need intact and safe. . . . When the war's over, perhaps we can be of some use in the world.' "[74]

Underground resistance groups show up in other types of fiction as well. A dystopian state arises in the magical world of Harry Potter (book 5, *The Order of the Phoenix*) when, as a means to control the populace, the magical government actively suppresses knowledge of the reawakening of the dark wizard Voldemort's campaign to ethnically cleanse the wizarding population of people without pure magical ancestry. The Ministry of Magic removes Dumbledore, the beloved head of Hogwarts School of Magic, and the minister, Cornelius Fudge, appoints his crony, Dolores Umbridge, as temporary Head of Hogwarts. Umbridge is paranoid and sadistic and sets out to make Harry and his friends' lives miserable. Knowing they will be persecuted for rebellious activity but also feeling that they must do something, Harry and his friends form a new and secret club, "Dumbledore's Army," to train one another in self-defense magic. They must keep their meetings a complete secret, as they could be expelled for such participation, but the value of the training, comradeship, and resistance makes it worth the risk.

FINAL THOUGHTS

Individuals *can* make a difference—we don't want to leave you with the impression that they can't. When enough people resist on a daily basis, it does begin to undermine the regime. And for the individual actors, small acts of resistance can keep the human spirit alive and help form needed connection with others. The takeaway message from this chapter, though, is that acting alone is unlikely to bring down a dystopian government. In the next chapter, we'll move into group efforts to bring down the regime. Fight on!

6

The Resistance Will Not Be Intimidated

*To fight and conquer in all our battles is not supreme excellence;
supreme excellence consists in breaking the enemy's resistance without fighting.*

—Sun Tzu

In the previous chapter, we looked at individual mechanisms for
surviving and resisting a dystopian government. Individual action
does not a successful resistance make. In fiction, our protagonist
may save the day—but they rarely do so singlehandedly. Individual action
can spark the revolution, but collective action is what really can topple the
dystopian regime. In the Hunger Games series, Katniss may push President
Snow's buttons, but she could never have brought the Capitol down on her
own—the same thing is true of Talley in *Uglies* or Emmet in *The LEGO
Movie*. So what is **collective action**, and how does it work? What should it
do, and why? Worry not—this chapter moves you from individual to collective resistance.

An individual mosquito is fairly easy to slap away, but have you ever been
surrounded by a cloud of the suckers? You can't slap away all of them. A
collective nonviolent resistance movement works
the same way. A good resistance movement will provide cover for its individual actors, who would be
immediate targets if working alone.

Dystopian fiction offers us some instructive examples of failed rebellions, and often the problem is that
no one joins in. Take the failed "soma uprising" in
Huxley's *Brave New World*. In this world, humans are
conditioned from birth to be happy and unthinking
drones, medicated by the government with soma.
John, raised in a different culture, finds the constant

> **Collective action** is
> simply when a group works
> together to accomplish a
> goal that one person, acting
> alone, would not be able to
> accomplish. Government
> (which provides for
> collective security, schools,
> defense, law and order,
> roads, etc.) and revolution
> (a sustained campaign to
> bring down the government)
> are both good examples of
> collective action.

drugging disquieting. His ill-fated protest involves commandeering a drug dispensary and throwing all the soma out the window; this does not sit well with the addicted masses or their corporate overlords. Instead of joining him, the Deltas try to tear him limb from limb. Poor John failed to understand the need for collective action and badly misjudged the situation. As long as the Deltas remained deeply addicted to the government-provided drug, they would not join the rebellion.

Free riding is the biggest problem that any collective action faces, and free riders are the big reason you hate group projects. First, the bigger the group gets, the more likely someone is to stop contributing to the group's goal (someone else will pick up the slack, right?). Second, if there's already a collective action taking place, then the work is getting done, so if you're risk averse/work averse, why join? Essentially, you have a group of people working toward a common goal and another group who want to see that goal attained but who aren't willing to join the action to make it happen. That second group is the free riders—they benefit from other people's participation in the collective action.

The problem for John, and for most nascent movements, is that collective action is (to put it mildly) often a miserable exercise in frustration. Writing in 1965, Mancur Olson delved more deeply into the challenges of collective action. Just because people have interests in common, Olson pointed out, does not mean they will organize together to achieve them.[1] Instead, individuals always have an incentive to **free ride** on the work of others; why join a movement when you could sit back, watch other people work hard, and then enjoy the same benefits? Free riders are just along for the ride; they get to the same destination, but without contributing gas money or sharing the driving.

This problem is exacerbated if there are high penalties for such movement activity; if you can avoid work *and* those penalties (say, death, jail, torture), why join a movement at all? The Deltas in *Brave New World*, conditioned as they were from birth to be nonrebellious and genetically manipulated to be not very smart, were never going to join John's failed revolution. Huxley's dystopian government involved a long-lasting and stable set of interlocking social, political, and economic systems, buttressed by some genetic engineering; it would not be toppled so easily.

MAMA, WHERE DO MOVEMENTS COME FROM?

This is where leaders and other key movement actors come in. Before a movement can become, well, a movement, it needs some thinking and some structure in place. To succeed, a movement must figure out how to articulate its central claims, convince others of their justice and rightness, and find ways to make the work of the movement not too difficult or over-bearing, so that ordinary people can participate. Laura Liswood, founder of the Council of Women World Leaders, likes to say that all successful movements must move through three phases, from the "unthinkable" to the impossible to the inevitable.[2]

So the first thing is that a movement must be *thinkable*. People must be able to imagine the change they want to see in the world. That may seem blindingly obvious, but sometimes it is hard to see oppression. Think about this: sexual harassment, domestic violence, sexual coercion by exploitative bosses, marital rape—for millennia, none of these were thought of as crimes, violations of women's human rights, discrimination, or even as problem-atic. Mostly, we didn't even have names for these things; moms everywhere told their daughters, "That's life, honey." The idea that these were wrong, harmful, even illegal, had to be *developed*, which women lawyers and activ-ists accomplished in the 1970s.[3]

A movement needs both theory and language behind it. High-commitment activists develop the thinking (theory and language) essen-tial in developing the movement's goals, strategies, and tactics and in get-ting others (who are not part of the inner core) to join in. For instance, the U.S. "women's liberation" movement of the 1960s and 1970s produced the ideas and language that went into the term "male chauvinist pig," which was a useful shorthand term that served both to draw attention to sexist male behavior and to call for it to change.[4] Terms like that one allowed "everyday activists,"[5] ordinary nonmovement women, to play a role in fight-ing back against the idea that abusing women was "just life." The women's movement is a great example of how language and theory together form the *message*—which is the bedrock on which a successful movement can then be built.

TIMING IS EVERYTHING

If your movement has any shot at winning, conditions must be favorable. Societal events produce what you might call "windows of opportunity" wherein a social movement might be successful.[6] These windows are constantly opening and closing, in accordance with current events and changing political conditions. You have to strike when a window is open if you want your movement to catch on; the political system, in other words, must be showing some vulnerability.

In the Jim Crow South, for example, World War II created such a window of opportunity for the American civil rights movement. The war's end brought the return of a cadre of black veterans, who had seen better integration and racial equality overseas.[7] At the same time, the United States was increasingly facing international pressures from the Cold War, and Russia actively used against the United States news reports of racial segregation, the poor treatment of African Americans, and other racial discrimination; the Russian and other countries' presses used these facts as evidence of U.S. hypocrisy and of the superiority of communism, which they claimed better created equality for all. Finally, the mass decolonization of Africa and Asia meant the formation of dozens of new countries run by nonwhite peoples; racial equality was front and center on the worldwide stage. Reports of officials from the new African nations being treated poorly on visits to the United States were a huge embarrassment.[8] All of this pressure forced the U.S. government into pro-civil-rights action that its leaders (Truman, Eisenhower, and other presidents) would likely not have taken otherwise, such as Truman's integration of the military in 1948 or Eisenhower's use of the army to integrate schools when Southern governors and angry mobs tried to block black children from entering.[9]

Yet simply having a window of opportunity is not enough; the movement also needs some organizational structure in place *and* a strong belief that things can change.[10] In the civil rights era, the movement had a strong organizational structure that included local NAACP (National Association for the Advancement of Colored People) chapters, black churches, and black colleges.

Next is the belief that things can actually change. And this is where the theory and language—the message—developed earlier is so critical; who's going to join a movement that they don't believe will work? As the political scientist E. E. Schattschneider noted back in 1960, "People are not likely to start a fight if they are certain that they are going to be severely penalized for their effort."[11] Or, to take it back to Laura Liswood's framing, the movement, before it can attract mass membership, needs to find a way to convince its participants that it is not *impossible* but *inevitable*. We're going to come back to how to attract members later on—but first we want to talk about what you're attracting them *to*.

BRAINS OVER BRAWN

When it gets down to having to use violence, then you are playing the system's game. The establishment will irritate you—pull your beard, flick your face—to make you fight. Because once they've got you violent, then they know how to handle you. The only thing they don't know how to handle is nonviolence and humor.

—John Lennon

Defining what you're asking people to join is pretty important. Although we've used the word "revolution" earlier, we do not mean *violent* revolution. Violent revolution works in fiction because fiction requires action, and wars move the plot dramatically. In real life, violent revolutions have a lower probability of success than do nonviolent ones.[12] You, therefore, want to bring people to your nonviolent resistance movement.

Regimes *want* protests to turn violent. Violence on the part of the resistance allows the regime to justify their own violence—after all, they're simply responding in kind.[13] They *want* opposition movements to attempt assassinations, plant bombs, kill civilians, and generally wreak violent havoc, so the government can gain points with the general population by "keeping order" (cracking down on the opposition). We see this in Gilliam's film *Brazil* (also implied in Orwell's *1984*), where the government uses the "terrorist" bombings to justify its continued oppression of the people. Indeed, it is a bonus for the regime if violent opposition causes the deaths of civilians because those deaths (intentional or not) mean that the opposition will lose the support of large portions of the population. The outrage may be so great that the opposition can actually end up generating more popular support for the government.[14]

John Lennon, lead singer of the Beatles and antiwar activist, summed it up pretty well—regimes will try to provoke violence because *then they know how to handle you.*[15] And don't forget, the government is *highly* likely to outgun you; they have weapons of war—you likely have light arms, at best. In Le Guin's novel *The Dispossessed*, the poor and oppressed of the fictional state of Benbili take up arms against an oppressive government, but our protagonist, Shevek, reads about the vast arsenal being amassed against them and feels sick to his stomach. He knows the Benbili rebels have no real chance of success.

Always remember: the regime controls the police and the military, so unless the opposition movement is being funded and armed by a very powerful country, the regime is better equipped and better trained than the opposition. Also, by resorting to violence, the resistance is likely to bring about a situation in which the regime looks like the *good guys*. It happened in Chile; an attempt by a spinoff group to kill the dictator, Pinochet, actually made people less likely to support the nonviolent resistance groups too.[16]

Nonviolent resistance has a *ton* of advantages, not the least of which is that nonviolence attracts more people than violence; in the resistance game, more people means a better chance of success.[17] People are less likely to sign on for violence for three basic reasons: **opportunity costs**, morality, and physical limitations. First, most of us have at least some moral objections to harming others—especially if we view those folks as innocent of wrongdoing. Second, in a dystopian state the penalties are high for any sort of resistance, but the penalty for revolution is often torture followed by execution. That's a pretty high opportunity cost.

Opportunity costs are basically the tradeoffs you make when you pick one option (opportunity) over another—if you pick option A over option B, you forgo the benefits you could have gotten if you'd gone with B. In this case, if you pick violence over nonviolence, the opportunity cost is likely to be your life.

Most folks aren't really keen on torture, death, or being tortured to death, so they're less likely to sign on for violence. Finally, violence requires some level of physical fitness and upper-body strength, which pretty much excludes a whole lot of people (often the elderly, the disabled, and lots of women). No one is saying women can't and don't engage in violence (they can and do), but it is fairly rare to see women actively involved in organized violent resistance movements. We're going to discuss the advantages of nonviolence in more detail later in this chapter, but the bottom line is that even though committing acts of violence against an oppressive government is appealing, it's very difficult to win a fight that will almost certainly be fought on your enemy's terms. Nonviolence forces the state to fight on *your* terms.[18]

STRENGTH THROUGH PEACE

During the Cold War, U.S. president Ronald Reagan often used the term "peace through strength," echoing world leaders as far back in history as ancient Rome's emperor Hadrian in the second century BCE.[19] The idea is that if everyone knows your state has massive military strength (and is prepared to use it), no one will attack you—hence peace is a result of strength. The unspoken implication of "peace through strength" is that anyone who isn't willing to use violence (or the threat of violence) to achieve their goals is weak. We, along with many notable advocates of nonviolence, reject that notion and instead declare "strength through peace." As Mahatma Mohandas Gandhi, the leader of India's nonviolent campaign for independence, famously said, "nonviolence is the weapon of the strong."

When the state starts brutal crackdowns on nonviolent protest, it takes incredible strength of will to remain committed to nonviolence. There are multiple examples of such strength of will from Gandhi's campaign for Indian independence. His followers were so committed to nonviolence that they did not defend themselves from horrific police brutality. Gandhi developed a method of nonviolent resistance called *satyagraha*,[20] which translates, approximately, as "firmness relying on truth as essence of being." People who practice *satyagraha* believe that it is their duty not just to pursue a better life for themselves but to use nonviolence to advocate for social justice.[21] That said, nonviolent resistance (also called civil resistance, nonviolent struggle, political defiance) is not the same thing as **pacifism**.[22]

As with many philosophies, **pacifism** can be interpreted many ways. Absolute pacifists reject all violence on moral grounds, arguing that there is no morally defensible use of force. In contrast, contingent pacifists are fine with some forms of violence (self-defense or protection of civilians, for example) but oppose war or militaristic violence.

Nonviolent resistance occurs when unarmed people apply political pressure in the form of nonviolent political acts, including (but not limited to) strikes, boycotts, sit-ins, protest marches, civil disobedience, picketing, and the like.[23] Nonviolent activists don't need to be committed to philosophical pacifism. In explaining the difference between the two, the sociologist and nonviolence advocate George Lakey writes, "One can see the difference when one realizes that most pacifists do not practice nonviolent resistance, and most people who practice nonviolent resistance are not pacifists."[24] Even Gandhi, who is often perceived as an absolute pacifist,[25] was careful to note that the *satyagraha* movement was not a pacifist endeavor.[26] In a situation where violence would have likely failed, Gandhi used nonviolent tactics as a *weapon* against the tyranny of British rule.

Gandhi didn't invent nonviolent resistance, but we're starting with him because his movement changed how people *do* nonviolent resistance in the modern era. Before Gandhi, groups used techniques like noncooperation with government officials, general strikes, and protest marches to varying

Consent of the governed is the idea that the government has power so long as the people agree to be governed. If the people withdraw their consent, then the government no longer has the power to rule. At that point, a new government, one to which the people consent, must be formed.

degrees of success, but their tactics were fairly limited, and there wasn't typically a unifying principle that bound the protesters to nonviolent action.[27]

Gandhi changed the game first by placing emphasis on both strategy (the goal and the plan for achieving it) and tactics (the techniques that will be used to achieve the goal). Gandhi's was not a one-size-fits-all approach to resistance; he experimented with different tactics to determine what worked best in different contexts. As you'll see shortly, that type of adaptability is vital to the success of a widespread nonviolent resistance movement. Second, Gandhi based his approach on the principle of the consent of the governed: if enough people withdraw their consent, then the government *must* fall. It cannot continue without support from the people.[28] Third, and most importantly, he married the principle of the consent of the governed with the idea that when people are shown the truth, their hearts and minds can be swayed; thus you could push people to withdraw their consent from the government by showing them the true face of an oppressive and brutal government. This is the basis of *satyagraha* and the principle around which his followers organized their nonviolent action.

WE ARE MADE BY HISTORY

Nonviolent resistance has a long history.[29] An important example comes from the first recorded mass nonviolent action, the *Conflict of the Orders* (that is, classes) in ancient Rome.[30] In 494 BCE, the plebeians (the nonslave working class) shut down the city to protest their ill-treatment at the hands of the city's upper class, the patricians.[31] Plebeians (like the "reds" in Aveyard's Red Queen series or the "proles" in Orwell's *1984*) ran the shops, grew the food, and made the things, but they had few political rights. They were conscripted into the military, but their farms and businesses often failed while they were off serving in the military. They had to pay taxes to fund the wars they were being sent to fight, but if they couldn't pay their taxes (when their farms and businesses failed), they were placed in debt bondage until they worked off the tax debt.

The plebeians appealed to the government to put an end to these practices but got nowhere. When their appeals failed, the plebeians stopped working and left Rome in protest.[32] It didn't take the patricians long to realize that they were going to have to make concessions if they wanted the city to function again. They set up a "tribune" of plebeians, which was essentially an assembly that functioned as a check on patrician power. It took more than two hundred years of struggle (and a few more secessions) for the plebeians to achieve all of their goals, including a written code of law to which the plebeians consented. A written code of law ensured the Romans wouldn't be subject to vague and arbitrary rules imposed by their rulers.[33] Sound familiar? You might think of, say, the U.S. Constitution, or even the English Magna Carta, which shared this goal.

Why, you might be asking yourself, is this super-ancient history relevant today? It's not just relevant; it's essential! People tend to think of consent of the governed as a fairly modern principle, yet the plebeians demanded it, albeit in limited form, circa 450 BCE—more than two thousand years before

Figure 6.1 Engraving of the Revolt of the Plebeians (c. nineteenth century).
Source: iStock.

John Locke gave us the vocabulary to talk about the concept and nearly 2,400 years before Gandhi developed the principle of *satyagraha*. The plebeians demanded a voice in the creation of that first set of written laws *and* consented to being governed according to those laws. Over two hundred years of nonviolent struggle by the plebeians helped lead to the first codification of Roman law, and Roman law is the foundation on which the majority of legal systems in the world were built.[34] The world's first recorded nonviolent protest movement ultimately resulted in helping establish the principle we now call rule of law, meaning that societies should be governed by law and not by the whims of individual leaders.[35] If *that's* not relevant here, we're not sure what is.

WE SHALL OVERCOME

In the last chapter, we talked a lot about individual resistance. Individual civil disobedience—deliberately breaking laws considered to be immoral or unjust—is typically motivated by the individual's moral or religious beliefs. For example, the poet Henry David Thoreau, an antiwar activist and ardent abolitionist, refused to pay taxes because his taxes helped fund the U.S. war against Mexico and supported slavery.[36] Thoreau believed that civil disobedience was a matter of individual conscience. He wasn't attempting to start a larger movement.[37] Like Thoreau, many people who practice individual civil disobedience have no intention of radically transforming society; they simply feel that they cannot in good conscience follow an unjust law.

In contrast, *collective* nonviolent action aims at societal transformation. Collective nonviolence is when a group of people commit themselves to putting political pressure on society through nontraditional political protests—it's about remedying societal injustices and righting political wrongs.[38] During the civil rights movement in the 1950s and 1960s in the United States, protesters didn't sing "*I* shall overcome," even though that was the original lyric of the song.[39] They sang "*We* shall overcome" because even a person as committed, persuasive, and dynamic as the leader of the movement, Dr. Martin Luther King Jr., couldn't overcome the systemic oppression of African Americans on his own. King and other leaders of the civil rights movement were well versed in both the theory and practice of

Figure 6.2 Civil rights march.
Source: Public domain, via New York Public Library.

nonviolent action—they even traveled to India to learn directly from Gandhi.

We can't get you a personal audience with Gandhi, but we do think it's important to understand not just that nonviolence works but *why*. In the next section, we'll give you the basic theories of nonviolent action, and in the next chapter we'll get into specific tactics that can be used to combat a dictatorial dystopian regime.

THE JIU-JITSU IS STRONG

Jiu-jitsu is a martial art in which the defender uses the attacker's strength against him, countering indirectly rather than head-on.[40] Richard Gregg, a social philosopher, termed Gandhi's argument *moral jiu-jitsu* because nonviolence in the face of brutality knocks the soldiers and police off balance (morally speaking) and can cause them to reconsider their violence against the protesters.[41] The modern godfather of nonviolent resistance, Gene Sharp, reimagined the *moral* jiu-jitsu premise as *political* jiu-jitsu.

Sharp's premise is that nonviolence doesn't change the hearts and minds of the regime or its followers, but the optics of brutally beating peaceful protesters puts pressure on the regime both internally and externally. The regime looks bad, which shifts public opinion and throws the regime off balance politically, and if it looks bad enough externally, regimes can lose foreign aid or trade deals.[42] Political jiu-jitsu is one of the many reasons dictators work very hard to control the media; if the violence isn't visible, then the public isn't affected by it, and the government isn't knocked off balance.

Of course, Sharp would be the first to tell you that political jiu-jitsu doesn't work 100 percent of the time.[43] For one thing, not all regimes are sensitive to the optics. If they don't care how it looks, the regime isn't going to hold back. We see this in Ursula K. Le Guin's *The Dispossessed*. In one of the few examples of collective nonviolent resistance in dystopian fiction, the underclasses of the state of A-Io stage a mass protest, whereupon the government promptly sends in helicopter gunships and mows the protesters down. There were no television cameras, so no one outside of the protest could see what was happening. *Optics, shmoptics.*

For another thing, the success of political jiu-jitsu is somewhat dependent on the regime determining that attacking the protesters could weaken the regime rather than strengthening the government's position.[44] In Le Guin's novel, the A-Io government was not worried about backlash, especially since there were no news reports about the massacre of unarmed protesters. Given today's instant-communications culture, which takes place particularly through social media rather than traditional news, it is harder to hide repression, and the visibility puts pressure even on some pretty obstinate dictatorships. Even North Korea makes propaganda materials to demonstrate how idyllic life is there; they want to control how they're seen.

THE REVOLUTION WORKS IN THE MOVIE

Of course it works in the movie—it has to, or you lose the audience. The fact that it works in fiction helps feed the idea that violent resistance to bad government is a normal thing (whether it is an *effective* thing is a whole other issue). Other contributing factors are that (a) the violent resistance movements are the ones you see in the news and that (b) even a lot of

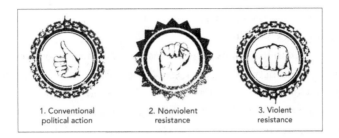

Figure 6.3 The political action continuum.

Source: Made by the authors, based on K. Schock, "The Practice and Study of Civil Resistance," *Journal of Peace Research* 50, no. 3 (2013): 277–90.

people who study conflict for a living would tell you that political action is a continuum and that violent resistance is what you keep in your back pocket for when the situation is dire and there's no other choice.[45] The simple form of that continuum looks like figure 6.3.

The problem with the standard political-action continuum is that it pretty much assumes violence is both inevitable and somewhat normal.[46] Today's fiction writers certainly seem to have taken this one to heart, since we see this progression in most recent dystopian fiction. Just remember that the violent revolution works in the movie, book, and on TV because the writers control the script! In contrast, scholars and practitioners of nonviolent resistance argue that moving toward violence is neither inevitable nor normal. Not only does the government abandon all restraint in the face of violent resistance, but violence makes it harder to attract people to your cause.[47]

Throughout this and the next chapter, you'll see examples of nonviolent resistance movements that were successful—the Indian independence campaign and the U.S. civil rights movement are two such campaigns. We're political scientists, though, so a handful of cases won't necessarily convince us that nonviolence actually works. To feel much more confident in that assessment, we would have to look at lots of cases of both nonviolent *and* violent resistance and compare success rates. Fortunately, other political scientists have helpfully done that for us. For example, Erica Chenowith and Maria Stephan analyzed 323 violent and nonviolent resistance campaigns between 1900 and 2006, examining the success and failure rates of both types.[48]

Their research finds the following:

1. Not only have the numbers of nonviolent campaigns gone up, but their success rates have, too.
2. From 1940 to 1949, nonviolent campaigns had about a 40 percent success rate; between 2000 and 2006, the success rate hit 70 percent.
3. A nonviolent campaign is almost two times more likely to have some measure of success (partial or full) than a violent one.
4. Nonviolent campaigns are numerically larger than violent campaigns—on average, larger by about 150,000 people.
5. Campaigns that are committed to nonviolence have a far greater chance of getting security forces to defect from the regime, compared to violent campaigns.

Nonviolent resistance really can be effective—even in the face of massive government crackdowns—if you do it right.

THE ELEMENTS OF SUCCESSFUL NONVIOLENT RESISTANCE

There are three crucial elements of successful nonviolent resistance: mobilization, resilience, and leverage. The short version is that your movement has to be able to (1) recruit a lot of people (and get money and materials), (2) use a variety of tactics *and* bounce back from losses, and (3) leverage your successes to undermine the regime's support. There's a fourth element, when government viciousness backfires, but that's more of a bonus than a necessity. Let's start with the three key things.

Mobilization: A trickle can become a flood

We've already told you that having people aplenty is necessary if you want your resistance to have any chance of succeeding. People can be mobilized (brought into the movement) from above (elites rallying the people) or below (grassroots movements coming from the people). Either way, the key is to get them on your side. But mobilization against a dystopian regime is a scary proposition. It's not a simple thing to convince people to join the movement; they have to see that the benefits of success are worth the costs (actual and potential) of participating in the resistance. There will be a lot of people who want to see the regime fall but who aren't willing to risk their necks by working against the government. If you can lower the risk—which you've already done to some extent by choosing nonviolent approaches—some people will join (trickle). When those people join, that lowers the risk further, which encourages even more people to join (flood).[49]

While ideally everyone will run right out to join the resistance, they won't—even if they agree in principle with what the resistance is doing. (Think back to that "free rider" problem.) *Mobilization* is about finding enough people and resources to sustain the resistance despite the nonaction of those damn free riders. Having more people also tends to diversify the resistance movement, meaning that the state can't stop the resistance simply by clamping down on one group.[50] Mobilization is necessary if you're going to be successful, but it's not the only thing you'll need.

Resilience: When cutting off the head doesn't kill the snake

There are a couple of aspects to being a resilient movement. The first is that the movement has to be able to survive the loss of its top leadership.[51] The authorities will go after the leaders first, on the theory that the group will fall apart once they're gone. Plus, by publicly taking out the leaders (either via arrest/detention or murder) the regime sends a powerful warning to the opposition's rank and file.[52] That's why, in the original *Star Wars* (1977), the Empire takes Princess Leia into custody—they can torture her into giving up the Rebel Alliance, and then they can kill her to send a message about what happens when you defy Emperor Palpatine (insert evil laugh here).

Your resistance movement has to be organized in such a way that cutting off the head doesn't kill the snake. While we're not advocating the violence, we do appreciate the diffused structure of the Rebel Alliance. It wouldn't have fallen apart without Leia because there were a lot of committed rebel leaders, all of whom were clear on the plan for taking down the Empire. We see the same thing in Jack London's *The Iron Heel*; Ernest Everhard was the principal architect of the Second Revolt, but the antioligarchy movement had so many capable leaders that it was able to carry on after Everhard's arrest and murder.

The second part of being resilient is the ability to change up your tactics to counter the new methods of repression that the regime will come up with. This was one of Gandhi's strengths; he had an arsenal of nonviolent tactics that he could use in different ways to fit different situations.[53] Tactical resilience connects back to the mobilization of diverse populations, too—bringing in different groups brings in different perspectives, which tends to be good for tactical innovation.[54]

On a related note, in a nonviolent movement part of being resilient is making sure that the whole movement, not just the leadership, understands the principles of nonviolent resistance. Everyone needs to be committed to the same principles so that the movement doesn't resort to violence when the leaders are silenced.

Leverage: Small forces can move large weights

Leverage is about using power to make something move—like when you use a jack to lift a car.[55] In the case of nonviolent resistance, the movement gains leverage to (re)move the regime by targeting the groups that support the state—particularly the police and military (a.k.a. the security apparatus).[56] If you can get the security apparatus to **defect**, then you've destroyed their most important source of power and oppression.[57]

With respect to the security apparatus, "**defect**" means that they refuse to carry out the regime's violence. The security apparatus is part of the larger state bureaucracy—the public workers who do all of the work that makes government run (collect taxes, issue permits, drive buses, try cases, etc.). Getting all of those government workers to defect would cause an immediate collapse of the government because there would be no one left to do the work that makes government run.

To extend our Star Wars example: in *The Force Awakens* (2015), Finn witnesses a massacre. It weighs on his conscience; he escapes from the First Order and eventually meets up with the Resistance. He defects. In real life you need a *lot* of soldiers and police officers to defect to bring down an oppressive regime. During the 2011–2012 Arab Spring, Egyptian soldiers repeatedly protected protesters from other security forces and refused direct orders to shoot. When it became clear he had lost the military, Egypt's strongman leader Hosni Mubarak stepped down as prime minister.[58]

How do you get the state's security forces to defect? Each situation will be different. How loyal are the security forces? Are they actually getting paid? Are the police well integrated into their communities? Are military commanders popular with troops and/or citizens?—but there are a few common elements.

The first set of tactics relates to *moral* jiu-jitsu: appeal to the morality of the individual members of the security forces.[59] If the population is religious, for example, resisters can put security officers' eternal souls on the line by putting clergy at the front of the movement. If there are strong moral norms in a state, resisters can use those norms to set up a moral quandary for soldiers (the soldiers have to ask themselves "do I do A, which violates the moral basis of society, or B, as I've been ordered?").[60] Finally, make it personal—the broader and more diverse your movement is, the more likely it is that movement members have kinship or other ties to the security forces and/or the regime. When such relationships exist, there is more hesitation on the part of the security forces.[61]

The last tactic is related to *political* jiu-jitsu: make the cost of violent crackdown high by ensuring a wide broadcast. Had foreign journalists not been present to witness the epic police brutality against Gandhi's followers, the British government would have had complete control of the flow of information, and no one outside of India would have learned the truth about British rule. Likewise, Dr. Martin Luther King Jr. and other leaders likely deliberately chose Birmingham in 1963 for a major civil rights campaign, knowing that the police chief there, "Bull" Connor, would likely overreact—and he did. The pictures of fire hoses and attack dogs being turned on nonviolent children and innocent bystanders galvanized the nation, especially Northern white liberals who had not realized the extent of Jim Crow oppression.[62] (This gets into the idea of "backfires.")

When government crackdowns are well publicized, the broader ramifications—such as the loss of military aid and generally looking bad—are another part of making the security apparatus hesitate.[63]

Optional: Backfires (karma really is a bitch)

Historically speaking, governments have had few constraints on their behavior; most of the time they can get away with repressive tactics. But every so often, a regime's violence **backfires** on them and causes such outrage that it weakens the regime. This is why broadcasting the regime's brutality is important. Unfortunately, just broadcasting the violence isn't enough to make a backfire happen.[64]

To create a backfire, the violence perpetrated by the state has to be viewed as somehow unjust—either out of proportion or targeting people who are innocent or unable to defend themselves. Harm to children fits

Backfires are situations in which the regime's use of violence rebounds on them—where having used violence created a situation that's worse for the regime than it would have been had they just left it alone. The opposition typically uses the backfire as leverage to undercut both domestic and foreign support for the regime.

both categories and is viewed as especially reprehensible. Also, the resistance has to maintain strict nonviolent discipline to retain the moral high ground. Finally, the unjust actions of the state have to be seen by a sympathetic audience that is willing to express outrage.[65] When these three conditions are met, people who were previously either neutral or passive supporters of the resistance are mobilized. In some cases, regime supporters even defect.[66] Backfires help build two of the necessary conditions for movement success, mobilization and leverage, thereby increasing the odds that the movement will achieve its goals.

We see hints of potential backfire in Atwood's *The Handmaid's Tale* (this is more pronounced in the Hulu adaptation), in which it's implied that the Canadians are horrified by *everything* about the Republic of Gilead. We don't know a ton about the resistance ("Mayday") in the story, but we do know that they run an underground railroad of sorts, ferrying fertile women up to the Canadian border; the implication in the book is that they are not a violent resistance. We do know, though, that the Canadian press reports on the atrocities taking place in Gilead. (The television adaptation depicts an escaped Aunt, a woman appointed to monitor Handmaids, giving details about the Handmaid program to the Canadian press in episode 4). The stories seem to have a backfire-type effect—not only does Canada help the U.S. government-in-exile, but the United Nations levies sanctions on the Republic of Gilead.

In the nonfiction realm, we saw the backfire dynamic at play in Burma (now Myanmar) in 2007.[67] At that time, Myanmar and North Korea were about on par with civil liberties: there were none. That's where the Buddhist monks come in. As in most Buddhist countries, monks are highly respected, even revered, in Burma. About four hundred monks decided to take to the streets to protest new, draconian economic policies—and people felt pretty good about it because even the junta wouldn't mess with monks, right? Wrong. The military immediately fired on the monks, and those who weren't killed were rounded up and sentenced to hard labor in prison camps.

It was a massive miscalculation; attacking monks was a step way too far for most Burmese people. This kicked off the Saffron Revolution (so called for the color of the monks' robes), a series of nonviolent protests that forced the junta to transition to civilian government, even though the protesters were unsuccessful at fully ousting the regime. Burma is still not really a democracy at this point, despite holding elections. The former junta leaders and the military have tremendous power, and the state is known for persecuting and killing ethnic minorities. Most recently, the government has been accused of the attempted genocide of the Rohingya, a Muslim minority group.[68]

FINAL THOUGHTS

Revolutions seem spontaneous in films; they just happen, without anyone having to work for years and years. In contrast, real resistance movements are just that: work. It is no easy thing to overcome the collective-action dilemma, especially if the opportunity costs of nonconformity to the regime are high. It is up to you and your movement to create space, language, ideas, music, solidarity, and a new incentive structure that lowers the costs and raises the rewards for others to join. Our first and most important dictum is that your revolution must practice nonviolence. It also needs to take advantage of the political opportunities available to you and time its moves to take advantage of and create new such opportunities. Beyond these foundational lessons, you should know about the four elements of successful nonviolent resistance campaigns: mobilization, resilience, leverage, and careful use of backfires. If you have learned those lessons, you are ready to move along to chapter 7 to learn specific resistance moves.

7

Disintegrating the Oppressor

A goal without a plan is just a wish.

—Antoine de Saint-Exupéry

Spontaneous nonviolent *action* happens all the time, but a successful nonviolent resistance *movement* takes planning. In the novel *All Rights Reserved*®, where you have to pay copyright owners for every word you speak, the protagonist Speth made a spontaneous decision to go silent; others followed her lead, but since they couldn't communicate with one another, they couldn't form a concerted movement. What they needed was a plan, which is what we want you to think about in this chapter. In particular, your plan (which should include—surprise!—strategies and tactics) needs to do a few key things. In this chapter we will set these out as six major stages: (1) laying the groundwork, (2) launching the campaign, (3) maintaining solidarity and nonviolent discipline, (4) political jiu-jitsu, (5) achieving success, and (6) redistribution of power. We suggest that these things are necessary, in this order, for your successful nonviolent movement to avoid falling into some of the common traps of failed revolutions. And the greatest trap of all is violence.

As the last chapter explained, your movement needs to be and do a few key things. Above all it needs to be nonviolent. Dystopian fiction is rife with resistances (the Rebel Alliance in *Star Wars* spring to mind), but usually these movements use violence. But for most of the revolutions in dystopian fiction, it's pretty easy to think through how they could have used nonviolent resistance to greater effect. In box 1, we walk you through how a nonviolent movement would likely have resulted in a far better outcome in the Hunger Games series (although, with our scenario, the books probably wouldn't have been international bestsellers or a hugely successful movie franchise starring Jennifer Lawrence.)

One of the few successful nonviolent resistances in dystopian fiction is the "Defense Council" members in *The Fifth Sacred Thing*, by the ecofeminist sage Starhawk. Set in California in the middle of the twenty-first century, the action moves between San Francisco (an egalitarian "ecotopia" driven by sustainable energy and local agriculture) and Los Angeles (a capitocracy and the seat of power of the authoritarian "Stewards," who control the country by monopolizing water). But water is one of the "sacred things," and *"no one has the right to appropriate them or profit from them at the expense of others. Any government that fails to protect them forfeits its legitimacy."*[1] So when the invading Millennialist army comes for San Francisco, nine old women stand in their path nonviolently, daring anyone to kill them. The soldiers balk at killing the old women, effectively defecting, and San Francisco is at least initially spared corporate control.

Before we move on, we have to warn you that the fiction is sadly lacking in this chapter. It's not that we just skipped it—it's that (a) there's just not a lot of nonviolent resistance in dystopian fiction, and (b) even if there were, the planning side of things is unlikely to make it into the storyline. Planning, although necessary, isn't all that exciting. We've included a few works of fiction, but we pretty much rely on real-life examples throughout. But here's the good news: even in real life, humans are capable of extraordinary feats, and our examples feature some seriously badass people.

PLAN TO WIN, PREPARE TO WIN, EXPECT TO WIN

So how do you win against government?[2] Beyond a commitment to nonviolence, you will need to employ the strategies and tactics that create and maintain the key elements of a resistance movement: mobilization, resilience, leverage, and (hopefully) backfires against the state. Gene Sharp, the godfather of nonviolent resistance, has laid out a six-stage model, using all of these elements, for building your nonviolent resistance movement.[3] Sharp admits this is an idealized model, since every situation will be different. But it gives the basics of how nonviolent resistance should work.[4] For each stage, we'll give you a brief explanation and a few examples of how it works. Most of the examples of long-term, successful, nonviolent campaigns to resist bad government come from real life, but we've also found a few in dystopian fiction.

BOX 7.1: WHAT IF DISTRICT 13 HAD ORGANIZED A NONVIOLENT REVOLUTION?

The state structure in the Hunger Games series makes for a great example of what might have been had the resistance tried nonviolent protest. The state is divided into twelve districts, ruled by the Capitol. In book 1, the citizens of District 12 are going along with life as normal, including sending their tributes to the Games. In book 2, our heroine, Katniss, becomes the Mockingjay, and we see a few small acts of symbolic nonviolent resistance, but by the end of book 2, Katniss's beloved District 12 has been destroyed and a full-on rebellion is coming. Book 3 is all about that rebellion. In book 3, it becomes clear that an outside group from the lost District 13 manipulated everything to make Katniss the face of the resistance in order to get the districts to rally around her.

Once the districts were in open revolt, the Capitol's gloves came all the way off. No more restraint of any sort. As a result, the revolution was extraordinarily violent, and the Capitol completely devastated many of the districts. Untold numbers of people died or were displaced from their homes—all so that District 13 could take control. Of course, it's pretty clear by the end that District 13 isn't going to be much better than the Capitol. (Side note: when violent revolutions succeed in overthrowing the hated government, they're likely to result in a new dictatorship. We'll come back to that in chapter 8.) Now, was mass death and destruction the only way the trilogy could end? No. It most certainly was not.

The Capitol's leaders were never benevolent dictators. The Capitol's rule was brutal and oppressive, and resisting it was hazardous to your health (and to your genetic makeup—who wants to be turned into a mutation?). Because of that, it was hard for District 13 to recruit the other districts to fight. The Capitol's iron grip seems pretty convincing, until you think through a point that is made more than once in the books: The Capitol doesn't make or grow *anything*. It is completely dependent on the districts for everything. That, in and of itself, is a serious amount of power at the districts' disposal.

Now, imagine this: what if instead of plotting a violent overthrow of the Capitol, District 13 had sent emissaries to each district and put in the work to convince the other districts to engage in strategic nonviolent resistance? Instead of physical warfare, the districts could have engaged in economic warfare. Factory workers could have collectively walked off the job, agricultural workers could have refused to harvest, and transportation workers could have refused to move the trains.

If enough people had refused to cooperate with the Capitol, they could have brought down President Snow with far less bloodshed. That's not to say the Capitol wouldn't have spilled some blood (they'd go in hard and fast in an attempt to terrify the districts back into submission), but they eventually would have run out of food and ammunition. A coordinated noncooperation campaign among all of the districts could have *disintegrated* the Capitol (that's a technical term that we discuss toward the end of the chapter) with far fewer casualties or displacements.

STAGE 0: GETTING YOUR HEAD IN THE GAME

This one isn't technically one of Sharp's stages, but he does discuss the importance of mental preparation. To be involved in a movement like this, you have to come to terms with what committing to nonviolent resistance

Figure 7.1 Gandhi (1931).
Source: Public domain, via Wikimedia Commons.

will likely mean. The opportunity costs for nonviolent resistance are lower than for violent resistance, but those costs are still high. You, and the people close to you, have to be prepared to pay with either your freedom or your life. You must also have courage; rein in your fear so that you can enter into the movement confidently. Sharp says cowardice has no place in a nonviolent resistance movement. You can be scared, but you can't let fear control your actions.

There's no better example of mental preparation than Gandhi. A deeply philosophical man, Gandhi believed that nonviolence is the tool of the *mentally* strong, and he developed his philosophy of *satyagraha* accordingly.[5] He was well aware of the lengths to which the British would go keep India under British control; after all, the British considered India the "jewel in the crown" of the British Empire, and they were not about to give India up without a fight. Early in the planning process for his independence campaign, Gandhi became aware not just that Indian citizens weren't mentally prepared for a nonviolent campaign but that many members of his own political party, the Indian National Congress, weren't particularly committed to nonviolence, either. Gandhi regrouped, started a small campaign using only his most committed supporters, and then used the publicity from that campaign to demonstrate the power of nonviolence and attract more people to the movement.[6]

STAGE 1: LAYING THE GROUNDWORK

There's a common saying that "no plan ever survives contact with the enemy."[7] That doesn't mean you shouldn't make a plan. You have to do serious homework before you can make a plan, which means you have to have a good understanding of what's happening so that you're able to adapt when your plan goes south. You also have to prepare people for what's coming so they can participate when the movement swings into action or when its leaders are taken out. Our example for laying the groundwork comes from an episode early in the Indian campaign for independence: Gandhi's Salt March.

The back story

The British both taxed salt and forbade Indians from making it. To protest this restriction of a basic staple, Gandhi led a two-hundred-plus-mile march to Dharasana, the center of British salt making in India. At Dharasana, the protesters—in groups of fifty—directly approached the salt manufacturing and storage facility in an attempt to cross the fence. The American journalist Webb Miller documented what he witnessed: "Scores of native police rushed upon the advancing marchers and rained blows on their heads with their steel-shod *lathis* [batons]. Not one of the marchers even raised an arm to fend off the blows."[8] Although the Salt March did not end with a repeal of the repressive British salt policies, the movement did succeed at drawing international attention to British brutality in India. It also succeeded in a domestic backfire; British attempts to stop the salt protests were so violent that they generated considerable domestic support for Gandhi and his followers.

TACTIC: DO YOUR HOMEWORK

Information is essential to success. You need to be able to articulate the problem for the group, which means going beyond your own perceptions. You also must understand your side of the conflict. Do the problems affect more than one group in your society? Are the other groups potential allies? What would it take to get them to join you? What resources do you have? What resources could potential allies bring to the movement? Next, you need to know your enemy inside and out. How does the regime operate?

Who are the key players? What are their weaknesses? Do they have external support? What kind of internal support do they have? How are they likely to react to your movement? Don't stop there—get as much information on the regime as is humanly possible. Try not to tip your hand while doing so.

Gandhi's "homework" before the Salt March consisted of two things: knowing his enemy and taking the pulse of the Indian people. In his youth, Gandhi's family sent him to London to be educated as a lawyer. As a result, Gandhi had a good understanding of the British people and their government. He had also lived and campaigned in another British colony, South Africa; from that experience he learned how British colonial governments functioned, ruled, and reacted to protest.

In the years leading up to the Salt March, Gandhi traveled throughout India, meeting people and talking to them about their daily lives and problems. He met with people of all castes in an attempt to break down barriers in Indian society, as his travels had taught him that unless caste, religious, and gender-based barriers were demolished, nonviolent cooperation would be impossible.[9] He also met with people from different religions but found that mutual distrust among the religions might make it hard to rally people around a common cause. All of this preparation fed his plan for a nonviolent campaign to free India from British rule.

TACTIC: MAKE A PLAN

Start by clarifying your movement's objectives (the "why"); otherwise a plan cannot achieve them. Once the objectives are set, determine the "who," "what," "when," "where," and "how" of your struggle. Take into account what resources you have or could reasonably get your hands on; remember, this is strategic planning, not pie-in-the-sky dreaming. Think through the stages of your campaign and in what order you will tackle your objectives. Consider what form the state's responses might take and how you would handle whatever methods of repression they adopt.

Gandhi's overarching goal was to use nonviolence to force the British to free India. He worked through a political party, the Indian National Congress. He, along with other Congress leaders, mapped out a campaign of noncooperation that would proceed in stages. The Congress party provided him with a base of supporters and helped build local organizations throughout the country.

TACTIC: NARROW YOUR PLAN OF ATTACK

Approach your objectives sequentially rather than simultaneously to avoid spreading your people thin. An early victory energizes the base, so think about exploiting one of the regime's weaknesses early on to achieve one of the movement's goals; this will help with further mobilization.

Getting the British out of India was a huge goal; Gandhi and the Congress party had to decide what to tackle first. Gandhi thought it should be the British salt monopoly and salt taxes; this was an issue that affected all of India, but as it wasn't vital to the British control of India, the British wouldn't likely crack down too hard or too early. Congress leaders thought salt policies were unimportant, but Gandhi knew differently. Salt was essential to daily life, and the poor were being disproportionately harmed, which meant the policies were unjust. Waging a *satyagraha* against British salt policies would be something that could unify and mobilize Indians from all castes and religions while not prompting the British to crush the movement preemptively.

Figure 7.2 Gandhi and the Salt Marchers (1930).
Source: Public domain, via Wikimedia Commons.

TACTIC: AIR THE GRIEVANCES

Start educating the citizenry. They may not be aware of the full extent of the regime's brutality, so they may not be motivated to help your movement. Start a campaign to help people understand the issues fueling the resistance. Help them see why it's necessary and why nonviolent resistance has a good chance of succeeding, but don't sugarcoat the situation. You're trying to mobilize people to join the cause; they need to have the same understanding of the risks that you did before you started.

Gandhi didn't have the power of television, the internet, or even radio to communicate with the masses. He essentially didn't even have newspapers, either; they existed, but illiteracy rates were sky high. Gandhi's personal popularity, though, meant that Indians would turn out in droves to hear him speak. He also used the local networks forged by his party to take his message directly to the people.

TACTIC: GO PUBLIC

Sharp writes: "In the struggle to attain freedom, it is necessary to behave like free people."[10] As noted in the previous chapter, resistance groups often attempt to operate in secret to avoid censure (and worse). It makes sense, particularly at the beginning. At some point, though, secrecy becomes counterproductive to a mass movement. Secrecy creates divisions and paranoia that can ultimately doom the group to failure. Plus, if your actions are secret, you won't actually be able to create a mass movement—how would people know to join you? If you want to attract people to the movement and work together toward freedom, an open movement in which you openly state not just your goals but how you plan to attain them is crucial.

Gandhi wrote letters to the British government detailing the movement's grievances and plans for marching and raiding the salt facility. He gave his opponent the opportunity to remedy grievances before taking action, which cast his movement in a positive light: he played fair, opened a dialogue that could have led to negotiation with the British, and sent the message that he didn't fear British reprisals. While the Salt March was initially unsuccessful, the protest successfully rallied allies to the cause, unified different segments of society toward a common goal, and put the brutality of the British government in the national and international spotlight.

STAGE 2: LAUNCHING THE CAMPAIGN

The point at which you implement your plan and begin actively resisting collectively is a positive yet dangerous time. On one hand, the visibility of your action is likely to bring in followers. On the other hand, you're challenging the regime, and they *will* react. Whether that reaction is violent or not will vary depending on the stakes attached to your move. If the regime reacts violently, it's imperative that your followers react in a strictly nonviolent way. If they don't, your movement will crash before it ever gets off the ground. Even one violent participant can spoil the movement for everyone. Our stage 2 example is the Mothers of the Plaza de Mayo.

The back story

The Mothers of the Plaza de Mayo came together because their children had been disappeared by the military government in Argentina.[11] As noted earlier, the Argentine Dirty War (1976–1983) was exactly as advertised: dirty. The regime branded "anyone who opposes the Argentine way of life" a subversive—the military government's claims to legitimacy and moral authority rested, in part, on their claims of protecting Christian values and the Argentine family.[12] The security apparatus was given almost unlimited authority to deal with so-called subversives. Disappearing people was already a common practice in Argentina,[13] but its incidence rose drastically during the Dirty War. A group of fourteen mothers of the disappeared became determined to find their children. They began protesting each Thursday in front of the presidential palace on the Plaza de Mayo in the heart of Buenos Aires, and soon more joined them.

TACTIC: HELP, I'M BEING REPRESSED

If you did your planning well, you've considered what methods of repression the regime might use against you. It's likely that they'll try to control the media or plant false stories about your movement; it's up to you to counter that narrative with a positive message that brings attention to your plight. They're also likely to threaten you and your family, confiscate your property, ban gatherings, arrest and imprison you, and/or use violence against you.

It's up to you and your followers to make the regime's attempts at repression ineffective. That doesn't mean that you can stop them from ratcheting up the pressure on the group. Rendering the repression ineffective means that the group has to stick with its nonviolent protests even as the full weight of the government is brought to bear. It's easy to say you wouldn't give in, but think back through some of the real stories we told you in chapter 2 about government brutality—are you sure you wouldn't give in if, for example, the government were drugging people, loading them onto planes, and pushing them out over the ocean? If you're going to be effective, the movement must be committed to persisting despite the heavy toll the resistance may take on members. It is up to you to make sure that you've taken the pulse of the group and are not asking them to bear more than they are capable of bearing—and to backtrack if you've miscalculated either the government's response or your followers' tolerance.

In the case of the Mothers of the Plaza de Mayo, for the first few months after they began protesting, walking around the plaza with their children's names embroidered on white headscarves, the government paid little attention. That changed after the Mothers placed a Mother's Day ad in the newspaper asking the state and the Catholic Church for information about the disappeared. They followed with a petition asking for information; both requests were covered heavily by international media. With the spotlight on the Mothers, the military tried various repression techniques: planting false stories about the Mothers and calling them "las locas" (the crazy women), arresting them, and threatening them with death. Ultimately, the regime disappeared fourteen of the Mothers, trying to break the group's will to fight.[14]

The Mothers' resolve was instead strengthened by the regime's campaign of terror. As one said, "When everyone was terrorized we didn't stay at home crying—we went to the streets to confront them directly." Another added, "They thought we would be too afraid to go back to the square. It was difficult to go back . . . but we went back."[15]

Not only did they go back, but they also courted the media at every international event held in Argentina, telling reporters about their children, saying, "they took them alive, we want them returned alive." The Mothers made themselves as visible as possible, making it more difficult for the regime to oppress or disappear them. By the end of 1979, the group had hundreds of members all across Argentina. The regime stepped up its campaign against them, temporarily forcing them to abandon their protests in

Figure 7.3 Mothers of the Plaza de Mayo.
Source: Public domain via Wikimedia Commons.

the plaza, but the Mothers regrouped. Despite beatings by the police, the Mothers reclaimed their protest space in 1980 and were never forced out again. The Mothers by themselves did not bring down the regime, but they were a part of the events that led to the ultimate collapse of the Argentine military government in 1983.

STAGE 3: MAINTAINING SOLIDARITY AND NONVIOLENT DISCIPLINE

When a resistance campaign drags on, supporters may be tempted to leave the movement or, worse, turn violent. Gandhi understood this, noting that for those who were hopeless, harming the oppressor might feel like a restoration of the people's dignity.[16] Here, it's your job to make sure they feel well supported and appreciated so that they don't leave the cause. We don't just mean saying "thanks for your support." Keep in mind, your supporters have likely been targeted by the government, too. They may have lost jobs, been imprisoned and/or beaten—they may have even lost friends or family. If you're fighting a regime that controls most of the country's resources, resisting can make you hungry as well as weary.

At this point, people have given up a lot to help you bring down the regime, and the longer the situation lasts, the closer they may come to embracing violence. If you can keep their morale up and their commitment to nonviolence strong, then the regime is losing its battle to intimidate the movement. We'll use the 1965–1970 Delano, California, grape strike (and boycott) as our example for this stage.[17] Although the grape strike was not directed against government, it illustrates the importance of solidarity and nonviolent discipline.

The back story

Over the course of the twentieth century, unionization and regulation improved working conditions in most sectors of the American economy. The agricultural sector, and especially working conditions for migrant farm workers, was a significant exception. Unions had been attempting to organize workers for decades but got little traction. Law enforcement was typically all too willing to help growers keep workers in line via intimidation, force, and arrest. Despite these threats, in the summer of 1965 long-suffering Filipino and Mexican grape farm workers staged a walkout to protest their low pay.

The largely Filipino Agricultural Workers Organizing Committee (AWOC), led by Larry Itliong, quickly came to their aid and invited the largely Latino National Farm Workers' Association (NWFA)—led by the now-famous labor organizer César Chávez—to join the strike.[18] The collaboration between Itliong and Chávez was a huge development; for a century, growers had been pitting Filipino and Latino workers against each other to break strikes and prevent unionization (divide and conquer, you'll remember, is a classic tool of oppressors).[19] Concerned about the strength of their new union, NFWA leadership debated joining the AWOC strike until Helen Chávez, César's wife, simply asked, "Are we a union or not?" The leadership put the issue to a vote of the NFWA members, framing the strike as an issue of dignity and freedom. Most important to this example, before the vote César Chávez explicitly stated that this would be a "nonviolent struggle, even if violence is used against us."[20] On September 16, 1965, Mexican Independence Day, NFWA members voted yes to the strike and joined the AWOC on the picket lines a few days later.

TACTIC: EASE THE BURDEN

You can't prevent the suffering of your followers, and to be honest, people visibly suffering at the hands of the regime is an important part of gaining support and making nonviolence work. You can and should, however, attempt to take the edge off of people's suffering. Remember: you'll fail if you try to push people further than they can bear. First, make sure you're addressing morale issues. The state will try to isolate people; make sure they know they aren't alone. Hold mass meetings, prayer vigils, and rallies to bring your supporters together. Give them visible symbols that allow movement members to recognize one another—like the Mockingjay pin in the Hunger Games series or the white scarves of the Mothers of the Plaza de Mayo. Make sure that the rank and file have access to movement leaders and that the leaders are in the thick of the protests. When members have lost their jobs and don't have the means to feed or shelter their families, make every effort to provide food and shelter. In short: don't let your followers down. They rely on your leadership to keep going.

In the Delano grape strike, the migrant farm workers started out with almost nothing, which meant they had no resources to maintain the strike. Where would they get food or money while on strike? The Delano farm owners counted on that to break the strike and drive workers back into the fields. It didn't work not just because people all over the world supported the workers' actions but also because people from across North America sent in donations to help sustain the strike (including $5,000 a month from the United Auto Workers union).[21] Then, in 1966, the AWOC and NFWA merged to form the United Farm Workers organization, which began to receive assistance from unions large and small throughout the United States and Canada.[22]

TACTIC: STRENGTHEN THEIR RESOLVE

People will be far more inclined toward violence if they don't understand why maintaining nonviolent discipline is important to the movement's ultimate success. Educate people. Show them how nonviolence benefits the movement in terms of recruiting new members and influencing the general public to support the cause. Link nonviolence to the wider values of the community and demonstrate how violence would weaken the movement in the long run.

As the grape strike dragged on, farm owners stepped up their campaign against the strikers—evicting them from farm camps, beating them, and even spraying them with pesticides. The police did nothing to stop the violence against strikers. The local sheriff banned gatherings of more than five people and declared it illegal to use the Spanish word *huelga* (strike). These tactics backfired, first when a local clergyman was arrested for rallying the strikers and again when female workers, including Helen Chávez, were arrested for yelling *huelga* in the fields. (The women spent three days in jail, during which time they laughed and joked so loudly and defiantly that the jail workers got fed up and told them to be quiet.)[23] The national news took interest, helping Chávez raise considerable money to support the strikers.

Chávez had studied Gandhi and had witnessed the successes of the civil rights movement, so he knew nonviolence would show people that the strikers' cause was just. But progress was very slow. Although huge numbers of grape workers joined the strike, the growers brought in scabs (workers

Figure 7.4 Strike poster (c. 1965).
Source: Courtesy of UFW.

willing to cross picket lines) to work the grape vines. Since grapes were still being harvested, union leaders called for an international boycott of California table grapes in an effort to bring farm owners to the negotiating table. But between the violence against them and the slow progress, the strikers began to lose faith in nonviolent resistance.

Despite Chávez's best efforts to rally his troops, some of the strikers started to sabotage the farms and farm equipment—some even brought guns to the picket lines. Chávez, in his "Letter from Delano," declared: "If to build our union required the deliberate taking of life, either the life of a grower or his child, or the life of a farm worker or his child, then I choose not to see the union built."[24] Chávez announced he would fast until the strikers recommitted to nonviolent action. It took twenty-five days and thirty pounds, but the fast brought union workers to his side and reunified the movement. He broke his fast in front of the national media while surrounded by thousands of supporters and Senator Robert Kennedy.[25]

TACTIC: EMPOWER THEM TO LEAD

The people in your movement are not your soldiers; they are volunteers. People have to want to continue nonviolent resistance on their own if you're captured or killed. Prepare by educating everyone on nonviolent strategy and tactics, and on movement goals and positions, to ensure the organization will always have competent leadership.

In the wake of his fast, Chávez personally recruited hundreds of strikers and sent them across the United States and Canada to organize an international boycott of California grapes. Marc Grossman, César Chávez's longtime spokesman, speechwriter, and personal aide, explains how Chávez empowered workers to lead the boycott:

Hundreds of strikers and their families, many of whom had never traveled outside California's Central Valley, picked up their belongings and traveled to organize the international grape boycott in cities across the U.S. and Canada. The boycott, a strategy Cesar learned from studying Gandhi and Dr. King, had never before been applied to a major labor-management dispute. So there was little "training." One grape striker taking off for a distant city asked Cesar, "How do you boycott?" He replied, "I don't know but you'll figure it out." They did, and recruited millions of people who joined La Causa by boycotting grapes and picketing supermarkets.[26]

The boycott worked; millions of people in the United States, Canada, and Western Europe refused to buy scab grapes. In 1970, five years after the Delano strike started, the farm owners signed their first union contract; they'd lost millions of dollars as a result of the boycott. The effectiveness of the grape strike and boycott is especially stunning in light of the political star power that opposed it. The governor of California, Ronald Reagan, made it the policy of the California state government to discredit the movement, and soon-to-be president Richard Nixon attacked the grape strike from the campaign trail and then from the Oval Office, even using the power of that office to quadruple shipments of California grapes to U.S. soldiers in Vietnam.[27]

STAGE 4: POLITICAL JIU-JITSU

As described in chapter 6, political jiu-jitsu is about knocking the regime off balance politically. Since governments are set up to deal with violence, they struggle to respond effectively to nonviolent resistance. There is a veritable arsenal of nonviolent methods at your disposal. Sharp has helpfully divvied the methods up into three main categories: protest and persuasion, noncooperation, and intervention. Our examples for this stage come from the Liberian Women in Peacebuilding Network's Mass Action for Peace, the antiapartheid campaign in South Africa, and Czechoslovakia's protest against Russian invasion.

TACTIC: PROTEST AND PERSUASION TECHNIQUES

Protest and persuasion techniques are typically symbolic and aimed at demonstrating opposition. Methods include parades, vigils, speeches, petitions, leaflets/pamphlets, symbols of resistance, public prayer, and more. People using these tactics are mobilizing the public but also suggesting an implicit threat that more serious action will occur if demands aren't met. Here we provide three examples: direct petitioning, prayer/worship, and the threat of public disrobing.[28]

The back story

Liberia endured nearly a decade and a half of civil war between 1989 and 2003. To call this war devastating is an understatement. More than 250,000 Liberians were killed in the war, tens of thousands more were mutilated, and an estimated 40,000 women were systematically raped.[29] The intentional targeting of women during the conflict was the catalyst for the founding of the Liberian Women in Peacebuilding Network's (WIPNET) Mass Action for Peace, a grassroots movement of women peace activists. The WIPNET women used every tactic they could think of, ultimately earning a 2011 Nobel Peace Prize for their spokeswoman, Leymah Gbowee,[30] for her contributions to "nonviolent struggle for the safety of women and for women's rights to full participation in peace-building work."[31]

And although it is not exactly dystopian fiction, we do have an excellent fictional parallel for the Liberian women's campaign: *Lysistrata*, an ancient Greek play by Aristophanes in which the title character convinces other Greek women to withhold sex from their husbands until the men negotiate an end to the decades-long Peloponnesian War. Although the play is a comedy, its underlying premise is deadly serious. These women had no

Figure 7.5 The Women of Liberia protest for peace.
Source: https://ipfs.io/ipfs/QmXoypizjW3WknFiJnKLwHCnL72vedxjQkDDP1mXWo6uco/wiki /Women_of_Liberia_Mass_Action_for_Peace.html (uncredited photo).

recourse through the usual channels of political participation. In a highly patriarchal society, they had few rights compared to male citizens and probably did not therefore have a lot of resources with which to mount a protest campaign. In both of these ways, the ancient Greek women led by Lysistrata were very much like the modern-day women of Liberia (who actually did go on a sex strike); both groups used what they had and were able to make a huge improvement in their countries.

Public prayer

Although there were divides between Liberia's Christian and Muslim communities, the fact that the fighters targeted all women and girls brought together women from both religions. WIPNET's leader Leymah Gbowee convinced the women to work together, asking, "Does the bullet know Christian from Muslim?"[32] They met daily to sing and pray in a field beside a prominent fish market that the president of Liberia, Charles Taylor, passed regularly. As Taylor's car passed, the women unfurled their banner: "The women of Liberia want peace! now!"[33] They expressed unity by wearing all white and forgoing accessories that indicate social class. By emphasizing shared convictions and praying together, the women sent the message that their faith would sustain their protest; they would not be silenced.

Direct petitioning

When no contact was forthcoming from Taylor's presidential palace, the women marched to parliament to protest, giving Taylor three days to respond to their demands for peace. The women returned to the field beside the fish market, continuing to pray, sing, and hold their banner where the president could see it. A week after their second trip to parliament, they received word that the president would see them.

Public disrobing

The women managed to get both President Taylor and the rebel warlords to meet for peace talks in Accra, Ghana. Liberian WIPNET leaders traveled to Accra and mobilized Liberian women refugees in Ghana to gather outside the talks to keep pressure on the men.

> We are tired of war, we are tired of running, we are tired of begging for bulgur wheat, we are tired of our children being raped. We are now taking this stand . . . because we believe as custodians of this society, tomorrow our children will ask us "Mama, what was your role during the crisis?"
> —Leymah Gbowee, public address to Liberian president Charles Taylor

The pressure wasn't working, however; the women felt the men weren't seriously attempting to bring peace to Liberia. The women staged a sit-in, locking arms so that the men couldn't leave the talks. Men tried to leave, some even resorting to climbing out of windows, but the women were resolute. The men were not getting past them. In parts of Africa, it is a curse to see a married or elderly woman deliberately disrobe, so the women threatened to strip themselves naked if the men kept attempting to leave before a ceasefire was signed.

Outcome

The women brought the warring factions to the table and made sure they stayed there. With the help of pressure from the international community, peace accords were signed on August 18, 2003. The WIPNET activists went on to help elect Africa's first woman president, Ellen Johnson Sirleaf.

TACTIC: NONCOOPERATION

Noncooperation is by far the largest of Sharp's categories of nonviolent action; most of the tactics involved in nonviolent action require some level of noncooperation with the regime. That makes sense when you consider that the fundamental premise of nonviolent resistance is withdrawing support from the state. People withdraw their support by not cooperating with the state. Noncooperation can take three basic forms: social, political, and economic. Our major examples for this tactic come from the resistance against apartheid in South Africa in the 1980s and include selective social boycotts, withdrawing from government educational institutions, and strategic use of multiple forms of economic noncooperation.

The back story

The territory that became South Africa was initially colonized by the Dutch in the mid-1600s and for hundreds of years was run by the Dutch and then the British as a slave society. By the early 1920s, the white government had adopted segregation laws, but they really hit their stride in 1948 when they implemented a new policy called apartheid, which translates to "apartness" in English. Under the apartheid regime, every race had its place.

White Europeans (about 20 percent of the population) were at the top of the social and political order, owning 80 percent of the land—the best and most productive lands, naturally.[34] But white rule in South Africa was dependent on African labor, and eventually resistance formed.

Africans' struggle to end the apartheid regime took place over several decades, and not all of the struggle was nonviolent. Hopelessness and rage sometimes erupted. However, much of the struggle was nonviolent; as Desmond Tutu—the African archbishop of the Anglican Church in Cape Town—declared, the movement needed to be nonviolent in order to stand up to the "harsh scrutiny of history."[35] Here, we highlight three noncooperation nonviolent collective-action techniques used by the resistance.

Selective social boycotts

Collaborators (Africans who cooperated with the powerful whites) were often reviled by the African community. In 1986, the African residents of a Johannesburg-area community called Alexandra had recently experienced a wave of violence; tired of the bloodshed, community organizations banded together to undermine their local governing council. As a part of their strategy, they employed a selective social boycott, during which the community ostracized Africans who collaborated with the white government. One account indicates that local merchants refused to sell goods to members of the council, taxis refused to take them as passengers, women broke up with their police-officer boyfriends, and the mayor's parishioners (he was also a pastor) boycotted church services.[36]

Withdrawal from government-run education

The South African government set up two educational systems, one for Africans and one for whites.[37] The state made no pretense of the systems being equal—they spent an estimated ten times as much on white students as they did on African students.[38] The system for the African education system was designed to (a) impress upon Africans that they were inferior to whites and (b) train African youth for a lifetime of subservience to whites. School boycotts were a regular method by which young Africans protested the conditions and content of their education.

The January 1984 walkout initially looked like any other small protest, confined to a handful of schools. However, larger issues in South Africa

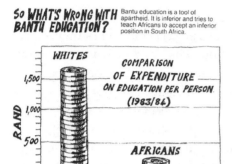

Figure 7.6 Comparison of South African per pupil spending.

Source: Reproduced from International Defence Aid Fund and UNESCO, *Fighting Apartheid: A Cartoon History* (London: International Defence and Aid Fund for Southern Africa and UNESCO, 1987).

converged with the initial school boycott, and by September more than 250,000 African students were on strike. Boycotts continued into 1985, until almost no young Africans were in school in any urban area. Finally, parents and teachers took matters into their own hands and created a National Education Crisis Committee, which worked with the students to address their concerns and establish a new curriculum outside the control of the government's Department of Education.

Strategic economic noncooperation

There are dozens of economic noncooperation tactics that can be used to resist a repressive regime, and Africans employed many of them against apartheid. Boycotts of white businesses became common after a famous one in 1985 in Port Elizabeth. The boycott put pressure on white businesses, but as one high-ranking white police officer noted, "If they don't want to buy, what sort of crime is it?"[39] Strikes were also popular methods of nonviolent protest. One of the most strategic uses of strikes came from the school boycott just discussed: The young school boycotters approached African trade unions to ask for their support. The unions agreed, staging a series of strikes alongside the school boycotters. At one general strike in 1984, an estimated combined total of 800,000 African youth and workers shut down South Africa's Southern Transvaal region for two days.[40]

Outcome

Nonviolent resistance by itself was not enough to bring down the South African apartheid regime. However, noncooperation with the government and white business placed enormous pressure on the regime, and the regime responded with increasing brutality. The world was watching, though, as the government's responses to nonviolent protest became increasingly harsh. A backlash slowly started to build in the international community. Celebrities refused to perform in South Africa, consumers forced their investment firms to cease investing with firms that did business in South Africa, and both the United States and the European Community (two of the largest economies in the world) imposed economic sanctions. Force was no longer enough to maintain the system. In 1990, the government released Nelson Mandela from prison and began negotiating with his African National Congress party to transition to democracy. Elections were held in 1994, with the ANC winning more than 60 percent of the vote and installing Nelson Mandela as president.[41]

TACTIC: NONVIOLENT INTERVENTION

Intervention requires taking the movement to the regime, which means it's riskier than the other categories of nonviolent resistance. The goal of intervention is in some way to disrupt (or even destroy) the oppressive structures inherent in the society. Methods of intervention include everything from sit-ins and physically obstructing government actions to setting up alternative societal systems, for example, transportation or banking networks. As you might imagine, the latter two (and other extreme forms of intervention) are not widely used.

Our two examples for nonviolent intervention come from the resistance to the Soviet invasion of Czechoslovakia in 1968: nonviolent obstruction and work-on without collaboration.[42] That second one is a mouthful—it just means that after an invasion, government workers stay on the job but treat the invaders as if they don't exist.

The back story

At the height of the Cold War, the Soviet Union enjoyed complete control over its satellite states, including Czechoslovakia. But in 1968, Czechoslovakia's government started making some serious reforms. "Socialism with a human face," they called it, and if these policies had been allowed to move forward, Czechoslovakians would have been freed from the control of the ruling Communist Party. These reforms were a huge threat to Soviet control over the rest of the communist bloc, so the Czechoslovakians couldn't be allowed to get away with their reforms. The Soviet Union invaded Czechoslovakia that August.[43]

The Soviets expected that the Czechoslovakian military would put up a fight, but the Czechoslovakian government ordered its military not to resist (fighting would have meant slaughter). At the same time, the government put out a radio statement imploring citizens not to resist Soviet troops. Ordinary Czechoslovakians took to the streets, with the national radio station exhorting them to remain calm and nonviolent.

Obstruction

As the Soviet tanks filled the streets, so did the youth of Czechoslovakia. On August 21, the youth of Prague acted as a human blockade to prevent tanks from moving. In another part of the city, they formed a human chain to prevent Soviet tanks and troops from crossing a major bridge. Sadly, not all attempts to stop the tanks worked; some youth were killed when the tanks opened fire on the crowds.

Figure 7.7 Citizens of Prague surround tanks during the "Prague Spring," August 21, 1968.

Source: Public domain via Wikimedia Commons.

Continuing to work

The military invasion was successful at gaining territorial control of Czechoslovakia, and the Soviet secret police (the KGB) took the Czechoslovakian leadership into custody. The country should have been under Soviet control—except it wasn't. The Soviets had a mess on their hands. Even the Czechoslovakian military was aiding the civil resistance. The military had secret radio stations that they turned over to the resistance, allowing the Czechoslovakians to continue to broadcast their defiance of Soviet occupation. The police, too, undermined the Soviet leadership. The police stayed on the job, not only ignoring Soviet attempts at control but using their police cars—lights and sirens blaring—to get anti-Soviet materials (printed by the state-run newspapers!) through checkpoints.

Outcome

In one sense, the resistance was a failure. The Czechoslovakian Communist Party leaders rolled back their reforms and were forced to allow Soviet troops to remain stationed in Czechoslovakia. In another sense, though, the people's resistance was successful; they forced the mighty Soviet Union to negotiate, which was an admission that Soviet military power had failed to subdue Czechoslovakia. In addition, moral jiu-jitsu swung into effect among the occupying troops; morale suffered, orders were disobeyed, and it seems all of the soldiers from the initial invasion were rotated back home (replaced by others) within a few days.

STAGE 5: ACHIEVING SUCCESS

Success can take a variety of forms, including partial victories. Sometimes, even just managing to get a seat at the table is a success. In Ursula K. Le Guin's *The Dispossessed*, the backstory is a nonviolent resistance campaign that took place over a century before book's real story begins. The backstory starts with an old woman, Odo, on the planet Urras (Earth-like, with a habitable moon called Anarres). Odo conceived of an egalitarian, communitarian society without laws or private property. Odo's vision was compelling, captivating the imaginations of menial and service-sector workers on Urras. Even in space, low-wage workers do not fare well in a hypercapitalist economy that lacks a welfare state. A group of Odo's followers (the Odonians) began a walk-out that led to a worldwide strike and eventually a long-term movement that threatened the stability of key Urrasti governments. The Council of World Governments granted the Odonoians the moon to, as one character tells us, "keep us from wrecking their profiteering states and setting up the just society there."[44] Nevertheless, the movement, despite not liberating all of Urras's workers, is a partial success. The Odonians accept the near-barren wasteland of Anarres as their new home, and several hundred thousand people evacuate Urras to build their utopia there.

In the previous chapter we discussed some essential elements of success: mobilization, resilience, leverage, and (if you can manage it) backfires. But how do you actually *achieve* success? Sharp gives us four main pathways: conversion, accommodation, nonviolent coercion, and disintegration.[45] For this stage, we'll connect these pathways back to some of the examples we've discussed in this chapter.

TACTIC: CONVERSION

One of the myths about nonviolent resistance is that it primarily works by bringing the oppressor around to the movement's way of thinking—the oppressive regime has a change of heart as a result of the nonviolent campaign and decides that the movement's goals are worth embracing.[46] This does work occasionally, but it's the least common pathway to success.

We see elements of conversion in the success of the Liberian Women's Mass Action for Peace. Both the Liberian president, Charles Taylor, and the rebel warlords were persuaded to come to the negotiating table by the WIPNET women's argument that peace was far better for Liberia than the continuation of the carnage. After the peace accords were implemented, disarmament proceeded slowly. The WIPNET women intervened again, convincing the former combatants that the cash-for-guns program was worthwhile, and then when violence broke out during the disarmament, the women convinced the former combatants to remain calm and continue disarming.

TACTIC: ACCOMMODATION

When the oppressor accommodates the movement, that doesn't mean they've decided the protesters are right. It means they've realized that they are unlikely to win, so they decide to give in to at least some of the movement's demands. It's important to note that accommodation happens even though the oppressor still largely has the upper hand—it's just that the movement has made enough headway that the oppressor realizes it's a good idea to concede at least a few points. Often the oppressor is trying to rid itself of the nuisance that is the movement or trying to prevent further economic loss.

Grape growers lost tremendous amounts of money as a result of both the California farmworkers' strike and the international boycott. In 1969 alone, unharvested grapes cost the farm owners $3 to $4 million, grape sales tanked as some big grocery chains stopped selling nonunion grapes, and many American families refused to buy "scab" grapes.[47] The growers were finally feeling the strike and boycott where it hurt: their wallets. Although many were steadfastly antilabor (and still are today), the grape growers finally sat down with the union to hammer out a contract. They gave in to the workers' demands, with the new union contract providing for higher pay, medical benefits, seniority, and job protections.[48]

TACTIC: NONVIOLENT COERCION

When a movement is able to undermine the oppressor's ability to keep control, they've successfully achieved nonviolent coercion. Unlike in an accommodation situation, the oppressor here is making concessions because they have no other choice. It may be that the opposition is too big to control effectively, the society is shut down because of citizen noncooperation, and/or the oppressor's own security apparatus can no longer be trusted to repress the protesters. To be clear: the oppressor isn't giving up power, here. It's still in charge, but the nonviolent resistance has worked well enough that the oppressor has to concede defeat on some issues.

The Soviets in 1968 had the overwhelming military advantage. Even (or especially) if the Czechoslovakian military or citizens had mounted armed resistance, the Soviets would have easily been able to crush it. The invasion should have worked, and they should have been able to install the government of their choice with little fuss. However, the Soviets had absolutely no idea how to respond to nonviolent resistance. They were able to control the territory but not the people. Indeed, the Soviets reportedly weren't even completely able to control their own soldiers! Given those factors, they had no choice but to negotiate with the state they were occupying. They continued to occupy Czechoslovakia but had to negotiate a settlement, which included leaving the pre-occupation Czechoslovakian government largely in place.

TACTIC: DISINTEGRATION

A lot of the same forces we talked about in nonviolent coercion are present in disintegration. The oppressor's ability to repress the movement has been severely constrained, often because the regime has lost some of its sources of power—it may be that the security apparatus has fully defected, that the economy has significant problems, or that the elites and/or external supporters have turned on the regime. As with nonviolent coercion, it may be that the resistance has gotten too big to control or that so many citizens have withdrawn their support that the regime can no longer function. At this point, the oppressor has no real choice but to give up power completely.

The fight against South African apartheid was waged over several decades and with a variety of violent and nonviolent tactics. By the 1980s, the tactics were *mostly* nonviolent. Noncooperation was rampant. African citizens staged economic boycotts and general strikes, ostracized Africans who collaborated with the government, staged transportation strikes and school boycotts, refused to pay rents, and much, much more. The government's response was to ramp up their methods of repression, growing ever more violent against each new protest—yet the noncooperation was so widespread that they could not control the movement. Africans would no longer tolerate apartheid and white rule. When the international community levied sanctions, the regime lost a major source of external support. It became clear to the regime that they could not hold power indefinitely, so they worked with African leaders to transition from the apartheid regime to inclusive democracy.

STAGE 6: REDISTRIBUTION OF POWER

Chapter 8 is pretty much entirely devoted to rebuilding your state once you get rid of your oppressors, so here we're keeping this short. After your nonviolent resistance movement succeeds, you have to build something in place of the government you just tore down. Nature abhors a vacuum, so if you don't build something, someone else will—and it may not be to your liking. Here, dystopian fiction offers myriad cautionary tales. (The genre really is better at the negative stuff.) For example, the teenage heroines of both Suzanne Collins's Hunger Games and Veronica Roth's Divergent series both eventually rebel against the new dystopian government that has taken the place of the previous dystopian government. The key takeaway here is that your work is not done when you've toppled the dystopian government— you're going to have to work even harder in the next phase unless you want yet another bad government.

FINAL THOUGHTS

At this point, we hope you see why nonviolence is always a better option than armed revolution. This chapter has offered an *ideal* model of successful nonviolent resistance, with examples drawn from around the world (and the few we could find in dystopian fiction).

Next, we're going to talk about rebuilding your society in the wake of a dystopian regime—stage 6. This one is so big it needs its own chapter. But here's the bottom line: when *violent* resistance is successful, the resulting state is likely to be authoritarian.[49] In contrast, your organized and disciplined *nonviolent* movement is more likely to result in democratic governance. Remember: you want to do as much as possible to set your state up for democracy because democracy is the antidote to dystopian government.

Unfortunately, winning a revolution doesn't wipe people's memories clean; everyone will be dragging considerable baggage with them into the new—hopefully democratic—regime. Things we'll be exploring in the next chapter include how you go about strengthening society, how you build workable institutions, how you encourage political participation, and how to prevent your new state from backsliding into authoritarianism.

8

Can You (Re)build It? Yes You Can!

But in point of fact a tyranny often changes into a tyranny.

—Aristotle, *Politics*

ongratulations! The oppressive regime is out; you're in. In Hollywood, this is where the story would end, implying that all to come will be sunshine and roses. Yet many fictional dystopias are set in rebuilt postconflict/postcatastrophe worlds (George Orwell's *1984*, Veronica Roth's *Divergent*, Suzanne Collins's *The Hunger Games*, Lois Lowry's *The Giver*, and many more). Often these rebuilt societies are someone's utopian ideal . . . but in the absence of democracy, it's hard to avoid dystopian outcomes for large portions of the population. As we've argued throughout this book, democracy—slow and annoying and messy as it can be—is really the only cure for dystopia.

If you want a happily-ever-after ending, now is not the time to get complacent. In the chaos that follows a collapsed government, your society could go either way: democratic or dystopian. In particular, as Aristotle's quote indicates, defeated dictatorships have a way of giving rise to new dictatorships.[1] Remember from chapter 1 how instability can drive people to embrace the controlling (read: safe) arms of the authoritarian state? That's what you have to guard against. Think about *Divergent*: the heroes bring down an authoritarian state only to have to confront not one but two potential dictators. In the nonfiction category, in 2011 Egyptians ousted the thirty-year reign of Hosni Mubarak, but by 2013 the country had reverted to authoritarianism under the rule of President Abdel Fattah al-Sisi.[2]

The tyranny-to-tyranny scenario can be avoided but only with hard work and a strategic plan for democracy. To rebuild successfully, you will need to know some basics about democratic governance, specifically about rights, constitutions, and institutions. Above all, a democracy must embrace rule of law. This chapter will help you rebuild your country while avoiding the dismal fate of too many failed revolutions.

UTOPIA IS NOT THE GOAL

You're trying to build a better society, not a perfect one. People are human: they *will* disagree on what that society should look like. You have to embrace that conflict if you want to succeed in building a democratic society. To eliminate conflicting ideals from human society, you would need to erase memory and history (as in Lowry's *The Giver* and in *Divergent*), kill off all emotional attachments (as in Huxley's *Brave New World* and Bradbury's *Fahrenheit 451*), and give people a reason to be united as a group—which usually has massive negative consequences for the minority in order to benefit the majority.

"The Ones Who Walk Away from Omelas," a famous short story, is Ursula K. Le Guin's **utilitarian** thought experiment on the majority/minority tradeoff: what if you could have a completely perfect utopian city in which everyone is happy, but the tradeoff for perfection is that there *always* has to be one child suffering horribly? The Omelans have achieved the happiness of the vast majority of people, and the cost is the misery of just one small child. Would you make that trade? The ones who walk away refuse the tradeoff—and they are right to do so. Society cannot be based on the premise that the suffering of some is okay as long as most people are happy. Instead, you should build the best possible institutions to (hopefully) make society fair. The best way that we humans have come up with to do this is democracy. Democracy will never be perfect, but it's better than the alternatives—and it is best to think of it as promising a process but not outcomes. (The basic idea is that if the process is just, the outcomes will be better.)

This chapter walks you through the different ways you could set up a new democracy, with a few key caveats up front. First, we're assuming that your society is full of conflict. Think about it: at least *some* of your population was doing just fine and wanted to keep the dictatorship or the previous failed-state government, others joined your movement, while still others wanted violent revolution. When you have such

According to **utilitarian** philosophy, a good government is one that produces the greatest good for the greatest number of people. This sounds reasonable until you realize that certain interpretations of utilitarianism suggest you could murder someone because their organs would save the lives of six other people (one life for six).

When your society has deep divisions, **power sharing** allows representatives from all of the major groups to be involved in formal political decision making, especially at the executive level.

internal conflicts, **power-sharing** arrangements among groups is necessary.[3] And second, consider your context. If the government used violence to keep power, there would be massive damage to the physical environment, likely including a humanitarian crisis, and the economy would probably be toast, plus other serious complications that would make rebuilding difficult. Because of those difficulties, we will assume you toppled the government without mass destruction *and* you have a functioning market economy.[4] We're assuming we are rebuilding a society that has internal conflicts and multiple groups competing for control but has managed to free itself from an authoritarian regime without destroying everything in the process.

YOU DISINTEGRATED THE OPPRESSOR—NOW WHAT?

You need a plan for quickly implementing democratic institutions and getting citizen buy-in. One of your first announcements should be that you are forming a transitional government and that elections will be held in short order. If your country already has functioning political parties,[5] you could schedule elections quickly—but if there aren't political parties, people need some time to get organized. Democracy requires parties to structure the competition and (hopefully) provide voters meaningful choices. Box 8.1 explains why parties are so important to democratic society.

In the meantime, you need an exit plan for the remnants of the regime you just disintegrated (no, you *cannot* kill them). The end of the Divergent series' Chicago Experiment was relatively nonviolent; in negotiating the end of his mother's dictatorship, Four (a.k.a. Tobias) gives her a way to exit gracefully. To her credit, she takes it. It helped that she's his mother . . . chances are that your opponents won't exit so smoothly. Consider exile: the old guard hanging around will endanger your attempts at democracy.[12]

Institutions are the mechanisms through which governments exercise power. They include executives, legislatures, courts, etc. Institutions define the rules of the political game in each country.

Before the first elections, you'll need to work with a variety of community leaders to write a new constitution. In writing the new constitution, the rebuilding team will design key democratic **institutions**. These include defining a new system for sharing authority

BOX 8.1: IT'S MY PARTY, AND I'LL CRY IF I WANT TO

Democracy, E. E. Schattschneider famously wrote, is "unthinkable save in terms of parties."[6] We've already said that you'll need functioning political parties as you start your new democracy—but why? We know: people regularly complain that parties nominate bad candidates and/or don't represent "the people." Do we have to have them? The answer is yes, and for some good reasons. Parties are necessary to aggregate preferences among the population; that is, they help people figure out what they think (and why) and then band together over it. Parties are also essential in governing to avoid unstable majorities. How parties within a country relate to one another and share political power is what we call the "party system" in place at any given time.

Parties organize the political landscape through their three basic components; V. O. Key calls these the PO, the PIG, and the PIE.[7]

- Party organizations (PO) are what you probably just think of as "parties," but technically, the PO is how the party is structured and all of the stuff (campaigns, platform development) that happens outside government institutions.
- Parties in government (PIG) are the elected officials from each party; their job is to represent both their constituents and their party at the same time.[8]
- Parties in the electorate (PIE) are voters who consider themselves members of a party.

In a mass democracy without parties, politics easily devolves into either anarchy or a popularity contest based on looks and personality rather than policy. In Bradbury's *Fahrenheit 451*, for instance, the wife of our protagonist (Montag) and her friends demonstrate this danger beautifully:

"Sounds fine," said Mrs. Bowles. "I voted last election, same as everyone, and I laid it on the line for President Noble. I think he's one of the nicest-looking men who ever became president."

"Oh, but the man they ran against him!"

"He wasn't much, was he? Kind of small and homely and he didn't shave too close or comb his hair very well."

"What possessed the 'Outs' to run him? You just don't go running a short little man like that against a tall man. Besides, he mumbled. Half the time I couldn't hear a word he said. And the words I did hear I didn't understand!"

"Fat, too, and didn't dress to hide it. No wonder the landslide was for Winston Noble. Even their names helped. Compare Winston Noble to Hubert Hoag for ten seconds and you can almost figure the results."[9]

Parties ideally encourage non-candidate-centric behavior[10]—although sadly for Mrs. Bowles, they can't cure stupidity. But maybe they don't need to. A good party system should simplify and present alternatives in the form of candidates and policies such that the "semi-sovereign people" (in Schattschneider's phrase) can have clear propositions to which they can say simply "yes" or "no."[11]

between the central and local governments, deciding on the new democratic system, and building courts. Your goals are to write a constitution *and* have the outcome accepted as legitimate (so the government is not seen as the people's enemy).[13] Gain the trust of citizens through open and transparent negotiations during the transition. Do not be the pigs from George Orwell's *Animal Farm*, who kept the other barnyard animals ignorant so that they could change the rules whenever they wanted. (In fact, don't be pigs at all.)

WHAT'S THE POINT OF A CONSTITUTION?

Having a written constitution is essential if a new democracy wants to be perceived as legitimate both by its people and by other democratic states.[14] Ultimately, the goal is that, as the freedom fighter V puts it in James McTeigue's movie *V for Vendetta*, "People should not be afraid of their governments; governments should be afraid of their people."

At its core, every constitution does three basic things:

1. Establishes the country as a legal entity and sets out the principles on which the society is founded.
2. Creates the country's political institutions and defines the duties and responsibilities of each institution.
3. Sets limits on the power of the government and establishes **rule of law**.[15]

In short: the constitution is the ultimate authority in the country. It defines what the government is, the principles under which the government operates, and the limits on what the government can and cannot do. Because it does all of these very important things, the constitution is the highest law in the country.

Rule of law means not just that there are laws that people have to follow but that the government and *all government officials* have to follow the law, too. The law applies equally to everyone. Rule of law means that it isn't the whims of individual leaders that govern a country—the laws do.

Now, the dictatorship might have established a constitution—they do that to give themselves a veneer of respectability. Alternately, your state might have had a democratic constitution at some point in the predictatorial era. If you already have a constitution, do you need to write a new one? We have a handy flow chart, figure 8.1, to help you decide.

We're going to assume that you need a new constitution; most transitional states do.[16] As Machiavelli

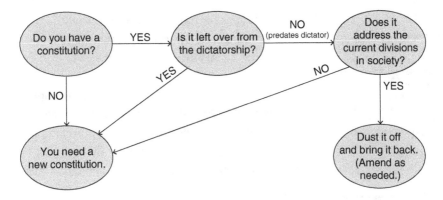

Figure 8.1 Do you need a new constitution?
Source: Graphic by the authors.

famously said (in *The Discourses*, not in *The Prince*), sometimes a country needs to "be brought back to its beginnings."[17] First, we'll look at the principles, like fundamental rights, that you should probably enshrine in your constitution. After that, we'll work on solving the institutional puzzle—how you decide which institutions are best for your particular situation—and we'll end with setting up a court system.

GIVE ME LIBERTY OR GIVE ME DEATH

In a democracy, the most important principles are typically civil liberties and civil rights. In that case, it might be helpful to define which liberties and rights are the most important to your society.

FUNDAMENTAL RIGHTS

Fundamental rights are the basis of democracy.[18] They come in two flavors: civil liberties and civil rights.

- Civil liberties protect you from government. They guarantee that the government cannot infringe upon your right to free speech, free exercise of religion, freedom of association, **due process**, etc.

Due process means that the state is *cannot* arbitrarily take fundamental rights from people. The government must have a legal/standard procedure for determining when and why a person's rights can be curtailed.
Equal protection means that the government *cannot* treat a particular group differently than other groups.

- Civil rights are things government *should* do to make sure everyone is treated equally and receives **equal protection** under the law.

Another important distinction is **negative rights** versus **positive rights**. Most of your civil liberties are *negative* rights; they define what the government *cannot* do (for example, it can't tell you what religion to be).[19] In contrast, *positive* rights are rights that help give people the capacity to participate in society on an equal basis to one another; the premise is that if only *some* people can fully participate in society, it's not really free. Positive rights include education, health care, and a social safety net.[20] Negative rights versus positive rights is the difference between *saying* everyone has equality of opportunity and *doing* something to ensure equality of opportunity.

The question for constitution builders is whether you want to stick strictly with negative rights in your constitution (the United States) or if you also want to also incorporate positive rights (Sweden, Portugal, South Africa). This is pretty important if your country has groups that have historically been marginalized—like women, racial/ethnic minorities, and/or indigenous peoples.

Negative versus positive rights: Imagine that it's a beautiful, sunny day and you're out sailing with friends. Suddenly, a rogue wave knocks you overboard, and the current carries you away from the boat.
Negative rights mean that no one has made a rule that if you fall out you're not allowed back on the boat, but no one's throwing you a lifeline, either. If you're a good swimmer and have the upper-body strength to pull yourself onto the deck, you'll be fine. If you're not much of a swimmer, well, good luck.
Positive rights mean that your friends will let you get back in the boat on your own if you can. If you need help, though, they're obliged to throw you a lifeline and then pull you back onto the boat—you have a positive right to assistance.

Why, you might ask, would some groups need something more than equal protection? This is an excellent question, and we'll counter it with two questions posed by U.S. president John F. Kennedy in 1963:

If [a person], because his skin is dark, cannot eat lunch in a restaurant open to the public, if he cannot send his children to the best public school available, if he cannot vote for the public officials who will represent him, if, in short, he cannot enjoy the full and free life which all of us want, then who among us would be content to have the color of his skin changed and stand in his place? Who among us would then be content with the counsels of patience and delay?[21]

Kennedy's question poses a thought experiment made famous in political theory by John Rawls (called the "Veil of Ignorance"): What if you didn't know some key things about yourself when you wrote the constitution— like your sex, your race/ethnicity, or your socioeconomic class? You might set things up more fairly, no?

MINORITY RIGHTS

Despite the fact that we all know that discrimination is widespread, there's a lot of controversy surrounding the specific inclusion of minority or women's rights in a constitution.[22] Dominant groups don't tend to think minorities should have "special" rights. Not seeing that they are advantaged by their dominant-group status is a key feature of "privilege," as in white privilege or male privilege.[23] Imagine the outrage in Huxley's *Brave New World* if anyone had tried to make the Deltas equal to the Alphas! While humans haven't gotten to the point of genetically engineered inequality, we are really good at creating inequality (remember *pigmentocracy* from chapter 4?). Our talent for creating inequality is why specific rights for minority groups are necessary—to protect them from persecution and help end their marginalization. The goal is to make ascriptive characteristics (like race, class, and sex) unrelated to political participation.

Many modern constitutions recognize that the mistreatment of minorities is so ingrained in society that minorities must have constitutionally guaranteed rights in order to overcome societal obstacles to full inclusion in society. A good example is minority rights in the Indian Constitution, explained in box 8.2.

Inclusion of minority rights in the constitution is important because constitutionally guaranteed rights cannot easily be taken away by future governments. This is because of *constitutional supremacy*—in any fight between the laws and the constitution, the constitution wins, and amending the constitution is usually difficult.

Women's rights

Have you ever wondered why, in Western societies, women adopt husbands' last names? It's a remnant of the historical practice of *patria potestas* (paternal power), the Roman legal principle of the primacy of the male

BOX 8.2: MINORITY RIGHTS IN THE INDIAN CONSTITUTION

India's constitution provides a good example of some of the complexities of including minority rights in a constitution. India's three-thousand-year-old caste system includes a group of outcastes—the Dalits—who are the lowest of the low, societally speaking. Even though Dalits are Hindu, the largest religious group in India, they're a protected minority because of their historical marginalization. Higher castes literally wouldn't touch a Dalit, hence the English name for the Dalits: "Untouchables."[24] Dalits were so reviled they were sometimes barred from walking down a road past a Brahmin (high-caste) neighborhood and temple.[25] If a Dalit drew water from a well, higher castes would no longer use the well. The practice of untouchability meant that Dalits were constantly subject to humiliation and abuse.

During India's transition from British rule to democracy, the drafters of the Indian Constitution decided that there was no way that lesser castes like Dalits would benefit from democracy unless they had positive rights.[26] The Indian Constitution was specifically written to encourage societal equality.

Figure 8.2 The Indian caste system.

Source: Graphic by the authors.

The situation of the Dalits was included in constitutional provisions that make it illegal for people to "perpetrate untouchability."[27] That means that it is unconstitutional to prevent Dalits from entering higher-caste temples, to abuse Dalits, to deny someone a job or place at school because they are a Dalit, and so on. Even this was not enough to help Dalits integrate into mainstream Indian society. So in another attempt to help Dalits achieve equality, in 1950 the Indian government introduced quotas for Dalits in government jobs and higher education.[28]

Despite these attempts at equality of opportunity, discrimination is still rampant. Many Dalits are able to get educated, but they are still often ostracized. Discrimination takes many forms, from smaller daily acts like higher-caste merchants who sometimes refuse to accept money directly from a Dalit to larger acts such as widespread violence against Dalits that the state rarely addresses.[29] If you imagine the Dalits' situation had there been no clear positive rights, you see why so many constitutions include them.

head of household over all members of that household. The Roman principle was applied throughout the Roman Empire and remained the root of marriage law in Europe. Once societies developed last names, the change of name became a quick and easy sign that a woman had moved from her father's control to her husband's.[30] It's the same principle that's at play in Margaret Atwood's *The Handmaid's Tale*—our protagonist is Offred and her fellow handmaid is Ofglen—literally "of Fred" and "of Glen" (their respective Commanders). As Box 8.3 indicates, societies will not spontaneously treat women equitably, which is why constitutionally defining women's rights is important.

Consider specific constitutional provisions that women must be treated equally before the law, as well as equality in these areas:

- Political/public life and rights
- Employment and economic rights
- Marriage, reproduction, family relations

Approaching the issue constitutionally puts women in a stronger legal position to fight for their rights.[31]

In a lawless society, everyone loses out—but women lose out as a group more than men. Dystopian fiction makes this point nicely (or, rather, horrifyingly). In the failed dystopias (usually postapocalyptic), the strong dominate the weak, and men usually dominate and oppress women. In Miller's *Mad Max: Fury Road*, women are basically cattle, kept either as "milkers" or breeders. We've told you at length about Atwood's *The Handmaid's Tale*, but the central fact the book highlights is that in the absence of good government, women are often parceled out to powerful men as property, both for their bodies and for the dowries they would bring. And this doesn't just happen in fiction—it's common throughout human history. Indeed, the anthropologist Gayle Rubin argues that the trading of women (wives, daughters, sisters) between male leaders as gifts and to cement alliances underlies the modern capitalist system.

In Emily St. John Mandel's novel *Station 11*, the failed state allows for all kinds of abuses of women and girls. In one "town" clustered around an old gas station and a hollowed-out Wal-Mart, a religious cult has taken hold, and the "Prophet" who runs the town has multiple child-wives. (The Traveling Symphony group at the center of the novel inadvertently rescues an eleven-year-old girl who wants to escape marrying him.) In a failed state, whether factual or fictional, the threats of rape and other male violence,

BOX 8.3: THE LONG HISTORICAL ARM OF *PATRIA POTESTAS*

In English Common Law (exported to British colonies), the *patria potestas* principle became *coverture*, under which a woman had no legal identity separate from her husband; she was "covered." Legally, man and wife were one person: *him*. This generally meant women couldn't enter into contracts without their husbands' permissions, couldn't own property, and had no standing in a court of law.[32] Legally, women weren't actually *people* in their own right.[33]

Although many states have now officially declared that women *are* people, the historical belief that that women are male property lives on in some unexpected (read: infuriating) ways. All over the world, women fight every day to keep their hard-won rights from being rolled back.

Canada: Are Women People?

A pivotal case in Canadian legal history is *Edwards vs. Canada*, known as the Persons Case because the question that five women (the Famous Five) brought before the Canadian courts was: Are women persons under the law? In the early twentieth century, women in most Canadian provinces could vote and stand for election, but the Constitution Act (1867) specified that only "qualified persons" (men) could be appointed to the Canadian Senate. The Famous Five took their case for personhood to court, and in 1929 (after many setbacks and appeals), the courts ruled women *were* "qualified persons" under the law. That means women fully became legal persons under Canadian law less than one hundred years ago (about the same time U.S. women finally gained the right to vote).

Figure 8.3 "Now That We Are Persons."

Source: Photo of "Now That We Are Persons," by Nellie McClung, from *Farm and Ranch Review* 25, no. 1 (1930) (Government of Alberta [Canada]).

It's My Body, Isn't It?

You might think that the right to control your own body is fundamental. For men, it is. For women, not so much. From forced pregnancies to female genital mutilation to marital rape, the law often denies women control over their own bodies. For example, under the law, husbands have traditionally had a marital right to sex, while wives have had no legal right to refuse—therefore, sex with an unwilling wife hasn't traditionally been considered rape.[34] In many parts of the world, marital rape is still legal; women in those areas have no right to control their own bodies. Marital rape was gradually outlawed in Australia, Canada, Ireland, the United Kingdom, and the United States between the 1980s and early 1990s and in France and Germany in the mid-1990s. Think about it: in many supposedly "advanced" democracies, married women were not seen as human beings with the right to say no until *the late twentieth century*.

sexual and domestic labor slavery, forced marriages, breeding in captivity, and other gendered oppression loom large. It is only rule of law with good institutions that can counter these, so set up your new government well!

SOLVING THE INSTITUTIONAL PUZZLE

Every new democracy has to figure out how to combine institutions so that they give the country a shot at successfully managing conflict and prevent violence. A constitution cannot do that on its own; it's a foundation on which people can—if they work at it—build a democratic society.[35]

We can't tell you which combination of institutions will be best—your country is bringing a lot of historical baggage with it on the long march toward democracy. That baggage (history, demographics, and culture) must shape your decisions regarding which institutions will work best; there may be things you want to change, but too much change can incur backlash from citizens.[36] Also, institutions don't operate in a vacuum—they're interconnected. That means you have to pick authority-sharing, democratic, and electoral systems that work well together and fit the situation in your society. Once you've decided those, we can move on to the courts.

RESPECT MY AUTHORITY

How you split the authority in your country has other constitutional implications. There are theoretically three ways you can split authority between

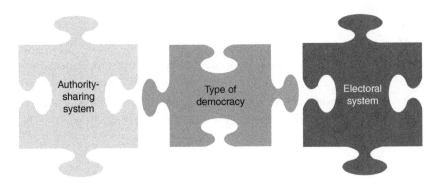

Figure 8.4 The institutional puzzle.
Source: Graphic by the authors.

different levels of government (for example, national versus local governments): unitary, federal, and confederal. We say "theoretically" because in practical terms, only the first two of those work well.

Every country has multiple levels of government—national, subnational (a.k.a. state/province), and local. What differentiates authority-sharing systems is how the hierarchy works among those levels. Whether you pick federalism or go with a unitary system will depend on context and the level of decentralization you think is best for your country.[37]

Unitary

Unitary systems are relatively straightforward: the vast majority of the power is concentrated in the central government (see figure 8.5). The emphasis in unitary systems is on efficiency, uniformity, and national unity.[38] The central government is ultimately responsible for all governance in the unitary state. It should, then, come as no shock to you that the vast majority of dystopian governments—in both fact and fiction—are unitary.

In a *democratic* unitary state, there's a very strong level of government accountability to the voters—it's not as if the central government can blame anyone else when there are problems.[39]

Devolution is when the central government gives some level of authority to a lower level of government. In unitary systems, central governments determine *if* they want to devolve authority and, if so, *how much* and *to which* subnational units. They do not have to give the same level of authority to all subnational units.

There *are* units of government outside of the central government, but any authority that they have is given to them—**devolved** to them—by the central government. What the central government gives it can also take back if it decides that a lower level of government should no longer have authority.[40]

Pros:

Unitary systems are great for smaller countries with relatively homogenous populations. They work well under these circumstances because a homogenous population means that there isn't a lot of rivalry between different groups, and since there aren't a lot of ethnic or religious divisions there's not usually much cultural variation across the different parts of the country.

Cons:

Unitary governments are often problematic in postconflict states—chances are that the centralization of power in the hands of one group was

Figure 8.5 Unitary authority sharing.
Source: Graphic by the authors.

a driver of the conflict in the first place. Unless the country commits to devolution from the outset, unitary systems leave little room for minority groups to be autonomous. This can exacerbate preexisting tensions.

Federal

Federalism isn't so simple. In a federal system, there is formal *decentral-ization*; authority is not concentrated in the national government. Federalism isn't overly popular for dystopian states because if you decentralize power, how do you keep your control over people? But if you start to look at popular dystopian science fiction, where the universe is really large and individual planets are small, you can see why a federalist system might be necessary. In the *Firefly* "Verse," the planets that form the Alliance all manage their own affairs, while the Alliance parliament makes policy for the Verse. The same is true in both *Star Trek* and *Star Wars*, although the former is highly utopian and the latter dystopian. But both showcase a federal system—in *Star Wars*, though, the intergalactic Senate has degenerated into a dictatorship that the Jedi and Rebel Alliance felt compelled to fight.

The defining feature of federal systems is that the *constitution*—not a central government—spells out the powers of the national and subnational levels of government. In turn, local governments get their power from subnational governments (see figure 8.6).

Because the national and subnational governments have their own constitutionally defined responsibilities and powers, the national government cannot curtail the authority of the subnational governments.[41] That said, in a federal system, the national government is more powerful than the subnational governments; in a fight between the national government and the subnational government, the odds are always in the national government's favor.

The beauty of federalism is that it allows people to be governed by elected officials who are closer to them, which means that different regions can develop different policies in accordance with local culture.[42] Cultural context always matters when it comes to institutional design and is especially important in governing a large and diverse area (like the galaxy).[43] From the outside, federal systems may all look the same, but there are often serious differences in how authority and responsibility are divided between the national and subnational governments. Even though the United States was instrumental in the implementation of federalism in post–World War II Germany, the U.S. and German federal systems have significant differences in how the levels of government relate to one another. These differences come from very different cultural, historical, and societal situations in each country.

Pros:

Conventional wisdom says that federalism works best in large/diverse countries like the United States and India. Federalism allows the different regions and the groups in those regions to have a high level of **self-determination**.[44] That high level of self-determination is what also makes federalism a popular choice for multiethnic countries, particularly in the wake of a conflict. Federalism also limits the possibilities for authoritarianism in the national government and gives subnational units a higher level of autonomy than they would have under a unitary system.

Self-determination is the ability of groups to determine their own political fate. Self-determination is sometimes thought to mean full independence, but a group can be self-determining within an already-existing state.

Remember: in a *unitary* system, the central government can give some level of autonomy to its regions, but what the central government gives, it can also take away. In a *federal* system, the constitution gives autonomy to the subnational units, and what the constitution gives, the central government cannot take away.

Cons:

Because the subnational units can pursue their own policies and cultural preferences, citizens' rights may depend on where they live.[45] For example, in Canada and the United States, women initially received the right to vote in some provinces/states but not in others. In both cases, the federal government had to step in to ensure voting rights for all women.[46] Other federal issues can be seen in one of the most famous fictional federations, the Galactic Federation of Free Alliances (the Federal Galactic Republic or the Galactic Alliance) in the original *Star Wars* trilogy. Corruption, inefficiency, and unhealthy competition for power all played a part in the downfall of the Galactic Alliance.

- Powerful local elites (like Jabba the Hutt) can misuse local/subnational levels of governance for their own gain.
- Federal systems can be inefficient and expensive. The national and subnational governments often duplicate efforts and/or create contradictory policies. Also, you have to pay for a lot more politicians and government workers, plus the buildings to house them all (think about the size and grandeur of the Imperial Senate building, with its floating platforms for each member).
- When there aren't enough resources to fund all levels of government effectively, local governments often get the short end of the stick because they have the least funding but the most day-to-day contact with citizens. Think about the scarcity on Luke Skywalker's home world, Tatooine, versus the abundance on the Republic's capital planet, Coruscant.

Other:

If you go with federalism, you have to decide how the subnational units get their preferences heard at the national level. One way to do this is with a *bicameral* national legislature, meaning the legislature has an upper house and a lower house. The subnational units in Germany, India, and the

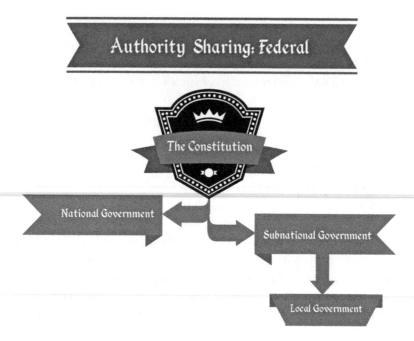

Figure 8.6 Federal authority sharing.
Source: Graphic by the authors.

United States are all represented through the upper houses of the national legislature.[47]

Confederal

We saved the worst for last. Confederations are a *really* unwieldy method of authority sharing. Like federal systems, there are two main levels of government: national and subnational units. Unlike in a federal system, however, in a *con*federal system the balance of power strongly favors the *subnational* governments (see figure 8.7). A famous example of how this failed is the Articles of Confederation, the precursor to the U.S. Constitution, which triggered the Revolutionary War with Britain but was nowhere near strong enough to sustain the new country once the war ended.

In a confederation, the subnational units have determined that there is a need for a little bit of higher-level coordination (usually for trade or security), so they craft a treaty (not a constitution!) to create a national

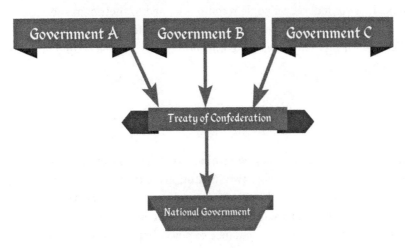

Figure 8.7 Confederal authority sharing.
Source: Graphic by the authors.

government that has very limited authority to act, has no electoral base of its own, and is largely dependent on the subnational governments for funding.[48] The power of the national government can be changed by agreement of the subnational governments, and the subnational units can leave the confederation any time they'd like.[49]

In other words, one subnational unit can hold the rest hostage. An inability to act (given the requirement of unanimity) and the lack of power to tax and spend usually put pressure on confederations to evolve into federations. For example, the United States and Switzerland both moved from confederal to federal states in response to difficulties in managing the country via confederal government.[50]

Pros:

In *theory*, confederations should work when there's a group of subnational units that share specific goals and agree to cooperate on those goals.

Cons:

In practice, the central government can't tax, spend, or make independent decisions; these issues tanked the confederal government of the United States that preceded the current federal system. Also, citizens have no real stake in a confederacy. People remain attached to their own subnational unit, they don't regularly interact with the confederal government, and there's nothing that makes the confederal government accountable to the citizens.

PICK THE FORM OF THE DEMOCRACY

The form of your democracy determines what type of legislature and executive you have and how those two institutions relate to each other. The legislature makes the laws; the executive implements the laws. The executive is also, in practical terms, the "face" that your country shows to the world.

Each country has its own balance of power between the legislature and the executive, but we can generally group democratic countries into three systems: presidential, semi-presidential, and parliamentary—and you can have a well-functioning country using any one of the three. That doesn't mean that they all have an equal chance of succeeding in every case—you'll still have to think carefully about which is best for your state's particular situation.

The **head of state** is typically a figurehead, someone who symbolizes the unity of the country but has little real power in governing, like the queen of England. Don't confuse head of *state* with head of *government*, which is the elected official who is responsible for governing the country. The United States (and much dystopian fiction) combines these two positions, but many countries separate them, for good reasons—the main one being that the symbolic figure representing the country can become tainted by actual involvement in partisan politics, thereby losing their unifying power.

Your type of **head of state**—monarch or elected official—determines whether your country is a *constitutional monarchy* or a *republic*. The Netherlands, Norway, and the United Kingdom are all constitutional monarchies; France, Germany, India, and the United States are all republics. Either way, these countries are *representative democracies* in which the voters delegate their power to elected representatives who are then empowered to make decisions on behalf of their voters.

PARLIAMENTARY DEMOCRACY

The defining feature of parliamentary democracy is that there is some degree of executive-legislative fusion; they are not completely separate institutions. The executive is accountable to the legislature, and the legislature is accountable to the people. This chain of accountability comes from how power is delegated from voters to the government: the voters elect the parliament, and the parliament then elects the head of government (the prime minister) to lead the executive.[51]

Some key aspects of a parliamentary system are:

1.   The prime minister is the head of *government*, but there are other ministers who help with governing the state. The ministers are referred to collectively as the *cabinet*. The head of *state* is typically either an elected (but ceremonial) president or a hereditary monarch.

2.   After the election, the leader of the largest party in parliament is invited to form a government. That leader becomes prime minister.[52] If the party has a majority in parliament, the whole cabinet comes from that party. If the party doesn't have a majority, the prime-minister-to-be reaches out to like-minded parties to see if they're willing to enter into a coalition with the largest party. Governments need a majority of the seats in the legislature in order to get anything done. Coalition governments are formed when no single party gets a majority and a group of parties join forces to run the country together.

3.   Each cabinet minister has responsibility for both a policy portfolio (justice, health, defense, etc.) and for the bureaucracy that implements those policies.[53]

4.   The legislative agenda—what the legislature takes up and when—is typically set by the cabinet. The cabinet ministers develop legislation and introduce bills to the parliament. Legislators are expected to vote with their party, which means that bills introduced by the cabinet almost always pass, since the cabinet ministers' parties control the majority.[54]

5.   The legislature has considerable power, though. It's responsible for putting the prime minister in power, so it can also remove the prime minister from power—usually with a *vote of no confidence*.[55]

6.   There is no fixed term of office in parliamentary systems. There's often a maximum number of years that you can go without having new elections, but elections are typically called as needed.

Pros:

Parliamentary government encourages coalitions and can be more inclusive than other forms, which is good for postconflict/divided societies. Also, the vote of no confidence means a bad government can be ousted before it does too much damage. Finally, in postconflict countries, people often expect changes to happen quickly, and that is possible in parliamentary systems, particularly when there's a majority government or a stable coalition.[56]

Cons:

Parliamentary government can be unstable, particularly in new democracies where parties are not strong and the coalitions between former combatants are fragile. The lack of separation of powers is also troubling, as it means that weak parliaments may not put a stop to executive abuses. Conversely, it also means that the parliament can be so strong that the cabinet fears being thrown out of power if it tries to make bold policy changes.[57]

PRESIDENTIAL DEMOCRACY

The defining feature of presidential democracy is that there is strict separation of powers between the executive and the legislature.[58] The chains of accountability are separate, too. The executive and the legislature are each accountable directly to the people because people vote independently for each office. This means that the president has a base of support separate from the legislature's base.

Some key items of note in a presidential system are:

1.   The president is the head of government (a.k.a. the chief executive) and, in many countries, also the head of state.[59]

2.   The president has a *cabinet* to advise on policy related to their portfolios and head the bureaucracies responsible for implementing policy.

3.   What the legislature takes up and when is set by the legislature, with little say from the executive. The president can try to persuade the legislature to take up particular issues, but even when the same political party controls both branches of government, legislative cooperation is not guaranteed.

4.   Legislation must be signed into law by the president. That means a president can control legislative outcomes by exercising the *veto*—the refusal to approve legislation passed by the legislature.[60]

5. A president cannot be removed from office by the legislature before a fixed term is up (unless the president does something illegal).[61]

Pros:

Presidential systems are extremely stable, thanks to their fixed terms of office; this is good for countries that have experienced instability. Voters directly elect both their chief executive and their legislators and therefore have more power to hold both accountable. Finally, the separation of powers means that the executive and the legislative branches can criticize each other without fear of bringing down the government, and each branch acts as a check on the power of the other.[62]

Cons:

A strong presidential executive can trend toward authoritarianism. Presidents are the leader of the entire country, which has prompted some presidents to abuse their power. Unless a president's abuses actually break the law, however, there's no way to remove him from office. Political *gridlock* is also a frequent problem: a stalemate in which policy does not get passed because the executive and legislative branches have different agendas. And the splitting up of power between legislative and executive, some scholars have suggested, divides accountability and weakens democracy.[63]

SEMI-PRESIDENTIAL DEMOCRACY

The defining feature of semi-presidential democracies is the dual executive: a prime minister and a nonceremonial president. As you may have guessed, this is a mixed system that combines features of parliamentary and presidential systems. There are many different ways to combine the systems, but generally the president is directly elected by the people, that president has constitutionally defined powers, and there is also a prime minister and cabinet that answer to the parliament.[64]

Some key items of note in a semi-presidential system are:

1. Technically, the prime minister is the head of government, but the president has more power than a typical head of state.[65]

2. The legislature elects and can dismiss the prime minister and cabinet, but the president can dissolve the legislature.[66]

3.   The powers of the president can be far different on paper than in practice; for example, Austria's president looks strong on paper but is weak in reality, while the French president looks weak on paper but is strong in reality.

4.   Some semi-presidential systems are closer to the presidential model; others are closer to parliamentary government.

Pros:

Semi-presidential systems have been used to great effect in postconflict states, since the dual executive can be a good method for power sharing. Like parliamentary systems, semi-presidential systems are good for inclusiveness while also allowing for more separation of powers than parliamentary government.[67]

Cons:

These systems can be confusing—who does what, who has power over whom? Plus, you may get the disadvantages of parliamentary systems (instability) plus the disadvantages of presidentialism (gridlock). The worst outcome is when the president and the prime minister come from different parties, which can result in a stalemate.[68]

ROCK THE VOTE

Picking an electoral system is arguably the most important part of your constitutional design.[69] We say arguably because some constitution builders focus on elections to the exclusion of the other elements of democracy.[70] That's problematic. Although voting is important, it isn't the only thing that matters in a democratic society—voting means nothing if your society lacks civil rights and civil liberties. North Korea holds "elections," for goodness' sake! Show of hands: who thinks North Korea is a democracy?

That said, you must have an electoral system if you want a functioning democracy. There are three families of electoral systems: plurality/majority, proportional representation, and mixed. Each family includes least a few options for conducting elections. We're going to discuss only the most common in each family, otherwise this chapter will never end. Figure 8.8 shows you which countries currently belong to which family of electoral systems.

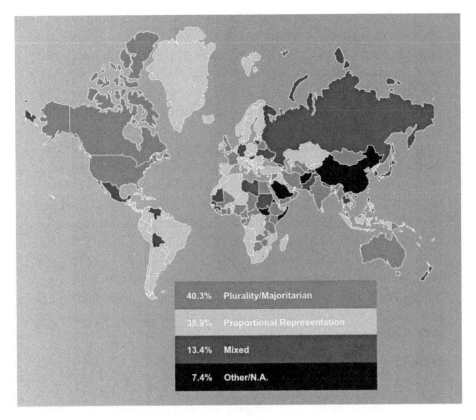

Figure 8.8 Electoral systems around the world.
Source: Made by authors from data from International IDEA, "Worldwide Electoral System Design Database: Electoral System Family," https://www.idea.int/data-tools/question-view/130357.

PLURALITY/MAJORITY

The basics: Each voter gets one vote. Voters cast their one vote for the candidate they prefer for each elected office. The candidate with the most votes wins. The system produces one winner, and that winner gets the office. That's because this family of voting methods is typically based on *single-member districts* (SMD) and *geographical* representation. Translation: the country is divided into electoral districts, each district gets one representative, and that representative's job is to represent the whole district. There are several ways to go about electing candidates in the plurality/majority category; we're going to talk about the two most common (accounting for more than 75 percent of all plurality/majority countries).[71]

1. *First past the post (FPTP)*: This is a *plurality* system in which a candidate doesn't have to get the majority of the votes to win—she just has to get the *most* votes. So, if we have five main ethnic groups and each puts up a candidate—one gets 15 percent of the vote, three with 20 percent each, and one with 25 percent—then the one with 25 percent of the vote wins. The system is simple, the votes are easily tallied, and people tend to understand it fairly well. The major problem is *wasted* votes—votes cast for candidates that didn't win. In our example, 75 percent of the constituents did not vote for the winner, thus 75 percent of the votes were wasted.

2. *Two-round system (TRS)*: This is a *majority* system in which the winner has to get a minimum of 50 percent plus one to win. If there are more than two candidates, such a majority doesn't typically happen in the first round of voting. A second round of voting—with only the top contenders on the ballot—is held to determine the winner. Like FPTP, it's fairly simple and people understand it. TRS is expensive, though. Your country has to hold two elections, usually in just a few weeks, and unless you make elections a national holiday, then people have to take time off from work to vote.

Party-system outcomes

Plurality/majority electoral systems typically lead to two-party systems in which the parties are relatively centrist (this is called "Duverger's Law"). We call them "catch-all" parties because they need to be able to "catch" the most votes. These systems narrow the political spectrum to two parties because voters **vote strategically**. These are single-member district/winner-take-all systems—if you vote for a small party, chances are high that either your vote is wasted *or* it helps create a **spoiler effect**.[72]

Strategic voting happens when you *want* to vote for a small-party candidate but you vote for the candidate of a specific large party because you fear a vote for your preferred candidate will have a **spoiler effect**. In other words, you correctly fear that voting for a small-party candidate will just take votes away from the large party that scares you least, thus ensuring a win for the large party that scares you most.

Pros:

Plurality/majority voting is simple and straightforward, and it typically results in single-party government. No pesky coalitions—just one party that can govern and an opposition that can check the power of the majority party. Advocates argue that it leads to better links and accountability between constituents and their representative because the representative is typically from the local area and can represent the district's best interests.[73]

Cons:

Electoral-systems experts rarely recommend plurality/majority systems for new democracies because *all* available evidence indicates that these systems are very hard to maintain, particularly in the wake of conflict.[74] They typically result in a lot of wasted votes, which can lead to renewed conflict in postconflict countries. Go back to our FPTP example, where the person with just 25 percent of the vote won and the other four groups get no voice in the new legislature. Would that seem fair or legitimate to the four groups who get nothing? Even in a stable country, plurality/majority systems are problematic:

- There's the spoiler effect we talked about earlier.
- Smaller parties can't compete, so people who prefer those small parties rarely have much of a voice in the political system.
- Third, since the main parties need to attract the most voters possible, they put forth the safest candidate possible—which largely excludes women and minorities.
- Plurality/majority systems are prone to **gerrymandering**, which gives one party a significant advantage over the other.

PROPORTIONAL REPRESENTATION

The basics: In a proportional representation (PR) system, voters vote for a *party*, and the party gets seats in the legislature based on the *proportion of the vote* it receives. If your party gets 30 percent of the vote, you get 30 percent of the seats in the legislature. This system is based on *multimember districts* and *ideological* representation. Translation: multiple people are elected from each district, and their role is to represent their voters' policy preferences. In some small countries, the entire country is the multimember district (Israel, the Netherlands, Namibia); in others, the districts correspond to provinces or regions (Argentina, Portugal).

Gerrymandering is when one political party intentionally draws the electoral districts in such a way that it actively harms the other party's chances of winning. Gerrymandering allows politicians to pick their voters rather than voters picking their politicians.

There are multiple forms of PR, but "list" is the most common type (accounting for 98 percent of PR countries).[75] In a list PR election, each party puts forth a list of candidates for the district. Voters vote for the party they prefer, and the party gets seats based on their share of the vote totals. List PR is easy to understand and typically results in few wasted votes, but a country must have at least a few organized political parties in order to make it work.[76] There are two varieties: closed- and open-list PR.

1. *Closed list*: In this version, your party's list is set—voters cannot change the order of the candidates on the list. Let's say your *district magnitude* (the number of legislative seats allocated to the district) is twelve, so each party fields a list of twelve candidates. If your party gets 25 percent of the vote, that's three of the twelve seats. The first three people on your party list get those seats, and voters cannot change the order of the list.

2. *Open list*: Again, the party puts out a list of candidates for the district. Rather than putting an X by the party you prefer, you find the list of the party you prefer and then put an X by one of the candidates on the list. This serves both as a vote for the party and as an indicator that you want a specific candidate to be at the top of the list. Once the votes are tallied, the lists are reordered based on the voters' preferences. Let's again say that your party gets three of twelve seats. Those seats still go to the top three candidates on the list; the difference is that in an open-list system, the list has been reordered based on voter preferences.

Party-system outcomes

PR systems tend to result in multiparty systems. While there may still be a little strategic voting, there's no spoiler effect.[77] Voters can confidently vote for smaller parties because they know there's a high likelihood that their small party will get at least a few seats in the legislature.

Pros:

Electoral-systems experts often recommend PR for emerging democracies because it has better political competitiveness outcomes (more groups have a shot at winning seats in the legislature). PR results in far fewer wasted votes than plurality/majority and is not very susceptible to gerrymandering. Plus, parties don't have to put forth the safest possible candidate; that's why women and minorities are both more likely to be elected in PR systems. Also, because PR does ensure that most political groups get representation, PR election results are perceived as fair and can increase people's trust in electoral outcomes.[78]

Cons:

Because parties rarely get an outright majority, PR often results in coalition governments. In well-established states, coalitions aren't usually a problem—they're typically coherent (parties have similar policy preferences) and fairly stable. But in new/postconflict systems, the coalitions may not be coherent, and the high level of compromise required to make the partnerships work can slow down the government. There is also an additional level of complexity to PR, which may require new countries to make more effort at educating voters if they want elections to run smoothly.[79]

MIXED SYSTEMS

The basics: Mixed systems have two electoral systems running in tandem; voters usually get two votes, one on the plurality/majority side of the ballot and one on the PR side of the ballot. Mixed electoral systems can be thought of as an attempt to get the best of both electoral worlds by combining the good parts of plurality/majority systems with the good parts of PR systems.[80] There are only two forms: mixed-member proportional (MMP) and parallel.

1. *Mixed-member proportional (MMP)*: In an MMP system, the legislature has district seats and proportional-representation seats. Importantly, the two systems are linked; what happens with the PR seats is dependent on what happens with the district seats. FPTP is frequently used to allocate the district seats, and the PR seats are set aside for parties that meet or exceed the country's threshold but got no district seats. This corrects for any disproportional results in the district seats and results in relatively proportional outcomes.

2. *Parallel*: In a parallel system, the legislature still has district seats and PR seats, and voters cast votes for each. The difference between parallel and MMP is that in a parallel system, the two votes aren't linked. What happens with the district seats has no bearing on what happens with the

PR seats. The lack of connection between the two means that the outcomes are less than proportional (but still more proportional than a fully plurality/majority system).

Party-system outcomes

Because they have a proportional component, mixed systems tend to result in multiparty systems. But because there is also a winner-take-all component, there's more strategic voting in mixed systems than in fully PR systems. The spoiler effect is limited, though, because smaller parties that are shut out of district seats can still win PR seats.[81]

Pros:

Mixed systems have many of the same advantages as PR systems while also having the same geographic-representation advantages of plurality/majority systems. People get to vote for a party and for a specific candidate, which gives them more input into who represents them than they would get in straight PR systems.

Cons:

In addition to the normal PR disadvantages, the main disadvantage of mixed systems is the complexity. Even in well-established MMP systems, voters don't always understand what each of their votes actually does for seat allocation. Also, mixed systems manage to combine the accountability problems of both PR and plurality/majority systems: you have legislators that are accountable to the party but less so to the voters, *and* you have legislators that are accountable to the voters but less so to the party. Differences in accountability create two classes of legislators, which can be problematic when they need to work together.[82]

THE SCALES OF JUSTICE

In a government of laws and not of men, no man, however prominent or powerful, and no mob, however unruly or boisterous, is entitled to defy a court of law.

—John F. Kennedy

Rule of law, and therefore democracy, is impossible without an *independent judiciary*. "Independent" means a court system that is not controlled by either the executive or the legislature. It doesn't necessarily mean "completely separate"; none of your institutions operate in a vacuum. The question is this: Does the judiciary have the ability to decide cases without interference from the executive and/or the legislature? You want a resounding *yes*, so we're going to look at how you get an independent judiciary (constitutionally) and what independence allows the judiciary to do (protect the constitution).

WHAT MAKES THE JUDICIARY INDEPENDENT?

The fundamental role of the courts is to adjudicate disputes, like state prosecution of crime, people suing the government, or people suing each other. Courts also make sure people's constitutional rights are not violated, serving as an important check on the other branches of government. However, the courts can't fulfill these functions effectively if they aren't largely independent from influence.

Your best plan for judicial independence makes it clear in the constitution that the courts are a separate and equal branch of the government. Constitution-building experts recommend that you define three things in your constitution to ensure that the courts are free from undue interference:

1. The process for selecting and appointing judges: More than one government institution should be involved in the selection and approval. That way, judges aren't beholden to the person/body who selected them. Many localities in the United States do elect judges, which we do not recommend. Elected or appointed, the *initial* selection is always a political process. The key thing is that judges should never be subject to *reelection*.[83] **Public opinion** can pressure them to make popular rather than just rulings.[84]

2. The length of judicial appointments: Longer terms of office—even lifetime appointments—create stronger judicial independence. Judges should make rulings without worrying about how those decisions will affect their job in the long run.

One of the most important decisions in U.S. history is the U.S. Supreme Court's 1954 decision in *Brown v. Board of Education*. The court ruled that segregation—separating black students and white students—is a violation of the Constitution's guarantee of all citizens' equal protection under the law. Would this have happened had the nine justices on the U.S. Supreme Court been elected? We can't know, but **public opinion** data from 1942 indicates that only 30 percent of white Americans approved of school integration. Since black Americans were regularly prevented from voting before 1965, white voters' opinions would have been what mattered to elected officials.

3.   Removing judges: You want to be able to remove someone corrupt from the judiciary, but you don't want judges removed for political reasons, so include more than one institution in the removal process. In some countries, the process requires cooperation between the legislature and the executive. Another option is to require that other members of the judiciary sign off.

EMPOWERING THE JUDICIARY:
CONSTITUTIONAL REVIEW

Judicial independence is crucial to one of the main tasks of the judiciary: constitutional review (*judicial review*, to Americans). If the government has in some way (law, action, or regulation) infringed upon people's constitutional rights or protections, then the courts have the power to void that law, action, or regulation.[85] The power to review constitutionality is what makes the judiciary an effective check on the actions of other institutions.

The American model: Concrete review

The practice of constitutional review began with an American case called *Marbury v. Madison* (1803), and for more than a century no other country gave its courts the power to review laws for constitutionality.[86] The American model centers on *concrete* review: the courts cannot rule on the constitutionality of a law or action unless someone has brought suit against a government official or agency, but any court can consider constitutionality.[87] The drawback of this model is that someone actually has to experience harm before the review can occur.

The European model: Abstract review

After World War II, European countries started to develop *constitutional courts*, the sole purpose of which is constitutional review.[88] Only the constitutional court can declare a law unconstitutional. The European model allows for *abstract* review, in which the court can decide on the constitutionality of a proposed law. The legal scholar Ran Hirschl explains that the difference in the two models "is between hypothetical 'what if' scenarios ('abstract' review) and judicial review that may take place only in the context of a specific legal dispute ('concrete' review)."[89] Until 2010, France only allowed abstract review,[90] but the problem is that the constitutional court can't strike down a law once it has gone into effect, meaning that the court can't remedy a situation where you only figure out a law is unconstitutional after it has been implemented.[91]

Most democracies see the considerable benefit of allowing both abstract and concrete review: prevent harm where you can, remedy harm once done.

MAKING IT ALL WORK TOGETHER

We can't stress enough how important it is that you think really carefully about how your democratic society will function. What are the tradeoffs that go along with each choice you make? Who benefits from which institutions? Will your new institutions work for your population? Huxley gives us a good example of democracy gone bad in *Brave New World*;[92] it illustrates *exactly* why people turn to authoritarianism if the hard work of a functioning democracy gets to be too much.

Each institutional choice that you make influences at least some of the others. If you pick a federal system, then you need to consider a bicameral (two-house) legislature. And if you have a bicameral legislature, you need to consider if the upper house (representing the subnational units) should be filled using a different electoral system than the one you use for other offices.

How do you know which institutions will work best? In short: you can't be certain. Even people who have made constitutional design their life's work can't be certain.[93] However, Andrew Reynolds, a political science professor who has advised on the constitutional design for more than a dozen countries, has a word of advice for would-be constitution builders: *alignment*.[94] The institutions you pick have to align across the board; they have to work with one another *and* within your social context.

Lessons from the "Cyprus Experiment"

Mustapha Mond, the Controller of the World State in Huxley's *Brave New World*, tells our heroes John and Helmholtz that they had tried a form of democracy in the early days, which failed miserably:

It began in A.F. 473. The Controllers had the island of Cyprus cleared of all its existing inhabitants and re-colonized with a specially prepared batch of twenty-two thousand Alphas. . . . The result exactly fulfilled all the theoretical predictions. The land wasn't properly worked; there were strikes in all the factories; the laws were set at naught, orders disobeyed; all the people detailed for a spell of low-grade work were perpetually intriguing for high-grade jobs, and all the people with high-grade jobs were counter-intriguing at all costs to stay where they were. Within six years they were having a first-class civil war. When nineteen out of the twenty-two thousand had been killed, the survivors unanimously petitioned the World Controllers to resume the government of the island. Which they did.

Democracy, as we have said, requires compromise—and perhaps humility as well. If everyone is equal politically, there must be some premise of social equality also; the World State's Greek-letter hierarchy system was incompatible with equality and therefore with democracy, particularly because the Alphas refused manual labor. But citizens in a functioning democracy need to respect *all* work as valuable; as the singer, actor, and all-around funny lady Bette Midler famously stated, "My idea of a superwoman is someone who scrubs her own floors."

Think about this scenario: a country has several ethnic groups, including a majority group that excludes the other groups from power. A temporary coalition forced the majority group out of power, but the coalition ended after the majority government collapsed. Under these circumstances, would a unitary authority-sharing system in a presidential democracy with FPTP elections be a good plan?

Indeed, that might be the *worst possible* set of institutions anyone could pick for a seriously fragmented postconflict society. The groups are coming out of a dictatorship (centralized power) under which they had no power, which makes reimposition of unitary government a bad plan. Federalism would be the obvious authority-sharing system, since each of these groups would benefit from autonomy. And neither FPTP nor presidential democracy are conducive to power sharing in a divided society—winner take all and coalitions unlikely? Recipe for disaster. Either parliamentary or semi-presidential democracies combined with some form of proportional elections would give you better representation for all of the historically marginalized groups.

To give this more context, we've drafted a Comparing Dystopias box that lays out what we think would be best for rebuilding the highly factionalized Chicago Experiment in Veronica Roth's book *Divergent* versus the institutional arrangements that highly factionalized Afghanistan went with in its 2004 constitution. Spoiler alert: it didn't go well in Afghanistan, because constitutions can't compete with people who are willing to bring back authoritarianism in order to attain or keep power.

State: The Chicago Experiment, *Divergent*

Freedom House Score (under the Faction system): 28 (not free)

Background: *Divergent* is set in the Chicago of a distant American future; in the wake of a second civil war, the U.S. government turned several large Midwestern cities into experiments in social engineering. To external observers, the Chicago Experiment was one of the strongest of the experiments. The government attributed this to the faction-based social structure they created for the experiment. Internally, however, the Chicago Experiment factions were on the brink of civil war. All-out war was prevented, but at the end of the series, Chicago was in the process of building a new society.

Social structure: The people of the Chicago Experiment are divided into five factions, plus a group of factionless who live in the city but are outcasts. The factions (and their primary traits) are Abnegation (selflessness and service), Amity (harmony and kindness), Candor (honesty and order), Dauntless (bravery and protection), and Erudite (knowledge and logic). Each faction lives in its own sector of the city, while the factionless are relegated to the ruined section of the city. The Abnegation faction was responsible for governing Chicago until the near–civil war.

Recommended institutional configuration:[95]

- *Federal authority sharing* would allow each faction to continue to control its own internal decision making. Given the federal system, it would be prudent to have a bicameral legislature in which the upper house represents the interests of the city's sections.
- A *semi-presidential democracy* has a dual executive that would allow the faction faithful and the factionless to share executive power.
- *Mixed-member proportional representation* would allow both a district-based vote and a proportional vote. Although MMP is more complex than PR or FPTP, citizens in the Chicago Experiment are likely to be literate, and there is a media system that can publish and distribute voter-education materials. Given that Chicago is relatively small and that some of the former faction members have moved outside of their original areas, a national list would be feasible for the proportional-representation portion of the ballot. The candidate that wins the plurality in the single-member district takes a seat, while the party-list vote would determine the number of seats each party receives in the legislature.
- Minority/women's rights: The Chicago Experiment included a number of women leaders, so women's rights are not of primary concern here. However, given the number of divisions in society and the city's recent history, it would be beneficial to enumerate and guarantee the basic rights of each group (factions, factionless, and newcomers to the city).

Predicted outcome: Our prediction for the Chicago Experiment is that the faction faithful would band together in the constitutional negotiations to try to keep the factions in control of the city. They'd likely argue for a unitary state and a presidential democracy with FPTP elections, as they would likely have the plurality of votes at this point. The factionless and newcomers would object but be outvoted. The number of wasted votes would be high in the first elections, but the internal divisions within the faction-faithful party would start to make themselves known. Infighting within the largest party could cause instability, and the factionless and newcomers could take advantage of that instability to take over the government (not that we're recommending a coup d'état). New democracies have to be flexible and willing to adapt their institutions as the situation changes. Ideally, citizens would push the government to hold a new constitutional convention and adopt more appropriate institutions.

State: Afghanistan

Freedom House Ranking (under Taliban Rule): 24 (Not Free)

Background: After its founding in 1747, Afghanistan—the crossroads between Central Asia, the Middle East, and South Asia—became of strategic importance to two of the major powers of the day: Britain and Russia. The British feared that the Russians had their eyes on British-controlled India and Britain's trade routes in Asia. Afghanistan was made a British protectorate and a buffer between Russian-controlled Central Asia and British-controlled South Asia (now India, Pakistan, and Bangladesh). Afghanistan declared independence in 1919. Successive Afghan rulers attempted to modernize and unify Afghanistan, to varying degrees of success. In 1979, the USSR invaded Afghanistan, beginning a long and bloody period of conflict. The United States backed Afghan freedom fighters against the Soviets. When the Soviets retreated from Afghanistan in 1989, they left a puppet government and widespread destruction. Tribal warfare ensued, with the Pashtun-led Taliban winning control of the state in 1994. They remained in power until the U.S.-led invasion of Afghanistan following the 9/11 attacks. A new constitution was adopted in 2004 as part of the effort to rebuild the country.

Social structure: Afghanistan is a multinational state, meaning that multiple nations (groups of people) live within the borders of the state. There are at least fifteen different ethnic groups in Afghanistan; the four largest are Pashtun (42%), Tajik (27%), Hazara (9%), and Uzbek (9%). Each group is concentrated in a different part of the country. The Pashtun, concentrated in the south and east, have historically dominated Afghan politics.

Recommended institutional configuration:

- Federal authority sharing would allow the largely self-governing ethnic communities a large measure of autonomy and would prevent one group from imposing its will on the others.[96]
- Parliamentary *or* semi-presidential democracy: A parliamentary system would allow for consensus government, which would be beneficial given the level of ethnic fragmentation but could lead to immobilism if coalitions are fragile. Semi-presidentialism would formally install a power-sharing executive that could ensure the major ethnic groups were all involved in executive decision making.[97]
- A proportional-representation electoral system (provincially based list) would allow voters to vote for the party of their choice in multimember districts. This would be a simple voting mechanism in a place where illiteracy rates are high and would have the benefit of allowing for ideological (or ethnic) representation by province (rather than having a national list like the Netherlands).[98]
- Minority/women's rights: Experts recommended that the constitution promote women's rights/women's equality and that it guarantee basic rights for each minority group.[99]

Actual outcome: The Afghan government did not take the experts' advice.[100] Instead, the 2004 constitution built a unitary state, centralizing all power in the capital (Kabul) but without having the resources to exercise control over the regions effectively.[101] The constitution set up a presidential system to keep power in the hands of the Pashtun tribe (which has ruled Afghanistan for the better part of 270 years). They also implemented a single *non*transferable vote (SNTV) electoral system; this system is so bad and so infrequently used that we didn't even discuss it in this book! It is ranked dead last by experts because it results in a huge number of wasted votes—over 70 percent in Afghanistan's first election. Of the candidates who *did* win, only about a third were from actual parties—the remainder were individual candidates, beholden to warlords, tribal leaders, and religious leaders.[102] That type of fragmentation (lots of people beholden to lots of different actors) is bad for governing and stability—which is evident in Afghanistan's 2017 ranking as the world's ninth most fragile state.[103]

BACK TO THE BAD OLD DAYS?

Democracies may die not at the hands of generals but of elected leaders—presidents or prime ministers who subvert the very process that brought them to power.

—Steven Levitsky and Daniel Ziblatt

We've said this a number of times, and we're saying it again: democracy is a hard form of government to maintain. We've talked about Aristotle's concept of *regime cycling*, and we've given you some examples—particularly from Latin America—where regime cycling has taken place. And, as we pointed out in the introduction to this chapter, many of the dystopias we've discussed in this book are set in places that were once democratic but are now authoritarian. Think about *All Rights Reserved®*, *Shipbreaker*, *The Heart Goes Last*, and a host of other modern dystopian novels in which there was once a democratic government, but it disintegrated into either chaos or authoritarianism.

Much of the concern in dystopian fiction has to do with income inequality (as discussed in chapter 3), the political dissatisfaction that creates, and the ways people express that dissatisfaction in democratic societies. In Sinclair Lewis's *It Can't Happen Here*, economic difficulties led to the American people to elect a demagogue who immediately did away with democracy—and many citizens celebrated its demise. In real life, think about how the Germans expressed their dissatisfaction with the Weimar Republic or how Russians expressed their dissatisfaction with the post–Cold War transition to democracy: they voted in Hitler and Putin, respectively. These are the well-known examples, but many a burgeoning democracy has fallen prey to authoritarian backsliding, and there is currently concern that established democracies may be heading backward, as we will now discuss.

U-TURN AHEAD: AUTHORITARIAN BACKSLIDING

It used to be that democracies died dramatic deaths at the hands of military juntas or violent coups d'état; during the Cold War, as Levitsky and Ziblatt tell us, "coups d'état accounted for nearly three out of four democratic breakdowns."[104] These days, though, coups are few and far between. Instead, democracies are more likely to die as a result of **authoritarian**

Authoritarian backsliding is when elected leaders engineer the weakening of democratic institutions to the point that the state is no longer democratic.

backsliding. The tactics leaders use to engineer such backsliding include increasing and unchecked violations of civil liberties, disregard for democratic norms, undermining of democratic checks and balances, and incessant attacks on the media.[105] These are all examples of what Levitsky and Ziblatt mean when they say that elected leaders can bring democracy down by subverting the very processes that brought them to power.

These days, we're talking about backsliding in well-established democracies because of a resurgence of **populism**.[106] As the gap between rich and poor has widened, so has political polarization—this has shown up in the growing popularity of populist politicians on both ends of the spectrum.

Populism is a political ideology that divides people into "the people" and "the elites." In this framework, the people are courageous and noble; they are the true citizens of the state. The elites, not so much; they're the enemy because they act in ways that harm the people. Populism is what can be called a "thin" ideology; it can be left wing or right wing, but populism can't stand up on its own. Left- and right-wing populists both inflame their followers with hateful rhetoric directed at whoever the populists have decided is "the elite."

In the early 2000s, after about two decades of stable democracy, a wave of left-wing populist electoral victories swept parts of Latin America. Left-wingers in Venezuela, Bolivia, and Ecuador won power by rallying the people against greedy capitalist elites and promising poor and indigenous communities that they would prosper under left-wing rule.[107] In Europe and the United States, on the other hand, there has been a string of right-wing populist successes—like Brexit in the United Kingdom, the inclusion of the far-right Freedom Party in Austria's government, the near-elections of Marine LePen and Geert Wilders in France and the Netherlands (respectively), and the election of Donald Trump in the United States. Right-wing populists also prey on people's economic concerns by playing up the role of immigrants and globalization in domestic unemployment.

We're all for the people ruling, but in a structured and democratic way, not a fearful populist way. The danger is that populism and democracy don't play well together: populism can very easily lead to authoritarian backsliding.[108] Democracy is about compromise and acceptance that the party or parties you oppose will sometimes be in power. Whether on the right or the left, populism is about winning at all costs because the other side is the enemy of the people. Democracy is about politicians and parties, the inclusion of diverse perspectives, and protecting minority rights. Populism is about a charismatic outsider leader who sidesteps the parties to go directly to the people, shuts down diverse perspectives whenever possible, and panders to the majority to the detriment of the minority. Treating the opposition as the enemy, shutting down dissenting voices, and mistreating minorities are all signs of authoritarian backsliding and demagoguery. As the professor of rhetoric Patricia Roberts-Miller puts it: "We don't have demagoguery in our culture because a demagogue came to power; when demagoguery becomes the normal way of participating in public discourse, then it's just a question of time until a demagogue arises."[109]

What does backsliding look like?

The political scientists Steven Levitsky and Daniel Ziblatt have developed a handy four-point test to determine if you've got an authoritarian-leaning populist government on your hands—here it is (almost verbatim):[110]

1. Do leading politicians overtly reject the rules of the democratic game?
2. Do leading politicians deny the legitimacy of the opposition?
3. Does the leadership seem to encourage or condone violence?
4. Is the leadership okay with suspending opponents' (including the media) civil liberties?

In a well-established democracy, you may think that these things don't matter too much; after all, you have a constitution and rights. How much harm can authoritarian leaders do within the confines of a strong democratic constitution?

Sadly, a *lot*. As Levitsky and Ziblatt point out, constitutions don't handle every potential situation, so democracies have developed democratic norms—the unwritten rules of the game. One of the reasons that democracies have traditionally worked, they argue, is that politicians have exercised restraint—but populist politicians are successful because they're not restrained. They get rewarded for violating democratic norms. That then translates to their behavior in office; they use their power to attempt to destroy their enemies and win at any cost. "Mutual toleration," that is, "not treating political rivals as existential enemies" but as fellow (loyal) citizens is chucked out the window.[111] This increases polarization across the board, and then large portions of the population begin to view other portions as the Enemy.

It gets worse if the leadership isn't just authoritarian leaning but actively trying to consolidate power. The warning signs here include packing key institutions with supporters (the courts and law enforcement), sidelining other major players (the media, the opposition), and trying to change how democracy operates (voter suppression, gerrymandering, changing the constitution).[112]

We will not go back!

The beauty of living in a well-established democracy is that society already has a number of mechanisms that will help you resist authoritarian backsliding. First, you likely have a robust *civil society*—all the organizations outside of government. These can be a great place to start mobilizing people to push back against the downhill slide to authoritarianism—but as we said in chapters 5 and 6, you'll need local organizations across your country to help get resistance going and stay going.[113] On that note, you're going to need to form coalitions—and Levitsky and Ziblatt warn that they do *not* mean coalitions composed solely of people who think exactly like you do about all of the major issues of the day.[114] Nope: you're going to have to embrace people who think differently on many issues but who agree that they prefer democracy to the alternative. You first have to get back to mutual tolerance; from there, you can go to resistance.

On resistance, the "unfreedom" expert Timothy Snyder says we should protect democratic institutions first and foremost because institutions don't protect themselves. They go down like dominoes unless each is defended from the beginning.[115] Pick an institution and defend it. Don't talk about attacks on "our institutions" unless you're making them yours by acting on their behalf. Follow the courts or the media, or even a single newspaper, and speak up on its behalf.

Protest will be important in this process, but it has to be protest with a goal. Is the goal to curb the backsliding? Is it to prompt lawmakers to use all legal means at their disposal to remove the authoritarian from office? Is the goal to vote all authoritarian-leaning politicians out of office? Once the goal is clear, people have to be willing and ready to take further action—particularly at the ballot box.[116] You'll definitely need to keep the pressure on the populists who are hijacking your government, and there's no better pressure than a massive turnout of the electorate. Court cases, bureaucratic challenges, ensuring that the opposition contests every seat in every election: all of these are things that you can do to resist the authoritarian backslide. And if these are insufficient, you have a guide to individual-level resistance, movement building, and nonviolent resistance right here in chapters 5 through 7.

FINAL THOUGHTS

Constitutions are a necessary but not sufficient step in consolidating your democracy. First, constitutions do not institutionalize themselves; you're going to have to do a lot of work to establish the constitution as the highest law in the land. Second, constitutions do not (and cannot) cover every contingency; this is why you have develop democratic norms, two of the most important being mutual toleration and restraint.[117] Finally, no democracy is unassailable; you will have to be vigilant in protecting your democracy from authoritarian backsliding.

Do not be surprised if your government seems to be backsliding; as the nineteenth-century British politician Sir John Dalberg-Acton warned, power corrupts, and absolute power corrupts absolutely. Power, once accrued, is often difficult to give up (just ask the Emperor in *Star Wars*). It's better not to let it accrue in the first place. Fight every step of the way when dictators and demagogues try to tell you their actions make you safer or more secure or that they know better than anyone else. The best wisdom is collective, and the best power is heavily checked and highly accountable.

Epilogue

Let me explain. No, there is too much. Let me sum up.

—Inigo Montoya, *The Princess Bride*

B y now we hope it is clear that it takes major work on the part of an independent, well-set-up government (one that has plenty of checks and balances of its own and enduring, legitimate institutions) to correct and restrain the worst impulses and effects of capitalism (and people). Left to itself and furthered by neoliberal economic policies, capitalism will cannibalize its own markets and destroy a lot of lives in the process, particularly when people (or parts of them) are treated as commodities.

Even the really, really rich people like Bill Gates and Warren Buffet cannot fix massive social problems on their own, though lord knows, a few of them keep trying. On the other hand, the new trend among the less philanthropically minded of the super-rich is building boltholes. Apparently, they're worried that society will break down and/or the world will end, so they're building giant underground bunkers (selling for millions of dollars apiece, by the way) and buying other off-the-grid hidey-holes to ride out the apocalypse.[1]

As this book has hopefully shown, individual solutions to collective problems just won't save you, but working together can be awful (and awfully difficult). In *Station 11*, a failed-state dystopia, the members of the Traveling Symphony have declared that "survival is insufficient," so they travel the country by foot performing concerts and Shakespeare. Even this small and dedicated company, who need one another for survival, have a hard time getting along: "Someone—probably Sayid—had written: 'Sartre:

Hell is other people' in pen inside one of the caravans, and someone else had scratched out 'other people' and substituted 'flutes.'"[2]

Yet as bad as other people (and flutes) may be, it is an unsafe world that is the real hell. As Hobbes famously said, life in a state of nature is nasty, brutish, and short. And for millions, this is still true; the failed states in which they live cannot protect them from terrible suffering and predation because it cannot enforce the rule of law, a critical function of good government. When this is the case, you need other people, and you need to work together with them. As Bernice Johnson Reagon, a veteran civil rights and feminist activist, put it, real coalition work often feels painful and upsetting: "You don't go into coalition work because you just like it. The only reason you would consider teaming up with somebody who could possibly kill you, is because that is the only way you can figure you can stay alive. . . . Most of the time you feel threatened to the core, and if you don't, you ain't doing no coalescing."[3]

It would be far simpler not to have to do all this work yourself but just to turn over the whole self-governance thing to someone else; benevolent dictatorship really is the ideal form of government in a lot of ways. There are only two problems with it: you can't be sure the authoritarian regime you get will be benevolent, and even if it is, you can't be sure it will stay that way. Dostoevsky, in the "Grand Inquisitor" section of his novel *The Brothers Karamazov*, hypothesized that human beings are weak and would readily trade away their freedom for security and bread. We very much hope he is wrong. And again and again, going back to ancient Rome and before, people have rebelled against unjust government; we can draw inspiration and strategic lessons from their actions.

What we do know is that any one person's or group's attempt at utopia has always failed, and these failures have always harmed people, sometimes unintentionally and sometimes in blissful ignorance of the damage. Attempting to simplify, control, and dictate real life, to solve other people's problems for them in the way you think is best, is what lands us in a real-life dystopia, and this is what dystopian fiction is warning us against. The best cure for dystopia that we know of is democracy, where no one person or group has a permanent advantage. Politics should provide an alternative to violence by creating peaceful transfers of power between groups; democracy is the only sustainable and just form of equality. This does not mean there will be no inequality, but it does mean that inequalities should rotate; *if the same one group is always screwed, you're doing it wrong.*

But democracy, friends, is fragile. History is littered with examples of failed attempts at something like democracy, and we still have not really figured it out. Even when we do seem to kind of get it right, or even partially right, it often does not work very well, because, well, we're human. How we should govern ourselves is the great, enduring, and still unsatisfactorily answered question of political science.[4] Having and keeping a republic is a lot of work—but it's worth it.

Keep up the hard work.

And may the Force be with you.

Notes

Introduction

1. Jonathan Barnes and Melissa Lane, *Aristotle's Politics: Writings from the Complete Works: Politics, Economics, Constitution of Athens* (Princeton, NJ: Princeton University Press, 2016).
2. Quoted in Ann Braude, *Sisters and Saints: Women and American Religion* (Oxford: Oxford University Press, 2007).
3. Based on Phillip K. Dick's classic dystopian novel of the same name.
4. Bruce Boston, "Dystopian Dusk," *Strange Horizons*, August 4, 2008, http://strange horizons.com/poetry/dystopian-dusk/.The genre isn't new, though—there are plenty of dystopian poems from bygone eras, like the two nineteenth-century female authors—Charlotte Smith ("Beachy Head") and Anna Barbauld (*Eighteen Hundred and Eleven*)—who each predicted dystopian British futures in verse. See Penny Bradshaw, "Dystopian Futures: Time-Travel and Millenarian Visions in the Poetry of Anna Barbauld and Charlotte Smith," *Romanticism on the Net*, no. 21 (2001).
5. Atchison was a metalhead in her youth. But you don't have to take her word for this; you can see either of the works cited here: Gerd Bayer, *Heavy Metal Music in Britain* (London: Routledge, 2016); Michael Harrison, "Factory Music: How the Industrial Geography and Working-Class Environment of Post-War Birmingham Fostered the Birth of Heavy Metal," *Journal of Social History* 44, no. 1 (2010): 145–58.
6. Carter F. Hanson, "Pop Goes Utopia: An Examination of Utopianism in Recent Electronic Dance Pop," *Utopian Studies* 25, no. 2 (2014): 403.
7. Martin T. Buinicki, "Nostalgia and the Dystopia of History in 2k's Bioshock Infinite," *Journal of Popular Culture* 49, no. 4 (2016): 722–37.
8. Freedom House, "Freedom in the World 2017 Checklist of Questions," https://freedom house.org/report/methodology-freedom-world-2017.

1. Malice in Wonderland

1. See, for example, Francis Bacon, *The New Atlantis* (1627).
2. Tony Burns, "Science, Politics, and Utopia in George Orwell's *Nineteen Eighty-Four*," in *Critical Insights: Dystopia*, ed. M. Keith Booker (Ipswich, MA: Salem Press, 2012); Fatima Vieira, "The Concept of Utopia," in *The Cambridge Companion to Utopian Literature*, ed. Gregory Claeys (Cambridge: Cambridge University Press, 2010), chap. 1.
3. Gregory Claeys, "The Origins of Dystopia: Wells, Huxley and Orwell," in *The Cambridge Companion to Utopian Literature*, 107. There are also at least three films called *Malice in Wonderland*, according to the Internet Movie Database (IMDB), and *Malice n Wonderland* is a pretty good Snoop Dogg album (not to be confused with similarly titled albums by Nazareth or Paice Ashton Lord).
4. Blaka Basu, Katherine R. Broad, and Carrie Hintz, eds., *Contemporary Dystopian Fiction for Young Adults: Brave New Teenagers* (New York: Routledge, 2013), 2.
5. Claeys, "The Origins of Dystopia," 108.
6. China Miéville, "'We Are All Thomas More's Children'—500 Years of Utopia," *Guardian*, November 4, 2016, https://www.theguardian.com/books/2016/nov/04/thomas -more-utopia-500-years-china-mieville-ursula-le-guin.
7. Thomas More, *Utopia*, ed. George M. Logan, trans. Robert M. Adams (Cambridge: Cambridge University Press, 2016).
8. Burns, "Science, Politics, and Utopia."
9. Burns, "Science, Politics, and Utopia."
10. Claeys, "The Origins of Dystopia."
11. Claeys, "The Origins of Dystopia."
12. Yevgeny Zamyatin, *We*, reprint ed. (New York: Modern Library, 2006), 3.
13. Stewart was ruling on a case involving obscenity, *Jacobellis vs. Ohio*. In his concurring opinion he wrote this now-famous explanation: "I shall not today attempt further to define the kinds of material I understand to be embraced within that shorthand description['hard-core pornography'], and perhaps I could never succeed in intelligibly doing so. But I know it when I see it, and the motion picture involved in this case is not that."
14. Larry Diamond, *The Spirit of Democracy: The Struggle to Build Free Societies Throughout the World* (New York: Macmillan, 2008), 66.
15. International Labour Organization, "Global Estimates of Modern Slavery: Forced Labour and Forced Marriage" (ILO, Geneva, 2017).
16. Robert Michels, *Political Parties: A Sociological Study of the Oligarchical Tendencies of Modern Democracy* (1911), trans. Eden Paul and Cedar Paul (New York: Hearst's International Library Company, 1915), 377.
17. Henry David Thoreau, "On the Duty of Civil Disobedience" (1849).
18. Side note: if a country puts "democratic" and/or "republic" in the short form of its name, the chances are high that it is neither. See the Central African Republic or the Democratic Republic of the Congo. The foregoing goes double if they add in "the

People's." See the People's Democratic Republic of (North) Korea or Lao People's Democratic Republic. The Republic of (South) Korea (since about 1987) is a notable exception to this rule.

19. There is some debate about this in the literature. We side with C. B. Macpherson, *The Political Theory of Possessive Individualism: Hobbes to Locke* (London: Clarendon, 1962).

20. Montesquieu, *The Spirit of the Laws*, trans. Thomas Nugent (New York: Hafner Library of Classics, 1949), 155.

21. Marc Hetherington and Jonathan Weiler, *Authoritarianism and Polarization in American Politics* (New York: Cambridge University Press, 2009).

22. Hetherington and Weiler point out that an authoritarian citizen would see George W. Bush as a legitimate leader because he frames things in black and white but not Obama since he's pretty comfortable with shades of gray.

23. Hetherington and Weiler, *Authoritarianism and Polarization*, 52, table 53.51.

24. Hetherington and Weiler, *Authoritarianism and Polarization*, 110.

25. Diamond, *The Spirit of Democracy*, 65–66.

26. Sarah Elizabeth Mendelson and Theodore P. Gerber, "Soviet Nostalgia: An Impediment to Russian Democratization," *Washington Quarterly* 29, no. 1 (2005): 88–89.

27. Diamond, *The Spirit of Democracy*, 154–60.

28. Diamond, *The Spirit of Democracy*, 154–60.

29. Diamond, *The Spirit of Democracy*, 154–60. Also see James Loxton, "Authoritarian Successor Parties," *Journal of Democracy* 26, no. 3 (2015): 157–70.

30. There's a solid argument to be made that illiberal democracies are simply competitive authoritarian regimes—kind of a hybrid government. See Steven Levitsky and Lucan A. Way, *Competitive Authoritarianism: Hybrid Regimes After the Cold War* (New York: Cambridge University Press, 2010).

31. Douglass C. North, John Joseph Wallis, and Barry R. Weingast, "A Conceptual Framework for Interpreting Recorded Human History," NBER Working Paper 12795, National Bureau of Economic Research, December 2006.

32. Diamond, *The Spirit of Democracy*, 296.

33. It is worth noting that King likely got this idea from the great abolitionist Frederick Douglass, who famously said: "Power concedes nothing without a demand. It never did and it never will."

34. Gene Sharp, *Waging Nonviolent Struggle: 20th Century Practice and 21st Century Potential* (Boston: Extending Horizons Books, 2005).

35. Richard Seymour, "Turkey's 'Standing Man' Shows How Passive Resistance Can Shake a State," *Guardian*, June 18, 2013, https://www.theguardian.com/commentisfree/2013/jun/18/turkey-standing-man.

36. Gene Sharp, *Sharp's Dictionary of Power and Struggle: Language of Civil Resistance in Conflicts* (New York: Oxford University Press, 2011), 270.

37. Pieter Verstraete, "The Standing Man Effect," *IPC Mercator Policy Brief* (July 2013): 1–11.

38. Sharp, *Waging Nonviolent Struggle*.

39. Professor Sharp, who died in 2018 at the age of ninety, was pretty much the godfather of nonviolent resistance. He has been described as "a dictator's worst nightmare," and his books are banned in several countries.

40. See Sharp, *Waging Nonviolent Struggle.*

41. Gene Sharp, *Power and Struggle: The Dynamics of Nonviolent Action, Part One* (Manchester, NH: Porter Sargent, 1973).

2. Defining Dystopia

1. James C. Scott, *Seeing Like a State: How Certain Schemes to Improve the Human Condition Have Failed* (New Haven, CT: Yale University Press, 1998), 5.

2. Scott, *Seeing Like a State*, 5.

3. George Orwell, "Letter to Noel Willmett, 18 May, 1944," in *George Orwell: A Life in Letters* (New York: Liveright, 2013).

4. Oceania is a fictional superstate that includes in its vast territory the island of Great Britain, now bleakly renamed Airstrip One.

5. Mary Beard, *Woman as Force in History: A Study in Traditions and Realities* (New York: Collier, 1971), 23. Also see Claudia Koonz, *Mothers in the Fatherland: Women, the Family and Nazi Politics* (New York: Routledge, 1987), xvii.

6. Peter Fritzsche and Jochen Hellbeck, "The New Man in Stalinist Russia and Nazi Germany," in *Beyond Totalitarianism: Stalinism and Nazism Compared*, ed. Michael Geyer and Sheila Fitzpatrick (Cambridge: Cambridge University Press, 2009), 302–44.

7. Interestingly, the premise of the "New Man" was rooted in the same belief in the positive power of science that we see in much of the utopian literature of the time. Science and technology could help make the "new man" a reality. See Fritzsche and Hellbeck, "The New Man in Stalinist Russia."

8. Koonz, *Mothers in the Fatherland*, 55.

9. German Labor Camp motto, as reported in the *New York Times*, September 26, 1937. Fritzsche and Hellbeck, "The New Man in Stalinist Russia."

10. Koonz, *Mothers in the Fatherland*, xxi.

11. David L. Hoffmann, "Mothers in the Motherland: Stalinist Pronatalism in Its Pan-European Context," *Journal of Social History* 34, no. 1 (2000): 35.

12. Hoffmann, "Mothers in the Motherland," 35.

13. Koonz, *Mothers in the Fatherland*.

14. Fritzsche and Hellbeck, "The New Man in Stalinist Russia."

15. Hoffmann, "Mothers in the Motherland." For more on Roosevelt, see Rebecca Edwards, *Angels in the Machinery: Gender in American Party Politics from the Civil War to the Progressive Era* (New York: Oxford University Press, 1997).

16. This was a universal concern among industrialized states; in some it started before World War I; in others it started in the postwar period. Almost all implemented pronatalist policies that encouraged the *right* women to have more babies. For example, Theodore Roosevelt encouraged all healthy white women to have at least four children. Edwards, *Angels in the Machinery*.

17. Mark G. Field, "Social Services for the Family in the Soviet Union," *Marriage and Family Living* 17, no. 3 (1955): 249.
18. Laurence Schneider, *Biology and Revolution in Twentieth-Century China* (Lanham, MD: Rowman & Littlefield, 2005), 5.
19. Harry Harding, *China's Second Revolution: Reform After Mao* (Washington, DC: Brookings Institution Press, 2010), 18.
20. Bradley K. Martin, *Under the Loving Care of the Fatherly Leader: North Korea and the Kim Dynasty* (New York: Macmillan, 2004), 374.
21. Elle Metz, "Why Singapore Banned Chewing Gum," *BBC News*, March 28, 2015, http://www.bbc.com/news/magazine-32090420.
22. Yongshun Cai, "Power Structure and Regime Resilience: Contentious Politics in China," *British Journal of Political Science* 38, no. 3 (2008): 411–32.
23. Yang Zhong, *Local Government and Politics in China: Challenges from Below* (New York: M. E. Sharpe, 2003), 3.
24. Diamond, *The Spirit of Democracy*, 236; Evelyne Huber, Deitrich Rueschemeyer, and John D. Stephens, "The Impact of Economic Development on Democracy," *Journal of Economic Perspectives* 7, no. 3 (1993): 71–86.
25. Bruce Bretts and Matt Roush, "Baddies to the Bone: The 60 Nastiest Villains of All Time," *TV Guide*, March 25, 2013.
26. Barbara Geddes, "What Do We Know About Democratization After Twenty Years?" *Annual Review of Political Science* 2, no. 1 (1999): 115, 121.
27. See Juan José Linz, *Totalitarian and Authoritarian Regimes* (Boulder: Lynne Rienner, 2000).
28. *Juche* basically means national self-reliance, independence, and worship of the ruling family, in particular the current leader. See Kongdan Oh and Ralph C. Hassig, *North Korea Through the Looking Glass* (Washington, DC: Brookings Institution Press, 2004), vii.
29. Michael Wahman, Jan Teorell, and Axel Hadenius, "Authoritarian Regime Types Revisited: Updated Data in Comparative Perspective," *Contemporary Politics* 19, no. 1 (2013): 25.
30. Wahman, Teorell, and Hadenius, "Authoritarian Regime Types Revisited," 25.
31. Geddes, "What Do We Know About Democratization," 115, 121, 124.
32. A military coup d'état that then results in the installation of a single dictator, like Ghaddafi in Libya, becomes a personalist regime. Geddes, "What Do We Know About Democratization."
33. With a few tiny periods of nonmilitary rule here and there.
34. Guillermo O'Donnell, "Reflections on the Patterns of Change in the Bureaucratic-Authoritarian State," *Latin American Research Review* 13, no. 1 (1978): 3–38.
35. *Grey Morning* is a film from 1969 that depicts a robot-led version of the Brazilian bureaucratic-authoritarian state; the director was almost immediately arrested by Brazilian authorities (according to IMDB).
36. Wahman, Teorell, and Hadenius, "Authoritarian Regime Types Revisited."
37. Larry Diamond, "Thinking About Hybrid Regimes," *Journal of Democracy* 13, no. 2 (2002): 21–35.

38. In M. T. Anderson's novel *Feed* (Somerville, MA: Candlewick, 2002), there's an elected government, but the capitalists are actually in control.

39. Katharine Adeney, "How to Understand Pakistan's Hybrid Regime: The Importance of a Multidimensional Continuum," *Democratization* 24, no. 1 (2017): 119–37; Marina Ottaway, *Democracy Challenged: The Rise of Semi-Authoritarianism* (Washington, DC: Carnegie Endowment, 2013).

40. Yes, we know you want us to group Iran and Saudi Arabia with the theocracies, but it's more complicated than that. You can easily say that they're a hybrid and a monarchy, respectively, each with an official state religion and a heavily religiously influenced legal code. The only *pure* theocracy really is the Holy See (Vatican City).

3. The Invisible Hand Strikes Again

1. Tom Moylan, "'The Moment Is Here . . . and It's Important': State, Agency, and Dystopia in Kim Stanley Robinson's *Antarctica* and Ursula K. Le Guin's *The Telling*," in *Dark Horizons: Science Fiction and the Dystopian Imagination*, Rafaella Baccolini and Tom Moylan (New York: Routledge, 2003), 135–36.

2. John Kenneth Galbraith, *American Capitalism: The Concept of Countervailing Power* (Boston: Houghton Mifflin, 1952).

3. Kembrew McLeod, *Freedom of Expression®: Resistance and Repression in the Age of Intellectual Property* (Minneapolis: University of Minnesota Press, 2007), 9.

4. *Steamboat Willie* was the first film starring Mickey and Minnie Mouse.

5. As McLeod intended, the irony of being able to trademark "freedom of expression" is staggering. Alana Horowitz, "The 15 Most Ridiculous Trademark Attempts Ever," *Business Insider*, April 8, 2011; McLeod, *Freedom of Expression®*.

6. "Who beats up on the GIRL SCOUTS, for the love of all that's holy?" McLeod, *Freedom of Expression®*, 19–21.

7. Smith originally wrote about the invisible hand in an earlier work, *The Theory of Moral Sentiments* (1759).

8. Smith *did* say that there are instances in which the government should intervene where the market would fail to correct/regulate, as in the case of monopolies. *The Wealth of Nations* isn't *all* rainbows and roses; Smith's is an admittedly flawed utopia.

9. David Harvey, *Spaces of Hope* (Berkeley: University of California Press, 2000), 7:175; quoted in Robyn McCallum, "Ignorant Armies on a Darkling Plain: The New World Disorder of Global Economics, Environmentalism and Urbanisation in Philip Reeve's *Hungry Cities*," *International Research in Children's Literature* 2, no. 2 (2009): 211.

10. Generally, we consider the mid-1700s (a.k.a. the eighteenth century) to the mid-1800s (a.k.a. the nineteenth century) to be the period of the first Industrial Revolution—give or take a few years on either side.

11. Gunnar Myrdal, *The Political Element in the Development of Economic Theory* (London: Routledge, 1953), 107.

12. Richard Simmons Jr., "Industrial and 'Condition of England' Novels," in *A Companion to the Victorian Novel*, ed. Patrick Brantlinger and William B. Thesing (Malden, MA: Blackwell, 2002), 336–52.

13. It was those conditions to which Carlyle was referring in the quote. Thomas Carlyle, *Chartism* (London: Chapman and Hall, 1842), 3.

14. John Foster, *Class Struggle and the Industrial Revolution: Early Industrial Capitalism in Three English Towns* (Routledge, 2003), 91–92.

15. See Foster, *Class Struggle and the Industrial Revolution*, 91–92.

16. World Bank, *World Development Indicators*, 2017, https://openknowledge.worldbank .org/handle/10986/26447.

17. Paul Mantoux, *The Industrial Revolution in the Eighteenth Century: An Outline of the Beginnings of the Modern Factory System in England* (1928; New York: Routledge, 2013); Alan Derickson, *Black Lung: Anatomy of a Public Health Disaster* (Ithaca, NY: Cornell University Press, 1998).

18. Mantoux, *The Industrial Revolution in the Eighteenth Century*.

19. Simmons Jr., "Industrial and 'Condition of England' Novels."

20. Karl Marx, *Capital: A Critical Analysis of Capitalist Production* (London: Appleton & Co.; Swan Sonnenschein & Co., 1889), 742.

21. Adam Schaff, "Marxist Theory on Revolution and Violence," *Journal of the History of Ideas* 34, no. 2 (1973): 263–70.

22. Marx gets a bad rap mostly because people associate him with horrible people like Stalin and Lenin, but he was a keen social observer, and his work contains a lot of good insights about exploitative labor practices and remains relevant to this day. The millions of deaths caused by so-called communist governments actually were inspired by Soviet and Maoist ideology and practices—not directly by Marx's writings. Marx may have been okay with violent revolution, but he did not advocate for governments slaughtering their citizens.

23. Robert Tombs, *The Paris Commune 1871* (New York: Routledge, 2014).

24. Donny Gluckstein, *The Paris Commune: A Revolution in Democracy* (Chicago: Haymarket, 2011), ix.

25. Vicente Navarro, "Why Some Countries Have National Health Insurance, Others Have National Health Services, and the United States Has Neither," *International Journal of Health Services* 19, no. 3 (1989): 383–404, Goran Therborn, "Classes and States Welfare State Developments, 1881–1981," *Studies in Political Economy* 14, no. 1 (1984): 7–41.

26. Peter Baldwin, *The Politics of Social Solidarity: Class Bases of the European Welfare State, 1875–1975* (Cambridge: Cambridge University Press, 1990).

27. Navarro, "Why Some Countries Have National Health Insurance"; Therborn, "Classes and States Welfare State Developments, 1881–1981."

28. Baldwin, *The Politics of Social Solidarity*.

29. Baldwin, *The Politics of Social Solidarity*.

30. Clay Jenkinson, in Ken Burns's documentary *The Roosevelts: An Intimate History* (2014).

31. Theodore Roosevelt, *Theodore Roosevelt, an Autobiography* (New York: Charles Scribner's Sons, 1913).

32. We're not counting H. G. Wells, who was more sci-fi, although *War of the Worlds* is debatable as dystopian fiction.

33. Jack London, *The Iron Heel* (1908; San Bernardino, CA: London Press, 2017), iii.

34. Barry Eichengreen and Peter Temin, "The Gold Standard and the Great Depression," *Contemporary European History* 9, no. 2 (2000): 202.

35. Some folks will tell you that the Soviets got stuck in what Marx called "the dictatorship of the proletariat," that is, the period between the overthrow of capitalism and the eventual withering away of the state. Those folks would be wrong. The political theorist Geoff Boucher explains that Marx looked at all governments as dictatorships of one class over the other(s) regardless of the type of government. So, instead of a "dictatorship" as we think of it, Marx meant that the dictatorship of the proletariat would be "the replacement of the nation state and private property with a participatory democratic social republic based on socialized property." Geoff Boucher, *Understanding Marxism* (Durham: Acumen, 2014), 37.

36. Erika Gottlieb, *Dystopian Fiction East and West: Universe of Terror and Trial* (Montreal: McGill-Queens University Press, 2001), 19, 119. Gottlieb reports that Hitler instituted a similar ban; she notes that "when the state engages the whole of organized society in testing a speculation about the future, there is no longer room for genuinely speculative literature."

37. Gottlieb, *Dystopian Fiction East and West*.

38. Vladimir Dudintsev, *Not by Bread Alone*, trans. Edith Bone (London: Hutchinson & Co. 1957).

39. Denis Kozlov, "Naming the Social Evil: The Readers of *Novyi Mir* and Vladimir Dudintsev's *Not by Bread Alone*, 1956–1959 and Beyond," in *The Dilemmas of De-Stalinization: Negotiating Cultural and Social Change in the Khrushchev Era*, ed. Polly Jones (London: Taylor & Francis, 2006).

40. Dudintsev's comment on dirty laundry comes from the epilogue (445); the comments from the publisher's note are on v.

41. Michael Wines, "Vladimir Dudintsev, 79, Dies; Writer Dissected Soviet Life," *New York Times*, July 30, 1998.

42. Gottlieb, *Dystopian Fiction East and West*.

43. Wines, "Vladimir Dudintsev."

44. J. Bradford de Long, Lawrence H. Summers, N. Gregory Mankiw, and Christina D. Romer, "How Does Macroeconomic Policy Affect Output?" *Brookings Papers on Economic Activity* 2 (1988): 433–94; Christina D. Romer, "What Ended the Great Depression?" *Journal of Economic History* 52, no. 4 (1992): 757–84; James R. Vernon, "World War II Fiscal Policies and the End of the Great Depression," *Journal of Economic History* 54 (1994): 850–68.

45. Francis G. Castles, *The Future of the Welfare State: Crisis Myths and Crisis Realities* (Oxford: Oxford University Press, 2004).

46. Sarwat Jahan, Ahmed Saber Mahmud, and Chris Papageorgiou, "What Is Keynesian Economics?" IMF, 2014, https://www.imf.org/external/pubs/ft/fandd/2014/09/basics.htm.

47. Keynes was fine with *some* inequality, just not the high levels typical of the period leading into the Great Depression. See Jonathan Kirshner, "Keynes, Legacies, and Inquiry," *Theory and Society* 38, no. 5 (2009): 527–41.

48. "If capitalist society rejects a more equal distribution of incomes . . . then a chronic tendency towards the underemployment of resources must in the end sap and destroy that form of society." John Maynard Keynes, "Some Economic Consequences of a Declining Population," *Eugenics Review* 29, no. 1 (1937): 13, 132.

49. David Harvey, *A Brief History of Neoliberalism* (Oxford: Oxford University Press, 2007).

50. Judith Squires, "Equality and Difference," in *The Oxford Handbook of Political Theory*, ed. John S. Dryzek, Bonnie Honig, and Anne Phillips (Oxford: Oxford University Press), 470–87.

51. Franklin Delano Roosevelt, "State of the Union Address to Congress, January 11, 1944," American Presidency Project, http://www.presidency.ucsb.edu/ws/index.php?pid=16518. Emphasis added.

52. John Maynard Keynes, *Tract on Monetary Reform*, reprint ed. (London: MacMillan and Co., 1924), 80.

53. John Quiggin, *Zombie Economics: How Dead Ideas Still Walk Among Us* (Princeton, NJ: Princeton University Press, 2012).

54. Harvey, *A Brief History of Neoliberalism*.

55. Reagan and Thatcher were not devotees of the atheist portion of Rand's philosophy.

56. Peter Fitting, "Utopias Beyond Our Ideals: The Dilemma of the Right-Wing Utopia," *Utopian Studies* 2, no. 1/2 (1991): 95–109.

57. Quiggin, *Zombie Economics*.

58. Lester K. Spence, *Knocking the Hustle: Against the Neoliberal Turn in Black Politics* (Brooklyn, NY: Punctum, 2015).

59. Examples include prisons, trash collection, education, utilities, toll roads—but keep in mind that not all of these happened in all countries.

60. Spence, *Knocking the Hustle*.

61. Harvey, *A Brief History of Neoliberalism*, 115.

62. J. Knight, "Updated Definition of Internationalization," *International Higher Education* 33 (2015): 3.

63. George Saunders, "The Semplica-Girl Diaries," *New Yorker*, October 15, 2012.

64. Ben S. Bernanke, "The Great Moderation," in *The Taylor Rule and the Transformation of Monetary Policy*, ed. Evan F. Koenig, Robert Leeson, and George A. Kahn (Washington, DC: Hoover Institution Press, 2004), chap. 5.

65. Quiggin, *Zombie Economics*.

66. GAO, "Financial Crisis Losses and Potential Impacts of the Dodd-Frank Act," Government Accountability Office, 2013, 17, 21, https://www.gao.gov/products/GAO-13-180.

67. Quiggin, *Zombie Economics*, 64.

68. Jacob S. Hacker, *The Great Risk Shift: The New Economic Insecurity and the Decline of the American Dream* (Oxford: Oxford University Press, 2008).

69. Keep in mind that as a result of globalization, a lot of American and European jobs were heading to cheaper locales. When the industry in your area collapsed, where were you supposed to get another job?

70. Hacker, *The Great Risk Shift*; Quiggin, *Zombie Economics*, 17.

71. Rebecca Mead, "Margaret Atwood, the Prophet of Dystopia," *New Yorker*, April 17, 2017.

72. Marx, *Capital*, 1:515.

73. John Maynard Keynes, "Art and the State," *The Listener* 16, no. 398 (August 26, 1936): 371. Keynes was *not* a fan of Marx—whom he called "dreary" and "out-of-date." See Keynes's 1934 "Letter to George Bernard Shaw," quoted in Jonathan Kirshner, "Keynes, Capital Mobility, and the Crisis of Embedded Liberalism," *Review of International Political Economy* 6, no. 3 (1999): 320.

74. B. I. Keeley, *Income Inequality: The Gap Between Rich and Poor* (Paris: OECD, 2015), 10–11.

75. Juliet B. Schor, *The Overspent American: Why We Want What We Don't Need* (New York: HarperPerennial, 1999); Juliet B. Schor, *Born to Buy: The Commercialized Child and the New Consumer Cult* (New York: Simon and Schuster, 2014).

76. Department of Justice, "Review of the Federal Bureau of Prisons' Monitoring of Contract Prisons," Office of the Inspector General, US Department of Justice, 2016.

77. *Dockery v. Epps*, U.S. District Court for the Southern District of Mississippi, filed 2013. See also the *Nation* series on private prisons by Seth Freed Wessler: https://www.thenation.com/special/private-prison-deaths/.

78. Laura Sullivan, "Prison Economics Help Drive Ariz. Immigration Law," *NPR*, October 28, 2010.

79. Sally Yates, "Justice Department Memo Announcing the End of Its Use of Private Prisons," U.S. Department of Justice, 2016.

80. The Sentencing Project, "Fact Sheet: Private Prisons in the United States" 2017, https://www.sentencingproject.org/wp-content/uploads/2017/08/Private-Prisons-in-the-United-States.pdf.

81. "Polluted Delhi Has 'Become a Gas Chamber,'" *BBC*, November 3, 2017.

82. NOAA, "What Is a Dead Zone?" https://oceanservice.noaa.gov/facts/deadzone.html.

83. Jane Mansbridge, "Presidential Address: What Is Political Science For?" *Perspectives on Politics* 12, no. 1 (2014): 8–17.

4. Strategies and Tactics of Dystopian Governments

1. An audio file of this famous speech is available at https://www.youtube.com/watch?v=bmhB6D1_AIc. Wels died in Paris in 1939, after fleeing first to Prague and then farther to escape the Nazi's purge of the Social Democrats. Rest in peace, Otto Wels.

2. Robert Conquest, *Stalin, Breaker of Nations* (New York: Penguin, 1992).

3. Hannah Arendt, "Reflections on Violence," *Journal of International Affairs* (1969): 1–35.

4. Niccolo Machiavelli, *The Prince*, trans. Harvey C. Mansfield (Chicago: University of Chicago Press, 1998), 66; emphasis added.

5. Jeremy Bentham's preserved body is on permanent display in the University College of London, as per his wishes, should you wish to pay your respects.

6. Michel Foucault sometimes can be a difficult and dense read, but if you're curious, he describes panopticism in much greater detail in chapter 3 of his *Discipline and Punish*, trans. Alan Sheridan (New York: Vintage, 1995).

7. Catherine Epstein, "The Stasi: New Research on the East German Ministry of State Security," *Kritika: Explorations in Russian and Eurasian History* 5, no. 2 (2004): 322.

8. See Christian Gierke, dir., *Stasi—East Germany's Secret Police* (2008).

9. The evidence indicates that the leftists did not view the Soviets as their allies and had no intention of seeking Soviet support—and that seems to have been pretty clear at the time (not just in retrospect). See John Charles Chasteen, *Born in Blood and Fire: A Concise History of Latin America* (New York: Norton, 2001).

10. Chasteen, *Born in Blood and Fire*, 277.

11. They weren't the only ones, mind you, but we don't have space to discuss all of Latin America. We picked these three because they are representative of the worst excesses of the military regimes of the era.

12. Chasteen, *Born in Blood and Fire.*

13. Mario Benedetti, "The Triumph of Memory," *NACLA Report on the Americas* 29, no. 3 (1995): 10.

14. Mark Danner, *The Massacre at El Mozote: A Parable of the Cold War* (New York: Vintage, 1994).

15. "El Salvador Told to Investigate 1981 El Mozote Massacre," *BBC World*, December 11, 2012; Danner, *The Massacre at El Mozote.* Danner lists the names of the dead on pages 280–304.

16. Marcia Esparza, Henry R. Huttenbach, and Daniel Feierstein, *State Violence and Genocide in Latin America: The Cold War Years* (New York: Routledge, 2009), 215.

17. Catherine Nolin Hanlon and Finola Shankar, "Gendered Spaces of Terror and Assault: The Testimonio of Remhi and the Commission for Historical Clarification in Guatemala," *Gender, Place and Culture: A Journal of Feminist Geography* 7, no. 3 (2000): 275.

18. Victoria Sanford, "From Genocide to Feminicide: Impunity and Human Rights in Twenty-First Century Guatemala," *Journal of Human Rights* 7, no. 2 (2008): 119; emphasis added.

19. Hanlon and Shankar, "Gendered Spaces of Terror and Assault."

20. Or so we think. For all we know, your flat screen TV might be watching you as you read this. Who knows?

21. Jennifer Gandhi and Ellen Lust-Okar Lust-Okar, "Elections Under Authoritarianism," *Annual Review of Political Science* 12 (2009): 403–22; Lily L. Tsai, *Accountability Without Democracy: Solidary Groups and Public Goods Provision in Rural China* (Cambridge: Cambridge University Press, 2007); Peter Ackerman and Jack DuVall, *A Force More Powerful: A Century of Nonviolent Conflict* (New York: St. Martin's, 2000).

22. Margaret Atwood, *The Handmaid's Tale* (New York: Fawcett Crest, 1985), 10.

23. Achille Mbembe, "Provisional Notes on the Postcolony," *Africa* 62, no. 1 (1992): 3–37.

24. Noah, who is the product of a black South African mother and a white European, was conceived in a time when race mixing (miscegenation) was illegal in that country (part of the apartheid policies), making his birth an actual crime. We cannot recommend his memoir highly enough: Trevor Noah, *Born a Crime: Stories from a South African Childhood* (London: John Murray, 2017).

25. Trevor Noah, quoted in Jethro Nededog, "Trevor Noah Compares Trump to South Africa's Scandalous President," *Business Insider Online*, November 16, 2016.

26. The low estimate is from Geoffrey Ponton, *The Soviet Era: Soviet Politics from Lenin to Yeltsin* (Cambridge, MA: Blackwell, 1994). The high estimate is from Aleksandr Solzhenitsyn, *The Gulag Archipelago* (New York: Thomas P. Whitney, 1974).

27. HistoryofRussia.org, 2017.

28. Daniel J. Leab, "How Red Was My Valley: Hollywood, the Cold War Film, and *I Married a Communist*," *Journal of Contemporary History* 19, no. 1 (1984): 66.

29. Bradley R. Simpson, *Economists with Guns: Authoritarian Development and U.S.-Indonesian Relations, 1960–1968* (Stanford, CA: Stanford University Press, 2008).

30. Kai Thaler, "Foreshadowing Future Slaughter: From the Indonesian Killings of 1965–1966 to the 1974–1999 Genocide in East Timor," *Genocide Studies and Prevention* 7, no. 2 (2012): 210.

31. Robert Gellately and Ben Kiernan, *The Specter of Genocide: Mass Murder in Historical Perspective* (Cambridge: Cambridge University Press, 2003), 290–91.

32. Although we have only mentioned the Serbs here, there were atrocities committed by all parties in this war—Serbs, Croats, and Bosnians. See Paul Bartrop, *Genocide: The Basics* (New York: Routledge, 2014), 84–85.

33. Max Levin and Robert A. Johnson, quoted in Evan Osnos, "Doomsday Prep for the Super-Rich," *New Yorker*, January 30, 2017.

34. Machiavelli, *The Prince*, chaps. 7–9.

35. George Orwell, *1984* (1949; New York: Signet Classic, 1977), chap. 7.

36. Chasteen, *Born in Blood and Fire*, 85.

37. Chasteen, *Born in Blood and Fire*, 85.

38. Chasteen, *Born in Blood and Fire*, 85; Edward Telles, *Pigmentocracies: Ethnicity, Race, and Color in Latin America* (Chapel Hill, NC: UNC Press Books, 2014).

39. Personal communication with Dr. Gregg B. Johnson, Valparaiso University.

40. Orwell, *1984*, chap. 5.

41. Larry Diamond, *The Spirit of Democracy* (New York: St. Martin's Griffin, 2008), 69–70.

42. As reported by CNN (https://www.cnn.com/2017/01/24/us/george-orwell-1984-bestseller-trump-trnd/index.html). Atwood's *The Handmaid's Tale* followed suit (http://www.independent.co.uk/news/world/americas/margaret-atwood-handmaids-tale-puritan-values-donald-trump-republican-party-abortion-a7575796.html), and the *New York Times Book Review* and other journalistic outlets began publishing long articles on dystopian fiction.

43. David King, *The Commissar Vanishes: The Falsification of Art and Photographs in Stalin's Russia* (New York: Metropolitan Books, 1997).

44. Based on the TV show *Firefly*, which featured the same premise and cast.

45. Anthony H. Cordesman, *Saudi Arabia Enters the Twenty-First Century: The Political, Foreign Policy, Economic, and Energy Dimensions* (Westport, CT: Greenwood, 2003), 2:292–93.

46. Christian Parenti, "Hugo Chávez and Petro Populism," *Nation*, March 24, 2005; Francisco Rodríguez, "An Empty Revolution—the Unfulfilled Promises of Hugo Chávez," *Foreign Affairs* 87, no. 2 (2008): 49–62.

47. Christian Joppke, "The Incomplete Turn to Human Rights Dissidence," in *East German Dissidents and the Revolution of 1989: Social Movement in a Leninist Regime* (London: Palgrave Macmillan, 1995).

48. This is some serious Big Brother–style word play. Even inmates thought the Soviets were mocking them. "If the Soviet [prisons] were to be called 'corrective institutions,' then the Cheka [secret police] should be renamed the 'Commission of Mutual Trust.'" Michael Jakobson, *Origins of the Gulag: The Soviet Prison Camp System, 1917–1934* (Lexington: University Press of Kentucky, 2015), 52. Side note: there were more categories of prisons, but Jakobson indicates that 70 to 80 percent of prisoners were in the "corrective" camps (106).

49. Jakobson, *Origins of the Gulag*, 141.

50. J. Arch Getty, "Trotsky in Exile: The Founding of the Fourth International," *Soviet Studies* 38, no. 1 (1986): 24–35.

51. Litvinenko, from his deathbed, directly accused Putin of ordering his death.

52. Diamond, *The Spirit of Democracy*; Alex Goldfarb, *Death of a Dissident: The Poisoning of Alexander Litvinenko and the Return of the KGB* (New York: Free Press, 2010).

53. Bartrop, *Genocide*.

54. Ben Kiernan, "The Cambodian Genocide, 1975–1979," in *Centuries of Genocide: Essays and Eyewitness Accounts*, 4th ed., ed. Samuel Totten and William S. Parsons (New York: Routledge, 2013), 317.

5. Individual Survival and Resistance

1. Albert O. Hirschman, *Exit, Voice, and Loyalty: Responses to Decline in Firms, Organizations, and States* (Cambridge, MA: Harvard University Press, 1970).

2. See, for example, the film *Defiance*, directed by Edward Zwick and starring Daniel Craig, based on the true story (Peter Duffy, *The Bielski Brothers: The True Story of Three Men Who Defied the Nazis, Built a Village in the Forest, and Saved 1,200 Jews* [New York: HarperCollins, 2004]) of the Bielski brothers and their gang, who helped to build a "Jerusalem in the woods" in the forests of Belarus, eventually helping save 1,200 Jews from the Nazis.

3. Francis Fukuyama, *Political Order and Political Decay* (New York: Farrar, Straus and Giroux, 2014).

4. Even radical suicide bombers are not "crazy"; there is usually a strategic logic and deep organizational context to their actions, and the movements behind these bombers have generally worked hard to weed out the truly crazy actors: "The organizers of suicide attacks do not want to jeopardize their missions by recruiting unreliable people." Robert J. Brym, "Suicide Bombing," in *The Social Movement Reader: Cases and Concepts*, ed. Jeff Goodwin and James M. Jasper (Malden, MA: Wiley Blackwell, 2015), chap. 22.

5. LaVerne Gyant and Deborah F. Atwater, "Septima Clark's Rhetorical and Ethnic Legacy: Her Message of Citizenship in the Civil Rights Movement," *Journal of Black Studies* 26, no. 5 (1996): 577–92.

6. Doug McAdam, *Political Process and the Development of Black Insurgency* (Chicago: University of Chicago Press, 1982).

7. *Time*, for example, calls the "Tank Man" photograph one of the hundred "most influential images of all time." "100 Photos," *Time.com*, http://100photos.time.com.

8. This section's title comes from *The Handmaid's Tale*—Offred finds the phrase "Nolite Te Bastardes Carborundorum" carved on her floor, and the Commander later gives her the translation: Don't let the bastards grind you down.

9. George Orwell, *1984* (1949; New York: Signet Classic, 1977).

10. Timur Kuran, "Preference Falsification, Policy Continuity, and Collective Conservatism," *Economic Journal* 97, no. 387 (1987): 642–65.

11. Margaret Atwood, *The Handmaid's Tale* (New York: Fawcett Crest, 1985), 86.

12. Atwood, *The Handmaid's Tale*, 10.

13. Atwood, *The Handmaid's Tale*, 89–90.

14. Atwood, *The Handmaid's Tale*, 10.

15. Viktor Frankl Institut, "Chronology," https://www.univie.ac.at/logotherapy/biography.html.

16. Frankl Institut, "Chronology."

17. Jane Mansbridge, "Presidential Address: What Is Political Science For?" *Perspectives on Politics* 12, no. 1 (2014): 8–17.

18. Fukuyama, *Political Order and Political Decay*, 3, drawing on Max Weber's definition.

19. Hannah Arendt, "Reflections on Violence," *New York Review of Books*, February 27, 1969.

20. William Penn, "First Frame of Government," http://law.jrank.org/pages/11667/Frame-Government-Frame-Government.html.

21. Mike Wright and David Urban, "Brutal and Inhumane Laws North Koreans Are Forced to Live Under," *Telegraph*, September 19, 2017.

22. Andrea Batista Schlesinger, *The Death of Why* (San Francisco: Berrett-Koehler, 2009).

23. Gregory Scott Katsoulis, *All Rights Reserved* (Vermaine: Harlequin Teen, 2017), 49.

24. Timothy Snyder, "20 Lessons from the 20th Century on How to Survive in Trump's America: A History Professor Looks to the Past to Remind Us to Do What We Can in the Face of the Unthinkable," *In These Times*, http://inthesetimes.com/article/19658/20-lessons-from-the-20th-century-on-how-to-survive-in-trumps-america.

25. Orwell, *1984*, 83.

26. Orwell, *1984*.

27. This is our scoring, using Freedom House guidelines. Freedom House scoring does not go back to the Soviet era. Given the similarities between the USSR and modern-day North Korea, and given that North Korea's 2017 score was a 3, we think our score is a reasonable estimation.

28. Christopher Andrew and Vasili Mitrokhin, *The Mitrokhin Archive: The KGB in Europe and the West* (New York: Penguin, 2000), 416–19.

29. Associated Press, "KGB Attempt on Solzhenitsyn's Life Reported," *Los Angeles Times*, April 21, 1992; Joseph Pierce, *Solzhenitsyn: A Soul in Exile*, rev. and updated ed. (San Francisco: Ignatius, 2011); Arkadiï Vaksberg, *Toxic Politics: The Secret History of the Kremlin's Poison Laboratory—from the Special Cabinet to the Death of Litvinenko* (ABC-CLIO, 2011).

30. Run an internet search on this: "First they came for the socialists . . ."

31. Snyder, "20 Lessons from the 20th Century."

32. David Livingstone Smith, *Less Than Human: Why We Demean, Enslave, and Exterminate Others* (New York: St. Martin's, 2011).

33. Simone de Beauvoir, *The Second Sex* (New York: Knopf, 1953). The word "otherness" has alternately been translated as "binarism" or "alterity" in some texts.

34. Marilynn Brewer, "The Psychology of Prejudice: Ingroup Love and Outgroup Hate?" *Journal of Social Issues* 55, no. 3 (1999): 429–44. See also Henri Tajfel, "Experiments in Intergroup Discrimination," *Scientific American* 223, no. 5 (1970): 96–103.

35. James Scott, *Seeing Like a State* (New Haven, CT: Yale University Press, 1998), 4, 3.

36. Scott, *Seeing Like a State*, 22.

37. Scott, *Seeing Like a State*, 6, 7.

38. Schlesinger, *The Death of Why*.

39. Sinclair Lewis, *It Can't Happen Here* (1935; New York: Signet Classics, 2014), 117.

40. In 2018, Netflix started a series called *We Speak Dance*, showing how dance "can be used as a political weapon symbolically and literally." See James Loke Hale, "'We Speak Dance': Netflix Series Shows How Dance Can Be a 'Weapon' for Empowerment—All Around the World," *Bustle*, December 28, 2017.

41. Xan Brooks, "Ai Weiwei: "Without the Prison, the Beatings, What Would I Be?" *Guardian*, September 17, 2017.

42. Jeffrey Vance, "The Great Dictator," Library of Congress, https://www.loc.gov/programs/static/national-film-preservation-board/documents/great_dictator.pdf.

43. Mel Brooks, quoted in "With Comedy, We Can Rob Hitler of His Posthumous Power," *Der Spiegel*, March 16, 2006.

44. Srdja Popovic and Mladen Joksic, "Why Dictators Don't Like Jokes," *Foreign Policy*, April 5, 2013.

45. Popovic and Joksic, "Why Dictators Don't Like Jokes"; also see Srdja Popovic, "The Power of Laughtivism: Ted Talk (Ted-X-Bg)," https://www.youtube.com/watch?v=BgaDUcttL2s.

46. Popovic and Joksic, "Why Dictators Don't Like Jokes."

47. Popovic and Joksic, "Why Dictators Don't Like Jokes."

48. Kali Holloway and Martin Mycielski, "Increasingly a Necessity: A 15-Point Guide to Surviving Authoritarianism," *Alternet.org*, December 17, 2017, https://www.alternet.org/2017/12/increasingly-necessity-15-point-guide-surviving-authoritarianism/.

49. Jon Sharman, "Pilots Stop 222 Asylum Seekers Being Deported from Germany by Refusing to Fly," *Independent*, December 5, 2017; also see Sabine Priess, "'Would You Like to Take This Flight with Us?'" *RBB-24*, June 12, 2017.

50. This section's epigraph is quoted in James Scott, *Domination and the Arts of Resistance: Hidden Transcripts* (New Haven, CT: Yale University Press, 1990), i.

51. James Scott, *Weapons of the Weak: Everyday Forms of Peasant Resistance* (New Haven, CT: Yale University Press, 1985).

52. Richard Wright, *The Ethics of Living Jim Crow: An Autobiographical Sketch* (1936; Los Angeles: Buk America, Inc., 2005).

53. Scott, *Weapons of the Weak*, xvi.

54. Scott Westerfeld, *Uglies Series: Uglies; Pretties; Specials; Extras*, boxed-set ed. (New York: Simon Pulse, 2012).

55. Ann D. Gordon, "The Trial of Susan B. Anthony," Federal Judicial Center, 2005, https://www.fjc.gov/sites/default/files/trials/susanbanthony.pdf.

56. Here she was interrupted by the judge and asked to stop speaking, but she kept right on going for several glorious more paragraphs full of excellent points; a full transcript can be found in Gordon, "The Trial of Susan B. Anthony."

57. Douglas Martin, "Natalya Gorbanevskaya, Soviet Dissident and Poet, Dies at 77," *New York Times*, December 1, 2013.

58. Albert O. Hirschman, "Exit, Voice, and the State," *World Politics* 31, no. 1 (1978): 101–2.

59. Annelise Orleck, "Soviet Jews: The City's Newest Immigrants Transform New York Jewish Life," in *New Immigrants in New York*, ed. Nancy Foner (New York: Columbia University Press, 2001), chap. 4.

60. Andrew Glass, "Castro Launches Mariel Boatlift, April 20, 1980," *Politico*, April 20, 2009.

61. Bradley Campbell, "During the Cold War, Buying People from East Germany Was Common Practice," PRI (Public Radio International), November 6, 2014.

62. Director Ridley Scott and the producing studio famously disagreed about the editing and ending of the movie, leading to the release of multiple "cuts." We strongly recommend the director's preferred version ("the final cut"), which does not include an unnatural Hollywood-style ending. See Alissa Wilkinson, "Which 'Blade Runner' Is the Best 'Blade Runner'?" *Vox.com*, October 4, 2017.

63. Srdja Popović and Matthew Miller, *Blueprint for Revolution: How to Use Rice Pudding, Lego Men, and Other Nonviolent Techniques to Galvanize Communities, Overthrow Dictators, or Simply Change the World* (New York: Spiegel & Grau, 2015).

64. Popović and Miller, *Blueprint for Revolution*. The slowdown is recounted in the documentary *A Force More Powerful* from 1999, made into a book by Ackerman and DuVall in 2000.

65. Jason Motlagh, "In Belarus, Clapping Can Be Subversive," *Atlantic*, July 21, 2011.

66. Maryna Rakhlei, "Public Demonstrations in Belarus: A Society Stirred," *Krytyka Polityczna* (Political critique), 2017, n.p. See also Kiryl Haiduk, Elena Rakova, and Vital Silitski, "Social Contracts in Contemporary Belarus," Belarusian Institute for Strategic Studies (2009).

67. Cassandra Santiago and Doug Criss, "An Activist, a Little Girl, and the Heartbreaking Origin of 'Me Too,'" *CNN*, October 17, 2017, http://www.cnn.com/2017/10/17/us/me-too-tarana-burke-origin-trnd/index.html.

68. Santiago and Criss, "An Activist."

69. Cara Buckley, "Can Anita Hill Fix Hollywood's Harassment Problem?" *New York Times*, December 20, 2017.

70. A prominent Ugandan LGBT activist, David Kato, was beaten to death in 2011; the official story is that a sex worker killed him. Kato's colleagues believe the motive was his sexuality and activism.

71. James Wan, "Meet the LGBT Activists Fighting Uganda's Anti-Gay Law," *Guardian*, July 31, 2014.

72. Michael J.Bosia, "Strange Fruit: Homophobia, the State, and the Politics of LGBT Rights and Capabilities," *Journal of Human Rights* 13, no. 3 (2014): 256–73; Tonny Onyulo, "Uganda's Other Refugee Crisis," Public Radio International, July 12, 2017.

73. Your beloved authors are memorizing as fast as we can!

74. Ray Bradbury, *Fahrenheit 451* (New York: Ballantine, 1953), 151, 152.

6. *The Resistance Will Not Be Intimidated*

1. Mancur Olson, *Logic of Collective Action: Public Goods and the Theory of Groups*, Harvard Economic Studies 124 (Cambridge, MA: Harvard University Press, 1965).

2. Laura Liswood quoted in Chana R. Schoenberger, "Quotas for Women on EU Boards: Good or Bad?" *Wall Street Journal*, May 17, 2012.

3. Catharine A. MacKinnon and Reva B. Siegel, *Directions in Sexual Harassment Law* (New Haven, CT: Yale University Press, 2003), introduction.

4. Jane Mansbridge and Katherine Flaster, "The Cultural Politics of Everyday Discourse: The Case of 'Male Chauvinist,'" *Critical Sociology* 33 (2007): 627–60.

5. Jane Mansbridge, "Everyday Activism," in *Wiley Blackwell Encyclopedia of Social and Political Movements*, ed. D. A. Snow et al. (Wiley-Blackwell, 2012).

6. Doug McAdam, *Political Process and the Development of Black Insurgency* (Chicago: University of Chicago Press, 1982). Also see Sidney Tarrow, *Power in Movement: Social Movements and Contentious Politics* (New York: Cambridge University Press, 1998).

7. Philip A. Klinkner and Rogers M. Smith, *The Unsteady March: The Rise and Decline of Racial Equality in America* (Chicago: University of Chicago Press, 2002).

8. Klinkner and Smith, *The Unsteady March*.

9. Klinkner and Smith, *The Unsteady March*.

10. McAdam, *Political Process and the Development of Black Insurgency*, chaps. 3, 5, 6, 7.

11. E. E. Schattschneider, *The Semisovereign People: A Realist's View of Democracy in America* (1960; Hinsdale, IL: Dryden, 1975), 8.

12. Erica Chenoweth and Maria J. Stephan, *Why Civil Resistance Works: The Strategic Logic of Nonviolent Conflict*, Columbia Studies in Terrorism and Irregular Warfare (New York: Columbia University Press, 2011).

13. Gene Sharp, *Power and Struggle: The Dynamics of Nonviolent Action, Part One* 10th printing ed. (Manchester, NH: Porter Sargent, 1973).

14. Gene Sharp, *Sharp's Dictionary of Power and Struggle: Language of Civil Resistance in Conflicts* (New York: Oxford University Press, 2011).

15. Richard B. Gregg, *The Power of Non-Violence*, 2nd ed. (1959; Read Books Ltd., 2013).

16. Shandra Bernath-Plaistad and Max Rennebohm, "Chileans Overthrow Pinochet Regime, 1983–1988," Swarthmore College, 2008, 2011.

17. Chenoweth and Stephan, *Why Civil Resistance Works*.

18. Chenoweth and Stephan, *Why Civil Resistance Works*.

19. Elizabeth Speller, *Following Hadrian: A Second-Century Journey Through the Roman Empire* (Oxford: Oxford University Press, 2003).

20. *Satyagraha* is the term for Gandhi's approach to nonviolent resistance, but it is also sometimes used to refer to an act of nonviolent resistance ("he started *a* satyagraha" or "the Salt Satyagraha").

21. Sharp, *Sharp's Dictionary of Power and Struggle*, 261–62.

22. Andrew Fiala, "Pacifism," *Stanford Encyclopedia of Philosophy*, https://plato.stanford .edu/archives/win2014/entries/pacifism.

23. Erica Chenoweth and Kathleen Gallagher Cunningham, "Understanding Nonviolent Resistance: An Introduction," Journal of Peace Research 50, no. 3 (2013): 271–76. See also Gene Sharp, *Waging Nonviolent Struggle: 20th-Century Practice and 21st-Century Potential* (Boston: Extending Horizons, 2005).

24. George Lakey, *Toward a Living Revolution: A Five-Stage Framework for Creating Radical Social Change* (Eugene, OR: Wipf and Stock, 2016), 82.

25. Lester R. Kurtz, "Gandhi and His Legacies," *Encyclopedia of Violence, Peace, and Conflict* (2008): 837–51.

26. From Gandhi's forward to Richard B. Gregg's "A Discipline for Non-Violence" (Pendle Hill, 1941), https://www.mkgandhi.org/ebks/a-discipline-for-nonviolence.pdf.

27. Sharp, *Power and Struggle*.

28. Sharp, *Power and Struggle*.

29. The quote that begins this section is from Dr. Martin Luther King Jr.: "We are not makers of history. We are made by history."

30. Geoffrey Ernest Maurice de Ste. Croix, *The Class Struggle in the Ancient Greek World: From the Archaic Age to the Arab Conquests* (Ithaca, NY: Cornell University Press, 1989).

31. Sharp, *Power and Struggle*.

32. The closest term we have to describe a widespread work stoppage is a "general strike." The translation for what the Romans called it is *secession*. It makes sense when you consider that the plebeians physically exited the city, thus seceding from Rome (temporarily). No one is exactly sure on the number of plebeian secessions, but historians are positive there were at least two and maybe as many as five.

33. Thomas Fortuna, "Plebeians Win Victory for the Rule of Law in Ancient Rome, 449 BCE. (See Also 494 Campaign)," Swarthmore College, 2011.

34. Geoffrey Samuel, *Epistemology and Method in Law* (New York: Routledge, 2016); Wayne R. Barnes, "Contemplating a Civil Law Paradigm for a Future International Commercial Code," *Louisiana Law Review* 65 (2004): 677.

35. Fortuna, "Plebeians Win Victory"; Daniel Kapust, "Skinner, Pettit and Livy: The Conflict of the Orders and the Ambiguity of Republican Liberty," *History of Political Thought* 25, no. 3 (2004): 377–401; Sharp, *Power and Struggle*.

36. Sandra Harbert Petrulionis, *Thoreau in His Own Time: A Biographical Chronicle of His Life, Drawn from Recollections, Interviews, and Memoirs by Family, Friends, and Associates* (Ames: University of Iowa Press, 2012).

37. Hannah Arendt, *Crises of the Republic: Lying in Politics, Civil Disobedience on Violence, Thoughts on Politics, and Revolution* (Houghton Mifflin Harcourt, 1972).

38. Kurt Schock, "The Practice and Study of Civil Resistance," *Journal of Peace Research* 50, no. 3 (2013): 277–90.

39. "We Shall Overcome" is a compilation of the music of a nineteenth-century spiritual sung by slaves, "No More Auction Block for Me," and lyrics adapted from a gospel song written in 1900, "I'll Overcome Someday," by an early gospel songwriter, Charles Tindley. Eileen Southern, *The Music of Black Americans: A History* (New York: Norton, 1997).

40. D. S. Hopkins, *What Is Jiu Jitsu? The Martial Arts and How to Understand Them* (First Edition Design Publishing, 2015).

41. Unfortunately, this often doesn't work the way Gandhi hoped it would—even Gregg's own recounting of the violence of the native police against the Salt Marchers showed that police violence increased in response to the passivity of the protesters. Gregg, *The Power of Non-Violence*; Brian Martin, *Justice Ignited: The Dynamics of Backfire* (Lanham, MD: Rowman & Littlefield, 2007).

42. Sharp, *Sharp's Dictionary of Power and Struggle*.

43. Sharp, *Waging Nonviolent Struggle*.

44. Martin, *Justice Ignited*.

45. Chenoweth and Stephan, *Why Civil Resistance Works*; Schock, "The Practice and Study of Civil Resistance."

46. Schock, "The Practice and Study of Civil Resistance."

47. Schock, "The Practice and Study of Civil Resistance."

48. Erica Chenoweth and Maria Stephan, *Why Civil Resistance Works*, 8–9, 7, 32–33.

49. Mark Granovetter, "Threshold Models of Collective Behavior," *American Journal of Sociology* 83, no. 6 (1978): 1420–43; Schock, "The Practice and Study of Civil Resistance."

50. Chenoweth and Stephan, *Why Civil Resistance Works*.

51. Kurt Schock, *Unarmed Insurrections: People Power Movements in Nondemocracies* (Minneapolis: University of Minnesota Press, 2005).

52. Martin, *Justice Ignited*.

53. Sharp, *Power and Struggle*.

54. Schock, *Unarmed Insurrections*; Chenoweth and Stephan, *Why Civil Resistance Works*.

55. See Joyce van Leeuwen, introduction to *The Aristotelian Mechanics: Text and Diagrams*, ed. Joyce van Leeuwen (Cham: Springer International, 2016).

56. Schock, "The Practice and Study of Civil Resistance."

57. Sharon Erickson Nepstad, "Mutiny and Nonviolence in the Arab Spring," *Journal of Peace Research* 50, no. 3 (2013): 337–49; Gene Sharp, *From Dictatorship to Democracy: A Conceptual Framework for Liberation* (New York: The New Press, 2012).

58. Nepstad, "Mutiny and Nonviolence in the Arab Spring."

59. Chenoweth and Stephan, *Why Civil Resistance Works*.

60. Nepstad, "Mutiny and Nonviolence in the Arab Spring."

61. Chenoweth and Stephan, *Why Civil Resistance Works*.

62. Jane Mansbridge and Shauna Shames, "Toward a Theory of Backlash: Dynamic Resistance and the Central Role of Power," *Politics and Gender Journal* 4, no. 4 (2008): 623–34.

63. The "loss of military aid" was a big part of the defection in Egypt—it was in part because the U.S. government publicly withdrew support from Mubarak; the military

knew that it was likely to lose not just U.S. military aid money ($1.3 billion annually) but also access to highly sophisticated weaponry. Nepstad, "Mutiny and Nonviolence in the Arab Spring."

64. Martin, *Justice Ignited*.

65. Martin, *Justice Ignited*.

66. Chenoweth and Stephan, *Why Civil Resistance Works*.

67. Srdja Popović and Matthew Miller, *Blueprint for Revolution : How to Use Rice Pudding, Lego Men, and Other Nonviolent Techniques to Galvanize Communities, Overthrow Dictators, or Simply Change the World* (New York: Spiegel & Grau, 2015), 126–27. Is it Burma or Myanmar, and does it matter? In 1962, a group of military officers overthrew the Burmese government and proceeded to rule the country until 2011 (we call this a military *junta*). For reasons too long to go into, in 1989, the junta changed the country's name to Myanmar. Basically Burma and Myanmar mean the same thing in the local language and you can use either.

68. See Eleanor Albert and Andrew Chatzky, "Backgrounder: The Rohingya Crisis," Council of Foreign Relations, https://www.cfr.org/backgrounder/rohingya-crisis.

7. Disintegrating the Oppressor

1. Starhawk, *The Fifth Sacred Thing*, http://starhawk.org/writing/books/the-fifth-sacred-thing/.

2. This section's title is part of a longer quote from the motivational speaker Zig Ziglar: "You were born to win, but to be a winner, you must plan to win, prepare to win, and expect to win."

3. All of the synopses in this section are adapted from two books: Gene Sharp, *Power and Struggle: The Dynamics of Nonviolent Action, Part Three* (Manchester, NH: Porter Sargent, 1973); and Gene Sharp, *Waging Nonviolent Struggle: 20th-Century Practice and 21st-Century Potential* (Boston: Extending Horizons, 2005).

4. Brian Martin, *Justice Ignited: The Dynamics of Backfire* (Lanham, MD: Rowman & Littlefield, 2007); Sharp, *Power and Struggle Part Three*; Sharp, *Waging Nonviolent Struggle*.

5. Richard B. Gregg, *The Power of Non-Violence*, 2nd ed. (1959; Read Books Ltd., 2013).; Martin, *Justice Ignited*; Peter Ackerman and Jack DuVall, *A Force More Powerful: A Century of Nonviolent Conflict*, 1st ed. (New York: St. Martin's Press, 2000).

6. Ackerman and DuVall, *A Force More Powerful*.

7. It's distilled from a longer quote: "Therefore no plan of operations extends with any certainty beyond the first contact with the main hostile force," by a nineteenth-century Prussian general named Helmuth von Moltke. Ralph Keyes, "The Quote Verifier," *Antioch Review* 64, no. 2 (2006): 256–66.

8. Quoted in Martin, *Justice Ignited*, 26.

9. The closest synonym for "caste" is "social class," but that's not exactly right, because there's a religious aspect to India's caste system, as well. The system technically divides Hindus into four castes, and the people who don't fit into those castes are outcasts

called Dalits, or "untouchables." The castes were rigidly segregated; it was forbidden to marry outside your caste—upper castes wouldn't even accept food from lower castes. The Indian Constitution now forbids discrimination based on caste, and people from different castes can intermarry as they see fit (legally), although social prejudice lingers.

10. Sharp, *Waging Nonviolent Struggle*, 369.
11. Ackerman and DuVall, *A Force More Powerful*; Joshua Paulson, "Mothers of the Plaza Mayo, Argentina 1977–1983," in Sharp, *Waging Nonviolent Struggle*, chap. 17.
12. See Paulson, "Mothers of the Plaza Mayo."
13. Ackerman and DuVall, *A Force More Powerful*, 270.
14. Ackerman and DuVall, *A Force More Powerful*, 276
15. Ackerman and DuVall, *A Force More Powerful*, 274.
16. Ackerman and DuVall, *A Force More Powerful*, 66.
17. John Gregory Dunne, *Delano: The Story of the California Grape Strike* (Berkeley: University of California Press, 1971); Hardy Merriman, "The California Grape Workers' Strike and Boycott, 1965–1970," in Sharp, ed., *Waging Nonviolent Struggle*, chap. 14. Also see the PBS documentary *Dolores*, about Dolores Huerta, a key UFW organizer: http://www.pbs.org/independentlens/films/dolores-huerta/.
18. It's so much more complicated than that, but given space limitations and our hope of keeping you interested, we've simplified. A lot.
19. Lorraine Agtang, "Commentary: UFW Is a Tribute to the Real Solidarity Achieved Between Latinos and Filipinos," *Northwest Asian Weekly*, December 20, 2013; Marc Grossman, personal communication with Amy L. Atchison, January 13, 2018.
20. Merriman, "The California Grape Workers' Strike and Boycott," 174.
21. The monthly $5,000 donation was started by then-UAW president Walter Reuther and continued monthly for many years. Grossman, personal communication.
22. Inga Kim, "The Rise of the UFW," *UFW.org*, 2017; Grossman, personal communication.
23. Grossman, personal communication.
24. César Chávez, "Letter from Delano," https://libraries.ucsd.edu/farmworkermovement /essays/essays/Letter%20From%20Delano.pdf.
25. Merriman, "The California Grape Workers' Strike and Boycott," 183.
26. Grossman, personal communication.
27. Merriman, "The California Grape Workers' Strike and Boycott," 185.
28. Abigail Disney and Leymah Gbowee, "Gender and Sustainable Peace," in *Psychological Components of Sustainable Peace* (Springer, 2012); Leymah Gbowee, "Effecting Change Through Women's Activism in Liberia," *IDS Bulletin* 40, no. 2 (2009): 50–53; Gini Reticker, *Pray the Devil Back to Hell* (Sausalito, CA: Fork Films).
29. This number is generally thought to be low, given the underreporting of rape. UN, "Background Information on Sexual Violence Used as a Tool of War," http://www.un .org/en/preventgenocide/rwanda/about/bgsexualviolence.shtml.
30. Shared with the first female president of Liberia, Ellen Johnson Sirleaf, and the Yemeni activist Tawakkul Karman.

31. Nobel Committee, "The Nobel Peace Prize for 2011 to Ellen Johnson Sirleaf, Leymah Gbowee and Tawakkul Karman—Press Release," October 2, 2011. Also see the documentary *Pray the Devil Back to Hell*.

32. Reticker, *Pray the Devil Back to Hell*.

33. Gbowee reports the banner's text, capitalization and all, in her book *Mighty Be Our Powers: How Sisterhood, Prayer, and Sex Changed a Nation at War*, an excerpt of which can be found at http://www.pbs.org/wnet/women-war-and-peace/features/the -president-will-see-you-now/.

34. Ackerman and DuVall, *A Force More Powerful*, 337.

35. Ackerman and DuVall, *A Force More Powerful*, 353.

36. Ackerman and DuVall, *A Force More Powerful*.

37. Joshua Paulson, "School Boycotts in South Africa, 1984–1987," in Sharp, ed., *Waging Nonviolent Struggle*.

38. Ackerman and DuVall, *A Force More Powerful*, 338.

39. Ackerman and DuVall, *A Force More Powerful*, 338.

40. Paulson, "School Boycotts in South Africa, 1984–1987," 236.

41. Ackerman and DuVall, *A Force More Powerful*, 367.

42. Sharp, "Czech and Slovak Defiance of Invasion, 1968–1969," in Sharp, ed., *Waging Nonviolent Struggle*, chap. 15.

43. Sharp, "Czech and Slovak Defiance of Invasion."

44. Ursula K. Le Guin, *The Dispossessed* (New York: HarperCollins, 1974), 44.

45. Sharp, "Four Ways Success May Be Achieved," in *Waging Nonviolent Struggle*, chap. 33.

46. Kurt Schock, "Nonviolent Action and Its Misconceptions: Insights for Social Scientists," *PS: Political Science and Politics* 36, no. 4 (2003): 705–12; Sharp, "Four Ways Success May Be Achieved."

47. Merriman, "The California Grape Workers' Strike and Boycott," 184.

48. Marshall Ganz, "Resources and Resourcefulness: Strategic Capacity in the Unionization of California Agriculture, 1959–1966," *American Journal of Sociology* 105, no. 4 (2000): 1003–62.

49. Steven Levitsky and James Loxton, "Populism and Competitive Authoritarianism in the Andes," *Democratization* 20, no. 1 (2013): 107–36; James Loxton, "Authoritarian Successor Parties," *Journal of Democracy* 26, no. 3 (2015): 157–70.

8. Can You Re(build) It? Yes You Can!

1. Steven Levitsky and James Loxton, "Populism and Competitive Authoritarianism in the Andes," *Democratization* 20, no. 1 (2013): 107–36; James Loxton, "Authoritarian Successor Parties," *Journal of Democracy* 26, no. 3 (2015): 157–70.

2. Freedom House, "Freedom in the World 2017 Report," https://freedomhouse.org/ report/freedom-world/2017/egypt.

3. Arend Lijphart, "Constitutional Design for Divided Societies," *Journal of Democracy* 15, no. 2 (2004): 96–109.

4. It *has* happened; see Czechoslovakia's 1989 Velvet Revolution—the government was toppled without mass violence or destruction. Tunisia's 2010 Jasmine Revolution was

also a peaceful ouster, and some small progress has been made toward democracy there.

5. See E. E. Schattschneider, *The Semisovereign People* (1960; Hinsdale, IL: Dryden, 1975); Arend Lijphart, *Patterns of Democracy: Government Forms and Performance in Thirty-Six Countries* (New Haven, CT: Yale University Press, 2012); Joseph A. Schumpeter, *Capitalism, Socialism, and Democracy* (New York: Harper & Brothers, 1942).

6. V. O. Key, *Southern Politics in State and Nation* (New York: Knopf, 1949); Schattschneider, *The Semisovereign People.*

7. Key, *Southern Politics in State and Nation*; V. O. Key, *Politics, Parties, and Pressure Groups*, 5th ed. (New York: Crowell, 1955).

8. John Aldrich, *Why Parties? A Second Look* (Chicago: University of Chicago Press, 2011); Kenneth Arrow, *Social Choice and Individual Values* (New York: Basic Books, 1951); Thomas Schwartz, *The Logic of Collective Choice* (New York: Columbia University Press, 1986).

9. Ray Bradbury, *Fahrenheit 451: A Novel* (1953; New York: Simon and Schuster, 2011), 93.

10. Thomas Patterson, *The Vanishing Voter: Public Involvement in an Age of Uncertainty* (New York: Vintage, 2009); Martin Wattenberg, *The Rise of Candidate-Centered Politics: Presidential Elections of the 1980s* (Cambridge, MA: Harvard University Press, 1991).

11. This idea and phrasing is from Schumpeter, *Capitalism, Socialism, and Democracy.*

12. Andrew Reynolds, *Designing Democracy in a Dangerous World* (Oxford: Oxford University Press, 2010).

13. Markus Böckenförde, Nora Hedling, and Winluck Wahiu, *A Practical Guide to Constitution Building* (Stockholm: International IDEA, 2011).

14. The United Kingdom doesn't have a written constitution per se, but (a) they aren't a *new* democracy, and (b) they have a written body of constitutional law (like the Magna Carta, the Acts of Union, or most any Act of Parliament) that has evolved over time into something like a constitution.

15. Dario Castiglione, "The Political Theory of the Constitution," *Political Studies* 44, no. 3 (1996): 417–35. For a wonderful exposition on the importance of the rule of law, see Timothy D. Snyder, *The Road to Unfreedom: Russia, Europe, America* (New York: Crown/Archetype, 2018).

16. Böckenförde, Hedling, and Wahiu, *A Practical Guide to Constitution Building.*

17. Niccolo Machiavelli, *Discourses on Livy* (Chicago: University of Chicago Press, 2009).

18. Böckenförde, Hedling, and Wahiu, *A Practical Guide to Constitution Building.*

19. I. Carter, "Positive and Negative Liberty," in *The Stanford Encyclopedia of Philosophy*, https://plato.stanford.edu/archives/fall2016/entries/liberty-positive-negative/.

20. David P. Currie, "Positive and Negative Constitutional Rights," *University of Chicago Law Review* 53, no. 3 (1986): 864–90.

21. John F. Kennedy, "Radio and Television Report to the American People on Civil Rights, June 11, 1963," John F. Kennedy Presidential Library and Museum, 1963, https://www.jfklibrary.org/archives/other-resources/john-f-kennedy-speeches/civil-rights -radio-and-television-report-19630611.

22. Böckenförde, Hedling, and Wahiu, *A Practical Guide to Constitution Building*.

23. Marilyn Frye, "Oppression: The Politics of Reality: Essays in Feminist Theory," reprinted in *Feminist Frontiers*, ed. V. Taylor, N. Whittier, and L. Rupp (McGraw-Hill Education, 1983); Peggy McIntosh, "White Privilege: Unpacking the Invisible Knapsack," *Peace and Freedom Magazine* (July–August 1989): 10–12.

24. Julie McCarthy, "The Caste Formerly Known as 'Untouchables' Demands a New Role in India," *Weekend Edition Sunday*, http://www.npr.org/sections/goatsandsoda/2016 /08/13/489883492/the-caste-formerly-known-as-untouchables-demands-a-new-role -in-india.

25. Richard B. Gregg, *The Power of Non-Violence*, 2nd ed. (1959; Read Books Ltd., 2013).

26. Böckenförde, Hedling, and Wahiu, *A Practical Guide to Constitution Building*.

27. Rather than defining *who* was an "untouchable," the framers of India's constitution defined what it meant to "practice untouchability" (i.e., to treat someone as an untouchable). Anupama Rao, *The Caste Question: Dalits and the Politics of Modern India* (Berkeley: University of California Press, 2009), 173.

28. "What Is India's Caste System?" *BBC News*, July 20, 2017, https://www.bbc.com/news /world-asia-india-35650616.

29. Barbara R. Joshi, ed., *Untouchable! Voices of the Dalit Liberation Movement*, Women in the Third World 209 (Atlantic Highlands, NJ: Zed, 1986), Rao, *The Caste Question*; S. Kumar, "Violence Against Dalit Woman and Constitutional Protection: An Analysis," *Asian Journal of Multidisciplinary Studies* 2, no. 1 (2014).

30. There were greater or lesser degrees of this throughout Europe, and it got quite complex in many ways, but the transfer of legal control of a woman from her father to her husband is the basic principle. For more on the complexities, see Thomas Kuehn, *Law, Family, and Women: Toward a Legal Anthropology of Renaissance Italy* (Chicago: University of Chicago Press, 1994), chaps. 8–10.

31. Böckenförde, Hedling, and Wahiu, *A Practical Guide to Constitution Building*, 125.

32. Claudia Zaher, "When a Woman's Marital Status Determined Her Legal Status: A Research Guide on the Common Law Doctrine of Coverture," *Law Library Journal* 94 (2002): 459. For the record: although women could own property in other systems, they couldn't enter contracts without the permission of a male guardian and had no legal standing in courts.

33. Rachel G. Fuchs, *Gender and Poverty in Nineteenth-Century Europe*, New Approaches to European History Series 35 (Cambridge: Cambridge University Press, 2005).

34. Jill Elaine Hasday, "Contest and Consent: A Legal History of Marital Rape," *California Law Review* 88, no. 5 (2000): 1373–505. See also Lily Rothman, "When Spousal Rape First Became a Crime in the U.S," *Time*, July 28, 2015.

35. Böckenförde, Hedling, and Wahiu, *A Practical Guide to Constitution Building*.

36. Reynolds, *Designing Democracy in a Dangerous World*; Jane Mansbridge and Shauna Shames, "Toward a Theory of Backlash: Dynamic Resistance and the Central Role of Power," *Politics and Gender* 4, no. 4 (2008): 623–34.

37. Böckenförde, Hedling, and Wahiu, *A Practical Guide to Constitution Building*.

38. Robin Boadway and Anwar Shah, *Fiscal Federalism: Principles and Practice of Multi-order Governance* (Cambridge: Cambridge University Press, 2009).

39. Pippa Norris, *Making Democratic Governance Work: How Regimes Shape Prosperity, Welfare, and Peace* (Cambridge: Cambridge University Press, 2012).
40. Paolo Beramendi, "Federalism," in *The Oxford Handbook of Comparative Politics*, ed. Carles Boix and Susan C. Stokes (Oxford: Oxford University Press, 2009).
41. Beramendi, "Federalism."
42. Daniel Halberstam, "Comparative Federalism and the Role of the Judiciary," in *The Oxford Handbook of Law and Politics*, ed. Gregory A. Caldeira, R. Daniel Kelemen, and Keith E. Whittington (Oxford: Oxford University Press, 2008), 153.
43. Böckenförde, Hedling, and Wahiu, *A Practical Guide to Constitution Building*.
44. Böckenförde, Hedling, and Wahiu, *A Practical Guide to Constitution Building*.
45. Böckenförde, Hedling, and Wahiu, *A Practical Guide to Constitution Building*.
46. Catherine L. Cleverdon and Ramsay Cook, *The Woman Suffrage Movement in Canada*, 2nd ed. (Toronto: University of Toronto Press, 1974).
47. Andrew Reynolds, Ben Reilly, and Andrew Ellis, *Electoral System Design: The New International Idea Handbook* (Stockholm: International Institute for Democracy and Electoral Assistance, 2008).
48. Beramendi, "Federalism."
49. Wayne Norman, "Federalism and Confederalism," in *The Routledge Encyclopedia of Philosophy* (Taylor and Francis, 1998), https://www.rep.routledge.com/articles/thematic/federalism-and-confederalism/v-1.
50. John McCormick, *Understanding the European Union: A Concise Introduction* (London: Palgrave Macmillan, 2014).
51. Kaare Strøm, "Parliamentary Democracy and Delegation," in *Delegation and Accountability in Parliamentary Democracies*, ed. Kaare Strøm, Wolfgang C. Müller, and Torbjörn Bergman (Oxford: Oxford University Press, 2003), chap. 3.
52. Unless no one is willing to join his coalition. In that case, the leader of the second-largest party is invited to form a government, she forms a coalition, and she becomes prime minister. This most recently happened in 2017 in New Zealand.
53. Michael Laver and Kenneth A. Shepsle, *Cabinet Ministers and Parliamentary Government*, Political Economy of Institutions and Decisions (Cambridge: Cambridge University Press, 1994).
54. Amy Atchison, "The Impact of Female Cabinet Ministers on a Female-Friendly Labor Environment," *Journal of Women, Politics, and Policy* 34, no. 2 (2015): 388–414.
55. Laver and Shepsle, *Cabinet Ministers and Parliamentary Government*.
56. Böckenförde, Hedling, and Wahiu, *A Practical Guide to Constitution Building*.
57. Böckenförde, Hedling, and Wahiu, *A Practical Guide to Constitution Building*; Paul Warwick, *Government Survival in Parliamentary Democracies* (New York: Cambridge University Press, 2007).
58. Böckenförde, Hedling, and Wahiu, *A Practical Guide to Constitution Building*.
59. Matthew Søberg Shugart, "Comparative Executive–Legislative Relations," in *The Oxford Handbook of Political Institutions*, ed. Sarah A. Binder, R. A. W. Rhodes, and Bert A. Rockman (Oxford: Oxford University Press, 2008).
60. David Samuels, "Separation of Powers," in *The Oxford Handbook of Comparative Politics*.

61. Samuels, "Separation of Powers."
62. Böckenförde, Hedling, and Wahiu, *A Practical Guide to Constitution Building*.
63. Böckenförde, Hedling, and Wahiu, *A Practical Guide to Constitution Building*; also see Juan J. Linz, "The Perils of Presidentialism," *Journal of Democracy* 1, no. 1 (1990): 51–69.
64. Samuels, "Separation of Powers."
65. Samuels, "Separation of Powers."
66. Böckenförde, Hedling, and Wahiu, *A Practical Guide to Constitution Building*.
67. Böckenförde, Hedling, and Wahiu, *A Practical Guide to Constitution Building*.
68. Böckenförde, Hedling, and Wahiu, *A Practical Guide to Constitution Building*.
69. Rein Taagepera, "Electoral Systems," in *The Oxford Handbook of Comparative Politics*.
70. Böckenförde, Hedling, and Wahiu, *A Practical Guide to Constitution Building*.
71. Reynolds, Reilly, and Ellis, *Electoral System Design*.
72. P. R. Abramson et al., "Comparing Strategic Voting Under FPTP and PR," *Comparative Political Studies* 43, no. 1 (2010): 61–90.
73. Reynolds, *Designing Democracy in a Dangerous World*.
74. Reynolds, *Designing Democracy in a Dangerous World*.
75. International IDEA, "Worldwide Electoral System Design Database: Electoral System Family," https://www.idea.int/data-tools/data/electoral-system-design.
76. Reynolds, Reilly, and Ellis, *Electoral System Design*.
77. Paul R. Abramson et al., "Strategic Electoral Considerations Under Proportional Representation," *Electoral Studies* 31, no. 1 (2012): 184–91.
78. Reynolds, *Designing Democracy in a Dangerous World*; Böckenförde, Hedling, and Wahiu, *A Practical Guide to Constitution Building*.
79. Reynolds, Reilly, and Ellis, *Electoral System Design*.
80. Reynolds, Reilly, and Ellis, *Electoral System Design*.
81. Reynolds, Reilly, and Ellis, *Electoral System Design*.
82. Reynolds, Reilly, and Ellis, *Electoral System Design*.
83. G. Alan Tarr, *Without Fear or Favor: Judicial Independence and Judicial Accountability in the States* (Stanford, CA: Stanford University Press, 2012).
84. H. H. Hyman and P. B. Sheatsley, "Attitudes Toward Desegregation," *Scientific American* 195, no. 6 (1956): 36. Also see Tarr, *Without Fear or Favor*.
85. Böckenförde, Hedling, and Wahiu, *A Practical Guide to Constitution Building*; Kluger, *Simple Justice: The History of* Brown v. Board of Education *and Black America's Struggle for Equality* (New York: Vintage, 2011).
86. Ruth Bader Ginsburg, "Looking Beyond Our Borders: The Value of a Comparative Perspective in Constitutional Adjudication," *Yale Law and Policy Review* 22 (2004): 329.
87. Ran Hirschl, "The Judicialization of Politics," in *The Oxford Handbook of Law and Politics*.
88. Ginsburg, "Looking Beyond Our Borders"; Hirschl, "The Judicialization of Politics."
89. Hirschl, "The Judicialization of Politics."
90. Böckenförde, Hedling, and Wahiu, *A Practical Guide to Constitution Building*.
91. Nicola Corkin, *Europeanization of Judicial Review* (London: Routledge, 2014).
92. Aldous Huxley, *Brave New World* (1932; London: Vintage, 1998), 151–52.

93. See, for example, Reynolds, *Designing Democracy in a Dangerous World*. Also see Böckenförde, Hedling, and Wahiu, *A Practical Guide to Constitution Building*.

94. Reynolds, *Designing Democracy in a Dangerous World*, 181–82.

95. Yes, we know that technically the Chicago Experiment is part of the larger United States—but fiction, as Samuel Taylor Coleridge once said, is all about the willing suspension of disbelief.

96. Reynolds, *Designing Democracy in a Dangerous World*; Andreas Wimmer and Conrad Schetter, "Putting State-Formation First: Some Recommendations for Reconstruction and Peace-Making in Afghanistan," *Journal of International Development* 15, no. 5 (2003): 525; Andrew Reynolds, "Constitutional Engineering and Democratic Stability: The Debate Surrounding the Crafting of Political Institutions in Afghanistan," in *Building State and Security in Afghanistan*, ed. Wolfgang Danspeckgruber and Robert P. Finn (Princeton, NJ: Lichtenstein Institute of Self-Determination, Woodrow Wilson School of Public and International Affairs, 2007).

97. Böckenförde, Hedling, and Wahiu, *A Practical Guide to Constitution Building*; J. A. Thier, "The Making of a Constitution in Afghanistan," *New York Law School Review* 51 (2006): 557.

98. Andrew Reynolds *Constitutional Engineering and Democratic Stability: The Debate Surrounding the Crafting of Political Institutions in Afghanistan* (2007); Reynolds, *Designing Democracy in a Dangerous World*.

99. Nusrat Choudhury, "Constrained Spaces for Islamic Feminism: Women's Rights and the 2004 Constitution of Afghanistan," *Yale Journal of Law and Feminism* 19 (2007): 155; Thier, "The Making of a Constitution in Afghanistan."

100. Surprisingly, they *did* include women's equality in the constitution and specified that "at least two female delegates must be elected from each province to the Wolesi Jirga (Council of People), the lower house of the national legislature." Choudhury, "Constrained Spaces for Islamic Feminism," 157.

101. Reynolds, *Designing Democracy in a Dangerous World*.

102. Shaun Bowler, David M. Farrell, and Robin T. Petitt, "Expert Opinion on Electoral Systems: So Which Electoral System Is 'Best'?" *Journal of Elections, Public Opinion, and Parties* 15, no. 1 (2005): 3–19; Andrew Reynolds, *Constitutional Engineering and Democratic Stability*, 62–63.

103. J. J. Messner, ed., *The Fragile States Index, 2017* (Washington, DC: Fund for Peace, 2017), 34.

104. Steven Levitsky and Daniel Ziblatt, *How Democracies Die* (New York: Crown, 2018). The epigraph for this section comes from page 3.

105. J. R. Dresden and M. M. Howard, "Authoritarian Backsliding and the Concentration of Political Power," *Democratization* 23, no. 7 (2016): 1122–43, Levitsky and Ziblatt, *How Democracies Die*.

106. Ben Stanley, "The Thin Ideology of Populism," *Journal of Political Ideologies* 13, no. 1 (2008): 95–110. Also see Cas Mudde and Cristóbal Rovira Kaltwasser, *Populism in Europe and the Americas: Threat or Corrective for Democracy?* (Cambridge: Cambridge University Press, 2012).

107. K. Weyland, "The Threat from the Populist Left," *Journal of Democracy* 24, no. 3 (2013): 18–32.

108. Weyland, "The Threat from the Populist Left."

109. Patricia Roberts-Miller, *Demagoguery and Democracy* (New York: Experiment Press, 2017); emphasis added.

110. Steven Levitsky and Daniel Ziblatt, "Author Q&A" (2018), https://www.penguin randomhouse.com/books/562246/how-democracies-die-by-steven-levitsky-and -daniel-ziblatt/9781524762933/.

111. Levitsky and Ziblatt, "Author Q&A."

112. Levitsky and Ziblatt, *How Democracies Die.*

113. Schattschneider, *The Semisovereign People.*

114. Levitsky and Ziblatt, "Author Q&A."

115. Timothy Snyder, "20 Lessons from the 20th Century on How to Survive in Trump's America: A History Professor Looks to the Past to Remind Us to Do What We Can in the Face of the Unthinkable," *In These Times,* http://inthesetimes.com/article/19658 /20-lessons-from-the-20th-century-on-how-to-survive-in-trumps-america.

116. Levitsky and Ziblatt, "Author Q&A."

117. Levitsky and Ziblatt, *How Democracies Die.*

Epilogue

1. Evan Osnos, "Doomsday Prep for the Super-Rich," *New Yorker,* January 30, 2017.

2. Emily St. John Mandel, *Station 11* (New York: Vintage, 2015).

3. Bernice Johnson Reagon, "Coalition Work," in *Home Girls: A Black Feminist Anthology,* ed. Barbara Smith (New York: Kitchen Table Women of Color Press, 1983), 356–57.

4. Jane Mansbridge, "Presidential Address: What Is Political Science For?" *Perspectives on Politics* 12, no. 1 (2014): 8–14.

Index